'Government space exploration is rapidly making way for privately-driven space commerce. *Above and Beyond* is an excellent treatise on the current state of the space enterprise and how it affects, and is affected by, commercial globalization trends.'

—David Alexander, PhD, *Director, Rice Space Institute, USA*

'A successful attempt to harness the convergence of divergent domains with lucidity, clarity and brevity. The analysis of the business of space is a thoughtfully dissected treatise on globalization which may serve as a compass for imagination, invention and innovation.'

—Dr Shoumen Datta, *Massachusetts Institute of Technology, USA*

Above and Beyond

The global space sector has always been regarded as a cutting-edge field, futuristic and at the forefront of innovation. In recent years, the sector has undergone massive change, giving rise to a high-technology niche worth over $330 billion in revenues worldwide and growing. That process, encompassing a greater and more diverse set of actors, has been described as the "democratization of space."

Above and Beyond: Exploring the Business of Space provides a comprehensive and current overview of the business of space and its distinctive competitive dynamics. The book explores the commercialization of space, taking the reader on a journey from the era of the Space Race up to the present and beyond. Focusing on both state and commercial actors, the book provides an exhaustive panoramic view of an area of growing human endeavour and ambition that is both informative and fascinating. As the business of space continues to develop and grow at a remarkable pace, the book offers a thoughtful and timely analysis of its past, present and future scenarios.

While providing a critical assessment of the business of space, this book offers valuable insights to academics, policy makers and anyone with a keen interest in the sector, as well as useful lessons from emerging commercial and traditional space actors that have broader applicability to other industries and their managers.

Louis Brennan is a Fellow of Trinity College and Professor within the Trinity Business School at Trinity College, Dublin, Ireland. He has published extensively in the fields of International Business, Operations and Technology Management.

Loizos Heracleous is Professor of Strategy at Warwick Business School, UK. He received his PhD from the University of Cambridge and a DSc from the University of Warwick for lifetime contributions to his field.

Alessandra Vecchi is Assistant Professor in the Department of Management at the University of Bologna in Italy, where she holds a Marie Curie Fellowship, and works as Senior Research Fellow at London College of Fashion at the University of London Arts, UK.

Above and Beyond

Exploring the Business of Space

**Louis Brennan, Loizos Heracleous
and Alessandra Vecchi**

Routledge
Taylor & Francis Group

LONDON AND NEW YORK

First published 2018
by Routledge
2 Park Square, Milton Park, Abingdon, Oxon OX14 4RN

and by Routledge
711 Third Avenue, New York, NY 10017

Routledge is an imprint of the Taylor & Francis Group, an informa business

© 2018 Louis Brennan, Loizos Heracleous and Alessandra Vecchi

British Library Cataloguing-in-Publication Data
A catalogue record for this book is available from the British Library

Library of Congress Cataloging-in-Publication Data
A catalog record has been requested for this book

ISBN: 978-1-138-09818-3 (hbk)
ISBN: 978-1-138-09820-6 (pbk)
ISBN: 978-1-315-10449-2 (ebk)

Typeset in Bembo
by Apex CoVantage, LLC

Contents

Figures

Tables

Above and Beyond: Exploring the Business of Space

Preface

Steven A. González

I believe we have entered a new era of space exploration which will redefine the business of space. An era built upon the foundation of the pioneering achievements of the international space agencies. As we collectively reach deeper and deeper into space, the opportunities and technologies that will be created in its wake will create new economies that were first conceived of as science fiction. For example, markets from space mining and in space manufacturing of superior optical fiber to tourist trips around the moon. The disruptions and discoveries of this era will not only impact business in space and but on economies of Earth as well.

This next phase of the human activity in space will see the emergence of space commerce. Every year we see new emerging companies created to leverage the resources in space or provide additional capabilities in space. These companies provide governments with increasing choices to access space and an incredible amount of information generated from the myriad of satellites in earth's orbit. Space commerce will increasingly look beyond government customers to other industries that can be transformed from the orbiting capabilities. The future business of space will not focus solely on the business "in" space but the commerce that is enabled through, in and because of space assets. Government and industry have created telecom and earth observation industries that are enabling new emerging markets to provide insights to terrestrial industries including energy, agribusiness and maritime trade. The United Kingdom's Satellite Applications Catapult is just one example of an organization helping new industries make use of and benefit from satellite technologies.

The interaction of space commerce with other forms of commerce on earth will create new opportunities for industries on earth. One example is a project intended to improve maritime vessel tracking from onboard the International Space Station (ISS). This project was funded by the Center for the Advancement of Science in Space (CASIS) and included the Greater Houston Port Bureau. The success of this project will provide greater insight into the transoceanic maritime trade.

The business of space is poised to take another leap forward as the number of spaceports continue to grow. It will create a competitive edge for those that can leverage this for their supply chain. Currently there is commerce through the ports, airports, rail and roads but those that are positioned near a spaceport may find an opportunity to transfer goods from one end of the globe to the other end in 4 hours. Towards this end an annual Global Spaceport Summit was launched in 2015 to bring together the spaceport community to discuss how they can work with one another as the various suborbital space vehicles mature.

Yet all of this would not be possible without the nearly 60-year evolution of the business of space from its roots in political competition to international collaboration and private/public partnerships. The authors' in-depth review of this evolution shines a light on the rich foundation that will propel us to the stars and create the space markets of tomorrow.

Steven González serves as the Technology Strategist in the Exploration Technology office at NASA Johnson Space Center, Houston, Texas.

Section I

Overview and trends

1 Introduction and background

The global space sector

Introduction

In this chapter we address the evolution of the global space sector outlining its most recent dynamics. We focus in particular on the dichotomy between space and globalization. To this purpose, the chapter comprises four sections. We describe the main theoretical foundations of the book in the second section by defining the concept of space from a globalization perspective. In the third section, we outline the dynamics of de-territorialization and re-territorialization as they are characterizing the sector. We trace the origins of space, from its early developments to the most recent dynamics of the business of space in section four.

The conceptualization of the business of space: a globalization perspective

Since the early 1970s, debates have raged throughout the social sciences concerning the process of "globalization", an essentially contested term whose meaning is as much a source of controversy today as it was some decades ago, when systematic research first began on the topic. Contemporary globalization research encompasses an immensely broad range of themes, from the new international division of labour, changing forms of industrial organization, and processes of urban-regional restructuring to transformations in the nature of state power, civil society, citizenship, democracy, public spheres, nationalism, politico-cultural identities, localities, and architectural forms, among many others. Yet despite this proliferation of globalization research, little theoretical consensus has been established in the social sciences concerning the interpretation of even the most rudimentary elements of the globalization process (e.g., its historical developments, its causal determinants and its socio-political implications).

Nevertheless, within this whirlwind of conflicting perspectives, a remarkably broad range of studies of globalization have devoted detailed attention to the problematic of space, its social production, and its historical transformation. Major strands of contemporary globalization research have been permeated by geographical concepts (e.g., "space-time compression", "space of flows", "space of places", "deterritorialization", "glocalization" the "global-local nexus", "supra-territoriality", "diasporas", "translocalities", and "scapes" among many other terms). Meanwhile globalization researchers have begun to deploy a barrage of distinctively geographical prefixes (e.g. "sub-", "supra-", "trans-", "meso" and "inter-"), to describe various emergent social processes that appear to operate below, above, beyond, or between entrenched geopolitical boundaries. In particular in social sciences, the recognition that social relations are becoming increasingly interconnected on a global scale necessarily problematizes the spatial parameters of those relations, and therefore, the geographical context in which they occur.

According to Friedman (1999) globalization is a new international system. It came together in the late 1980s and replaced the previous international system, the Cold War system, which had reigned since the end of World War II. Friedman defines globalization as the inexorable integration of markets, transportation systems, and communication systems to a degree never witnessed before – in a way that is enabling corporations, countries, and individuals to reach around the world farther, faster, deeper, and cheaper than ever before.

Several important features of this globalization system differ from those of the Cold War system. Friedman examined them in detail in his seminal book, *The Lexus and the Olive Tree*. The Cold War system was characterized by one over-arching feature and that was *division*. That world was a divided-up, chopped-up place, and whether you were a country or a company, your threats and opportunities in the Cold War system tended to grow out of who you were divided from. Appropriately, this Cold War system was symbolized by the Berlin Wall and the Iron Curtain.

The globalization system is different. It also has one overarching feature and that is *integration*. The world has become an increasingly interwoven place. Today, whether you are a company or a country, your threats and opportunities increasingly derive from who you are connected to. This globalization system is also characterized by a single word – *web*, the World Wide Web. So in the broadest sense we moved from an international system built around division and walls to a system increasingly built around integration and webs. In the Cold War we reached for the hotline, which was a symbol that we were all divided but at least two people were in charge – the leaders of the United States and the Soviet Union. In the globalization system we reach for the Internet, which is a symbol that we are all connected and nobody is quite in charge. While during the Cold War division caused rivalry and intense competition, in the globalization era there is the reality that we will all succeed only on the basis of collaboration. In this context, collaboration can assume many forms – from alliances to collaborative networks – and can involve a wide variety of actors.

Everyone in the world is directly or indirectly affected by this new system, but not everyone benefits from it, which is why the more it becomes diffused, the more it also produces a backlash by people who feel overwhelmed by it, homogenized by it, or unable to keep pace with its demands.

The other key difference between the Cold War system and the globalization system is how power is structured within them. The Cold War system was built primarily around nation-states. You acted on the world in that system through your state. The Cold War was a drama of states confronting states, balancing states, and aligning with states. And, as a system, the Cold War was balanced at the center by two superstates, two superpowers: the United States and the Soviet Union.

The globalization system, by contrast, is built around three balances, which overlap and affect one another. The first is the traditional balance of power between nation-states as we have many "super-powers". In the globalization system, the United States is seen as the sole and dominant superpower and all other nations are subordinate to it to one degree or another. The shifting balance of power between the United States and other states, or simply between other states, still very much matters for the stability of this system as it shifts from a uni-polar world dominated by the United States to a multi-polar world in which the United States is increasingly viewed as primus inter pares.

The second important power balance in the globalization system is between nation-states and global markets. These global markets are made up of millions of investors moving money around the world with the click of a mouse. Friedman calls them the Electronic Herd, and this herd gathers in key global financial centers – such as Wall Street, Hong Kong, London, and Frankfurt – which Friedman calls the "supermarkets". The attitudes and actions of the Electronic Herd and the "supermarkets" can have a significant impact on nation-states today, even to the point of triggering the downfall of governments and the consequent emergence of new dominant private actors and as we have experienced most recently the virtual collapse of the global economy.

The third balance that we have to pay attention to is the balance between individuals and nation-states. Because globalization has brought down many of the walls that limited the movement and reach of people, and because it has simultaneously wired the world into networks, it gives more power to *individuals* to influence both markets and nation-states than at any other time in history. Whether by enabling people to use the Internet to communicate instantly at almost no cost over vast distances, or by enabling them to use the Web to transfer money or obtain weapons designs that normally would have been controlled by states, or by enabling them to go into a hardware store now and buy a five-hundred-dollar global positioning device, connected to a satellite, that can direct a hijacked airplane – globalization can be an incredible force-multiplier for individuals. Individuals can increasingly act on the world stage directly, unmediated by a state. So according to Friedman we have today not only "many superpowers", not only "supermarkets", but also what Friedman calls "super-empowered individuals".

Table 1.1 summarizes the main arguments that allow Friedman to delineate the differences between the Cold War system and the globalization era. The dynamics that globalization entails and as they have been described by Friedman are well represented if we look at the evolution of the space industry. This section will review the evolution of the space industry by looking at its different stages – from the Cold War to globalization and their distinctive dynamics – in order to

Table 1.1 Friedman's Argument

• The Cold War System	• Globalization
• Division	• Integration
• Rivalry & Competition	• Many Superpowers
• Two Superpowers	• Collaboration
	• Supermarkets
	• Super empowered Individuals

Source: Adapted from Friedman, 2005.

provide a new conceptualization of the business of space that incorporates the globalization perspective.

De-territorialization and re-territorialization

Since the early 1970s, debates have raged throughout the social sciences concerning the process of globalization – an essentially contested term whose meaning is as much a source of controversy today as it was some decades ago, when systematic research first began on the topic. Contemporary globalization research encompasses an immensely broad range of themes, from the new international division of labour, changing forms of industrial organization (Cerny, 1995), and processes of urban-regional restructuring (Florida, 1996; Storper, 1995) to transformations in the nature of state power (Glisby & Holden, 2005), civil society (Van Rooy, 2004), citizenship (Castles & Davidson, 2000), democracy (Goodhart, 2001), public spheres (Bennett et al., 2004), nationalism (Hannerz & Featherstone, 1990), politico-cultural identities (Brenner, 1999); (Ferguson, 2005), localities (Amin, 2002), and architectural forms (Kobrin, 1997), among many others. Yet despite this proliferation of globalization research, little theoretical consensus has been established in the social sciences concerning the interpretation of even the most rudimentary elements of the globalization process (e.g., its historical developments, its causal determinants, and its socio-political implications). The notion of globalization as a catalyst for radical economic, political and social change is a recurring issue in the current academic literature. There is however a lack of consensus on the strength and the likely impact of globalization. This conceptual vacuum is well described by Scholte, who affirms that:

> in spite of a deluge of publications on this subject, our analysis of Globalization tends to remain conceptually inexact, empirically thin, historically and culturally illiterate, normatively shallow and politically naïve. Although Globalization is widely assumed to be crucially important, we generally have a scant idea of what, more precisely, it entails.
>
> (Scholte, 2000)

Nevertheless, within this whirlwind of conflicting perspectives, a remarkably broad range of studies of globalization have devoted detailed attention to the problematic of space, its social production, and its historical transformation. Major strands of contemporary globalization research have been permeated by geographical concepts ("space-time compression" (Luke, 1996), "space of flows" (Amin 2002), "space of places" (Brenner, 1999), "de-territorialisation" (Scholte, 2000), "glocalization" (Robertson, 1992), the "global-local nexus" (Friedman, 1999), "supra-territoriality" (Scholte, 2005), "diasporas" (Barker, 1999) and "scapes" (Brenner, 1999) among many other terms). Meanwhile globalization researchers have begun to rely on distinctively geographical prefixes (e.g. "sub-", "supra-", "trans-", "meso-" and "inter-"), to describe a set of emergent social processes that appear to operate across increasingly entrenched geopolitical boundaries. In social sciences, the acknowledgement that social relations are becoming increasingly interconnected on a global scale raises some interesting questions over the spatial parameters of those relations as well as the geographical settings in which they occur.

The contemporary era of globalization has been represented (Brenner 1999) as the most recent historical expression of an ongoing dynamic of continual de-territorialization and re-territorialization that has underpinned the production of capitalist spatiality since the first industrial revolution of the early nineteenth century. On the one hand, capitalism is under the impulsion to eliminate all geographical barriers to the accumulation process in pursuit of cheaper raw materials, fresh sources of labour, new markets for its products, and new investment opportunities. This expansionary, de-territorializing tendency within capitalism was clearly recognized by Marx, who famously described capital's globalizing nature as a drive to "annihilate space by time" and analyzed the world market at once as its historical product and its geographical expression.

On the other hand, as David Harvey has argued, the resultant processes of "space-time compression" must be viewed as one moment within a contradictory socio-spatial dialectic that continually molds, differentiates, deconstructs, and reworks capitalism's geographical landscape (Harvey, 1991). According to Harvey, it is only through the production of relatively fixed and immobile configurations of territorial organization including urban built environments, industrial agglomerations, regional production complexes, large-scale transportation infrastructures, long-distance communications networks, and state regulatory institutions that the capital circulation process can be continually accelerated temporally and expanded spatially. Each successive round of capitalist industrialization has therefore been premised upon socially produced geographical infrastructures that enable the accelerated circulation of capital through global space. In this sense, as Harvey notes, "spatial organization is necessary to overcome space".

This theoretical insight enables Harvey to interpret the historical geography of capitalism as "a restless formation and re-formation of geographical landscapes" in which configurations of capitalist territorial organization are incessantly created, destroyed, and reconstituted as provisionally stabilized "spatial fixes'" for each successive regime of accumulation (Harvey 1991).

From this perspective, the business of space can be seen as a presupposition, medium, and outcome of capitalism's globalizing developmental dynamic. Space is not merely a physical container within which capitalist development unfolds, but one of its constitutive key dimensions, continually constructed, de-constructed, and re-constructed through a historically specific, multi-scalar dialectic of de-territorialization and re-territorialization.

Building upon this theorization, Brenner (1999) understands Globalization as a double-edged process through which: 1) the movement of commodities, capital, money, people, images, and information through geographical space is continually expanded and accelerated ("de-territorialization"); and 2) relatively fixed and immobile socio-territorial infrastructures are produced, reconfigured, re-differentiated, and transformed to enable such expanded, accelerated movement ("re-territorialization"). Globalization therefore entails a dialectical interplay between the drive towards space-time compression under capitalism (the moment of de-territorialization) and the continual production of relatively fixed, provisionally stabilized configurations of territorial organization on multiple geographical scales (the moment of re-territorialization). The business of space and its geopolitical implications represent an emblematic example of this process by which de-territorialization and re-territorialization are taking place. To this end, Figure 1.1 illustrates these processes.

Figure 1.1 Territorialization, De-territorialization and Re-territorialization in space

In this context, territorialization happens on planet earth where the geopolitical boundaries of individual countries are established; de-territorialization happens mainly through space exploration and re-territorialization takes place by individual countries establishing their presence either in orbit through the establishment of relatively fixed organizational forms (i.e. like the establishment of a space station) or on other planets.

Origins of space

Human fascination in the world beyond the Earth's atmosphere predates even the pioneering astronomers of Ancient Greece. Great Stone Age structures such as Stonehenge are believed to have fulfilled astronomical (as well as religious) functions. Indeed, ever since humans first saw birds soar through the sky, they have wanted to fly. The ancient Greeks and Romans pictured many of their gods with winged feet, and imagined mythological winged animals.

The ancient fascination with the ocean of skies is illustrated in the legend of Daedalus and Icarus in which father and son escaped prison by attaching wings made of wax to their bodies. Unfortunately, Icarus flew too near the sun, the heat caused the wax to melt and he plummeted to the sea as a punishment for excessive daring. Chinese legend tells us of the first attempt to propel a man into space made in the 14th century by the Chinese official Wan Hu. He built a spacecraft with a chair, kites and 47 gunpowder filler bamboo rockets. There was a loud explosion followed by smoke and Wan Hu was never seen again (Burrows, 1999).

Early developments

During the centuries when space travel was only a fantasy, researchers in the sciences of astronomy, chemistry, mathematics, meteorology, and physics developed an understanding of the solar system, the stellar universe, the atmosphere of the earth, and the probable environment in space. In the 7th and 6th centuries BC, the Greek philosophers Thales and Pythagoras noted that the earth is a sphere. In the 3rd century BC the astronomer Aristarchus of Samos asserted that the earth moved around the sun. Hipparchus elaborated information about stars and the motions of the moon in the 2nd century BC. In the 2nd century AD Ptolemy of Alexandria placed the earth at the center of the solar system in the Ptolemaic system.

Not until some 1,400 years later did the Polish astronomer Nicolaus Copernicus systematically explain that the planets, including the earth, revolve about the sun. However, the scientific study of rockets, planes, and satellites was inaugurated in the Modern Era by the impressive study of flight by Leonardo da Vinci, one of the most versatile geniuses of the Renaissance. His surviving notebooks contain over 35,000 words and some 150 drawings that illustrate his theories, and his sketches indicate advanced ideas regarding the parachute and helicopter, neither of which existed at the time. Later in the 16th century the observations of the Danish astronomer Tycho Brahe greatly influenced the laws of planetary motion set forth by Kepler. Galileo, Edmund Halley, Sir William Herschel, and Sir James Jeans were other astronomers who made contributions pertinent to astronautics. The scientific breakthrough in designing spacecrafts came in the 16th and 17th centuries. Physicists and mathematicians helped to lay the foundations of astronautics with Johannes Kepler (1571–1630), the German mathematician figuring out the equations for orbiting planets and satellites and Isaac Newton (1643–1727) establishing the basic laws of gravitation which confirm that planets follow Kepler's equations. In 1654 the German physicist Otto von Guericke proved that a vacuum could be maintained, refuting the old theory that nature "abhors" a vacuum. In 1696, Robert Anderson, an Englishman, published a two-part thesis on how to make rocket moulds, prepare the propellants, and perform the calculations. In the late 17th century Newton formulated the laws of universal gravitation and motion. Newton's laws of motion established the basic principles governing the propulsion and orbital motion of modern spacecraft.

The 19th century brought about advanced research. The essential equations for rocketry were devised by a Russian school teacher Konstantin Tsiolkovsky (1857–1935). Tsiolkovsky concluded that space travel was a possibility and determined that liquid oxygen and hydrogen fuel rockets would be needed and that these rockets would be built in stages. His prediction came through 65 years later when the Saturn V Rocket facilitated the first landing of men on the moon. Tsiolkovsky also stated that the speed and range of a rocket were limited by the exhaust velocity of escaping gases (NASA, 2009). In America, Robert Goddard (1882–1945) constructed the world's first liquid fuelled rocket launch in 1926. Goddard, "the American father of modern rocketry" invented rocket technology and forged the same designs that were used by Germans during World War II. After a confirmation of their military might and strategic importance during the war, it was Hermann Oberth (1894–1989) who convinced the world that the rocket industry was something to take seriously in his highly influential and internationally acclaimed book *The Rocket into Interplanetary Space*. He was the only one of the three rocketry pioneers who lived to see men travel through space and land on the moon. Indeed, Oberth and a team of scientists directed by Wernher von Braun (1912–1977) developed and launched the German V2 rocket, the first rocket capable of reaching space. At the end of World War II, von Braun settled in the US where he played a crucial role in convincing the federal government to pursue a landing of men on the moon, and guided US efforts to success (NASA, 2009).

Literature has also greatly supported human interest in outer space. Greek satirist Lucian (2nd century AD) wrote about an imaginary voyage to the moon. Lucian was followed by French satirist Voltaire (*'Micromegas' – travels of inhabitants of Sirius and Saturn*), French writer Jules Verne (*From the Earth to the Moon*), British novelist H.G. Wells (*The first man in the moon, War of the Worlds*), Sir Arthur Clarke (*A Space Odyssey*) Isaac Asimov (*Nightfall*), and many others. Despite the scientific foundations laid in earlier ages, however, space observation and travel did not become possible until the advances of the 20th century provided the actual means of rocket propulsion, guidance, and control for space vehicles. The vivid interest in outer space and rapid technological progress that took place in the 20th century turned dreams into reality. Expendable rockets provided the means for launching artificial satellites, as well as manned spacecrafts. In the middle of the 20th century, space became the new frontier of international rivalry.

Soviet Union versus United States

From the brief historical outlook presented so far, it can be seen that the efforts to develop and launch rockets or spacecraft into space were gradually evolving from a personal fascination towards more strategic attempts initiated and financed by states to serve their potential military purposes. This was the first visible shift from "territorialization" to "de-territorialization" – while before embarking on any space activity, geopolitical rivalry between states would stem from asserting national borders on planet earth ("territorialization") the advent of the space exploration took geopolitical rivalry to another level ("de-territorialization").

The interstate rivalry reached its climax during the Cold War when the two superpowers, the USSR and the US, vied against each other using their space achievements to communicate their might and prestige. The Gromov Flight Research Institute was founded in 1941 in the USSR. The National Aeronautics and Space Administration (NASA) was created on 1 October 1958, 17 years later (BBC, 2009). The goal of space exploration and the conquering of space leveraged tensions between the USSR and the US to another level. On 4 October 1957, the USSR stunned the world by launching the first artificial satellite, Sputnik 1. In the context of the Cold War, that launch catalyzed a whole series of events, ranging from the founding of NASA a year later to efforts at improving education in the US, and the space race with its host of geopolitical implications (Dick, 2007).

American president Dwight Eisenhower knew that militarizing space would only accelerate the nuclear arms race. Consequently, on 1 October 1958 he brought together research laboratories developing rocket technology and put it under civilian control (NASA, 2009). In 1958, the US initiated its first man-in space programme, the so-called "Project Mercury". Known today as the space race for control of the heavens, this battle produced some of the greatest technologies and produced outer space heroes. 1957 saw the launch of the first man made satellite, Sputnik 1 by the Soviet Union. The United States responded in 1958 with the successful launch of Explorer 1. Both of these satellites were for purely scientific purposes. The space race was undoubtedly not just a quest for knowledge and scientific facts but a manifestation of the Cold War and to demonstrate US superiority over the Soviets. In the civilian sphere it was essentially a crusade for scientific prowess, proficiency, and to explore outer space with both satellites and humans, with the ultimate aim of landing on the moon. In a military capacity it was an extension of the arms race and the art of espionage, an investigation into rocket and artillery capabilities that had undergone research by German scientists long before the war propelled it to the fore. Since the space race was an integral part of the rivalry between the Soviet Union and the US both countries allocated large resources to the space industry. With the launch of Sputnik 1, the fear that it stirred, along with the realization that America did not have technological superiority in the field, quickly led to the formation of NASA by the US in July 1958. More importantly, a great public interest had been ignited into what would soon develop into a "star wars" era (Jones, 2004).

Once these milestones had been achieved, the goal then became manned flight. The Soviet Union launched the first man into space, the cosmonaut Yuri Gagarin, on 12 April 1961. Three weeks later, the United States levelled the playing field and launched its first astronaut Alan Shepard Jr. into space. Shepard was the first to manually control his spacecraft and he gave renewed hope to Americans within the Mercury project. Fifteen days after Commander Shepard's flight succeeded, President Kennedy issued the challenge to land a man on the moon by the end of the decade. He memorably said in his speech during a special session of Congress in 1961:

> I believe this nation should commit itself to achieving the goal, before this decade is out, of landing a man on the Moon and returning him safely to Earth. No single space project in this period will be more impressive to mankind, or more important in the long-range exploration of space; and none will be so difficult or expensive to accomplish.
>
> (Project, 2009)

This passage from John Kennedy's speech launching the space race in 1961 makes clear the importance that he attached to the propaganda aspects of the US space effort (Jones, 2004). According to Fisk (2008), the transformation of American society continued with President John Kennedy's remarkable pledge in 1961 committing the US to place a man on the moon and return him safely to earth before the decade was out. Perhaps the most revealing statements of Kennedy's intentions appeared later in the speech when he said, "a Moon landing would demand sacrifice, discipline, and organization: the nation could no longer afford work stoppages, inflated costs, wasteful interagency rivalries, or high turnover of key personnel" (Project, 2009). He also stated that: "every scientist, every engineer, every technician, contractor and civil servant must give his personal pledge that this nation will move forward, with the full speed of freedom, in the exciting adventure of space" (Project, 2009).

This endeavor was named the Apollo programme. Kennedy viewed the Apollo programme as an event that would transform the nation and according to Fisk (2008) it did. At the peak of the Apollo program, NASA consumed 4% of the federal budget; some 400,000 Americans worked on Apollo, including some 20,000 American industrial firms of all sizes. From Apollo, and all the other aspects of space that developed concurrently, the US vastly improved its technical workforce, and its sense of what technology can accomplish (Fisk, 2008).

After completing the first two initial objectives of sending a satellite and later a human to outer space, the race rapidly became one to get to the moon. This was achieved by the Soviet probe Luna 9 but the first manned mission to the moon was on 21 July 1969 when Neil Armstrong became the first human to set foot on the moon's surface as part of the Apollo 11 mission. His words on stepping out onto the lunar surface have since become iconic: "that's one small step for man, one giant leap for mankind" (Project, 2009). The Soviets were the first to orbit the earth, put both an animal and human into space and to reach the moon but because they failed to walk on it, the "race" is viewed by many to have been an American victory and the Soviet Union subsequently gave up the fight. The human landings on the moon were a set of signal historical events that impacted society, but it is not clear what the impact was or how long lasting it was (Jones, 2004). Even as the landings were taking place Congress decided to terminate the programme early, as the public lost interest and funding priorities changed (Dick, 2007).

The USSR achieved a series of successful lunar orbiters starting in 1966; three lunar sample returns in 1970, 1972 and 1976; and two Lunokhod rovers in 1970 and 1973. In 1971 the Soviets launched the world's first space station, Salyut 1. The Americans followed with Skylab in 1973 but it fell to earth five years later killing a cow in Australia.

The conquest of the heavens became the primary political challenge during the Cold War period. Finally, the space race ended in 1975 with the historic Apollo-Soyuz Test Project during which an American Apollo spacecraft docked with a Soviet Soyuz spacecraft above the earth for the first time. This began a new era of cooperative space ventures. Two of the space races original heroes were present on that mission. Legendary Mercury astronaut Duke Slayton, and the first man to walk in space, Alexei Leonov, shook hands on that day symbolizing an era of cooperation and the end of outer space animosities between the two great powers up to that point. Both countries had poured huge amounts of money into their space programmes, because many of the political and public opinion battles were being fought over superiority in space. Initially, space exploration was stigmatized by nationalistic ambitions that fueled international space races. The first step in international cooperation was realized with the US/USSR Apollo Soyuz test project (1975) (which provided valuable information on the synchronization of American and Soviet space technology, which would prove useful in the future Shuttle-Mir Program).

Throughout the 1980s many events took place that contributed to the development of the space industry. In April 1981, Robert L. Crippen and John W. Young made the first mission in NASA's space shuttle programme aboard the space shuttle Columbia. On 18 June 1983, Sally Ride became the first American woman in space with the launch of shuttle mission STS-7. On 30 August 1983, Guion S. Bluford, Jr. became the first black man in space aboard the space shuttle Challenger. The journey into space has not been without its tragedies. On 28 January 1986, the Challenger space shuttle exploded 73 seconds after take off with seven crew members aboard.

In 1986 the Soviet Union launched the first module of the MIR space station. This was continuously manned by cosmonauts until it's decommissioning in 2005. The latest station is the International Space Station (ISS). This collaborative effort between NASA and RKA ("Roskosmos" The Russian Federal Agency) started in 1998 and was completed in November 2000. Since this date the station has had a rotating permanent resident crew and has hosted five space tourists. Exploration has continued since the end of the space race. For example European Space Agency's (ESA) Aurora Programme intends to send a human mission to Mars no later than 2030 and Russia has announced announcement plans to build a permanently manned moon base.

However with the end of the Cold War era, space exploration budgets in both US and Russia shrank dramatically (Jones, 2004).

From space race to the business of space

The launch of the MIR space station in February 1986 played a major role in the transformation of the space industry. This was not only a significant landmark in the processes of "de-territorialization" and "re-territorialization" but it was a transformation characterized by a shift from fierce rivalry to global collaboration as seen today in many areas such as the Galileo Positioning System project[1] along with NASA's goal to put astronauts on Mars by 2030. Figure 1.2 depicts the main events of the space industry in relation to the processes of territorialization, de-territorialization and re-territorialization described so far.

The 1990s was to be a landmark decade for collaboration in the space industry. The former rivalry between the US and the Soviet Union was replaced by cooperation. In 1991 Cosmonaut Sergei Krikalev became the first Russian to fly aboard a US space shuttle. The following year, after travelling aboard a Russian

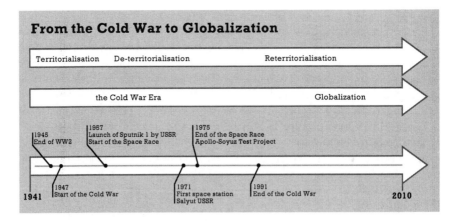

Figure 1.2 From the Cold War to globalization

Soyuz, US astronaut Norman Thagard along with Cosmonauts Vladimir Dezhurov and Gennady Strekalov spent 115 days on MIR. These events laid the foundations for future collaboration among nations, the most obvious manifestation of such collaboration occurred later in the 1990s when the first stage of the International Space Station was launched. The millennium has witnessed the continuation and expansion of the collaboration experienced throughout the previous decade. On 2 November 2000, the crew of Expedition One, astronaut Bill Shepherd and cosmonauts Yuri Gidzenko and Sergei Krikalev, docked at the International Space Station (ISS). They would be the first people to take up residence at the ISS, staying there for several months.

Global investment in satellite navigation systems has also been extensive in the 2000s. The US with the GPS system, Russia with its redevelopment of GLONASS (with the help of India), China developing Beidou and the European Space Agency with the earlier mentioned Galileo Positioning System, have all emerged as players in this sector of the industry.

Today, the space industry is still largely dominated by states. However, the United States and Russia are no longer the only "super-powers" in the industry; Europe, India, China, Japan, Brazil and Iran and other states have joined the Space Race. During the 1990s, the commercial space industry started to flourish and ties to the military lessened. Besides "super-powers" we also have "super-markets". In particular, the space market has expanded into new niche sectors: space tourism and travel, mining of resources, manufacturing opportunities, satellite technology, representing a shift towards privatization of the sphere. This new millennium is an important time in the history of space, not just for science, but also in the opportunities for business enterprise and commercialization.

States are still the major players and continue to cooperate in the field. The most prominent example of cooperation is the International Space Station (ISS). The United States, Russia, Canada, Japan and the European Space Agency (ESA) have all contributed to the station's construction. Space exploration has further strengthened the need for collaboration amongst the space players. Space exploration helps to define nations and their importance in the world. Countries that explore space are envied as cutting-edge nations possessing cultural vigour along with leading technologies. The number of countries involved in space exploration is growing steadily and we are entering a new era of historic significance, in which we will extend human presence beyond earth's orbit, both physically and culturally. Space exploration scores high on national players' agendas.

For example, with the substantial completion of the ISS in March 2011, plans for space exploration by the US remain in flux. Constellation, a programme for a return to the moon by 2020 was judged inadequately funded and unrealistic by an expert review panel reporting in 2009. The Obama Administration proposed a revision of Constellation in 2010 to focus on the development of the capability for crewed missions beyond Low Earth Orbit (LEO). This envisioned extending the operation of the ISS beyond 2020, transferring the development of launch vehicles for human crews from NASA to the private sector and developing technology to enable missions to beyond LEO. Similarly, ESA's exploration strategy in 2015 set the implementation of the Space Station programme and the Exo-Mars missions as the main focus for investments up to 2020. These programmes, together with investments in the development of lunar exploration products and the Mars Robotic Exploration Preparatory Programme (MREP), prepare for an international engagement in the space exploration endeavour for the post-2020 era, strongly leveraging on international cooperation opportunities.

In September 2010, it was announced that China is also planning to carry out explorations in deep space by sending a man to the moon by 2025. China also hopes to bring a moon rock sample back to earth in 2017, and subsequently build an observatory on the moon's surface. On 14 December 2013 China's Chang'e 3 became the first object to soft-land on the moon since Luna 24 in 1976. As indicated by the official Chinese Lunar Exploration Program insignia, denoted by a calligraphic moon ideogram (月) in the shape of a nascent lunar crescent, with two human footsteps at its center, the ultimate goal of the programme is to establish a permanent human presence on the earth's natural satellite. It was acknowledged that building a lunar base would be a crucial step to realize a flight to Mars and farther planets. However, since the whole project is only at a very early preliminary phase, no official moon programme has been announced yet by the authorities. Its existence is nonetheless revealed by regular intentional leaks in the media such as the Lunar Roving Vehicle that was shown on a Chinese TV channel during the 2008 May Day celebrations.

The Indian Space Research Organization (ISRO) also launched its Mars Orbiter Mission on 5 November 2013 which successfully entered into the orbit around Mars on 24 September 2014. India is the first in Asia and fourth in the world to perform a successful Mars mission. It is also the only one to do so on the first attempt and at a record low cost of $74 million. ISRO has so far launched 74 foreign satellites belonging to global customers gaining significant expertise in space technologies. In June 2016, India set a record by launching 20 satellites simultaneously. Recent reports indicate that human spaceflight will occur after 2017, on a GSLV-Mk III, as the mission is not included in the government's five-year plan.

However "de-territorialization" and "re-territorialization" are no longer the only drivers for the sector as private initiative is also progressively crystallizing in strength.

All the agencies mentioned previously have been government owned and operated. The past decade has seen another transformation of the space industry with the entry of private sector players. There is a shift emerging, from completely government funded projects, to privately funded projects. According to Suzuki (2007) during the 20th century, investment in space technology was at an infant stage and needed to be boosted by enthusiasm. Dreams and visions helped people support a significant amount of investment. However, 21st century space activity will be quite different from what it used to be, and must align with new social values. The social values of the 21st century are not just environmental and humanitarian, but also include efficiency of investment or, in other words, "value for money". In today's world, the financing of space is quite different from that of 1957. Private actors are beginning to invest in space and wealthy individuals are paying for their tickets to space, while national governments face severe constraints on their spending policy.

On one hand, the globalization of financial markets, the introduction of the single currency in Europe and neoliberal market-oriented policies have imposed a very narrow choice of policies on governments wanting to play with their budget. On the other hand, it is no longer necessary for a person with a dream of going to space to be a "national" astronaut; rather, s/he needs to be a millionaire. Also, private actors are investing in satellite systems through Public–Private Partnership (PPP) schemes in Europe (Brocklebank et al., 2000), and in the transportation system through the Commercial Orbital Transportation System (COTS) framework in the US (Sawamura et al. 1992). The role of state and national space agencies is adapting to this new social value of the efficiency of investment. It is not the state that looks after people's dreams but the market and private capital. Investment in space, therefore, needs to be more responsive to social needs because it needs to return benefits to taxpayers. Today, not all taxpayers appreciate the "progress" and "dream" aspects of space flight, but almost all taxpayers benefit from a better environment and safe navigation.

Thus, according to Suzuki (2007) it is imperative for everyone involved in space to recognize and understand that the name of the game has changed. Space activities need to adjust to the values of the 21st century, including "value for money". Those who are keen to go into space and believe in "progress" cannot depend on state-sponsored space activity. After all, many of the latest technologies and progressive ideas have been realized through market interactions. Space is becoming one of them.

As a result of this remarkable shift, some private enterprises have also ventured into the sector including SpaceX, Blue Origin, Virgin Galactic and Sierra Nevada. Amongst the most prominent companies is Space Exploration Technologies Corporation, better known as SpaceX, the aerospace company started by the founder of Tesla Motors Elon Musk in 2002. It designs, manufactures and launches advanced spacecraft to revolutionize space technology, with the ultimate goal of enabling people to live on other planets (SpaceX, 2016). It has been the first privately funded company to successfully launch, orbit and recover a rocket. With its reuse for future missions, this technology can greatly reduce the cost of space missions thus encouraging the development of commercial space transport services. Also, SpaceX has been the first private firm to send a spacecraft to the International Space Station. This accomplishment stemmed from a collaboration with NASA under NASA's Commercial Orbital Transportation Services (COTS) contract award and Cargo Resupply Services (CRS) contract award to coordinate the delivery of crew and cargo to the International Space Station.

Along with "supermarkets" we also have "super-individuals" as indeed, space travel is the final frontier for entrepreneurs. Until the 21st century, manned spaceflight was the preserve of government agencies and their contractors in what used to be called "the military". As the US aerospace journalist Michael

Belfiore recounts in his book, Rocketeers "a motley crew of business adventurers are investing hundreds of millions of dollars in private spacecraft" (Foust, 2003). The frontrunner amongst the private entrepreneurs was Burt Rutan, who has designed innovative aircraft since the 1960s. On 21 June 2004, his SpaceShipOne became the first privately funded craft to enter space (which starts at an altitude of 100km, according to the internationally accepted definition). Scaled Composites, Rutan's company, is building the fleet that Sir Richard Branson's commercial space venture Virgin Galactic will use to carry people into space for about five minutes at a cost of $200,000 each. It also has financial support from Microsoft (Branson, 2006). Aabar investments, the Abu Dhabi state-linked investment fund holds a 32% holding in Virgin Galactic. Many space entrepreneurs grew up at a time when it seemed reasonable for boys to assume that manned flights to the moon and beyond would be routine by the 21st century. They feel cheated by the way things turned out. Now they wish to use their wealth to make space tourism viable while they are around to enjoy it. As SpaceShipOne's creator, Burt Rutan, says private enterprise, not government funding, will conquer the final frontier. He presents his vision at cnnmoney.com in an interview given on the 24 February 2006 (CNN, 2006).

> Entrepreneurs have always driven our technical progress – and, as a result, our economy. They tend to be more innovative, more willing to take risks, and more excited about solving difficult problems. They seek break-throughs, they have the courage to fly them, and they know how to market them. They will now provide the solutions and the hardware needed to enable human spaceflight with an acceptable risk – at least as safe as the early airliners.
>
> (Rutan, 2006)

Elon Musk, Richard Branson's Virgin Galactic, Amazon CEO Jeff Bezos' Blue Origin, another space-oriented firm, all offer a fascinating glimpse of a new entrepreneurial fabric which is fostering a radically new business culture in the space sector. Entrepreneurs are thus embodying great pioneers enabling humankind to advance. Many of them are persuaded by Rutan's words. They fund prizes to stimulate research. For instance, the Orteig Prize was a $25,000 reward offered on 19 May 1919 by New York hotel owner Raymond Orteig to the first allied aviator(s) to fly non-stop from New York City to Paris or vice-versa. On offer for five years, it attracted no competitors. Orteig renewed the offer for another five years in 1924 when the state of aviation technology had advanced to the point that numerous competitors vied for the prize. In more recent times, the Ansari XPRIZE was a space competition in which the XPRIZE Foundation offered a US$10,000,000 prize for the first non-government organization to launch a reusable manned spacecraft into space twice within two weeks. It was modeled after early 20th-century aviation prizes, and aimed to spur development of low-cost spaceflight. The prize was won on 4 October 2004, the 47th anniversary of the Sputnik 1 launch, by the Tier One project designed by Burt Rutan and financed by Microsoft co-founder Paul Allen, using the experimental space plane SpaceShipOne. $10 million was awarded to the winner, but more than $100 million was invested in new technologies in pursuit of the prize. The fourth XPRIZE, the Google Lunar XPRIZE, was announced in September 2007. Google founders Sergey Brin and Larry Page are using company money to fund the fourth XPRIZE, to create a private race to the moon (Foundation, 2009). The challenge called for privately funded teams to compete in successfully launching, landing and then travelling across the surface of the moon while sending back to earth specified photo and other data. The XPRIZE would have awarded US$20 million to the first team to land a robot on the moon that successfully travelled more than 500 metres and transmits back high definition images and video. The XPRIZE offered the $20 million first-place prize until 31 December 2012, thereafter it offered $15 million until 31 December 2014. To provide an added incentive for teams to complete their missions quickly, it was announced that the prize would decrease from US$20 million to US$15 million whenever a government-led mission lands on and explores the lunar surface. The Chinese Chang'e 3 probe landed on the moon in December 2013. However, in November 2013, as the launch of the probe approached, it was agreed between the organizers and the teams to drop this rule. In 2015, XPRIZE announced that the competition deadline would be extended to December 2017 if at least one team could secure a verified launch contract by 31 December 2015. Two teams secured such a launch contract, and the deadline was extended. As of 2017 14 teams remain in the competition, with five teams, SpaceIL, Moon Express, Synergy Moon, Team Indus and Team Hakuto having secured verified launch contracts for 2017 (with SpaceX, Rocket Lab, Interorbital Systems, ISRO and ISRO respectively). The Google Lunar XPRIZE expires when all constituent purses have been claimed, or at the end of the year 2017, whichever comes first. NASA has started to award prizes under its Centennial Challenges scheme to spur technological development enabling lunar exploration. In the same vein the Northrop Grumman Lunar Lander Challenge has been running since 2006 while the Heinlein Prize, which honors the eponymous science fiction author, rewards progress in commercial space activities.

Conclusion

In this chapter we have addressed the evolution of the global space sector by outlining its most recent dynamics. We focused, in particular, on the dichotomy that exists between space and globalization. We introduced the main theoretical foundations by defining the concept of space from a globalization perspective, and the distinctive dynamics of de-territorialization and re-territorialization. We reviewed the origins of the sector from its early developments to the most recent dynamics of the business of space. Within this context, the emergence of the business of space is one of the direct consequences of globalization. The next chapter will deal with the opposite trend by which the emergence of the business of space the sector has also in turn facilitated and enabled some of the dynamics of globalization ultimately leading to the fraying of globalization.

Note

1 The Galileo Positioning System is a European project in which countries such as China, Israel, Ukraine, India, Morocco, Saudi Arabia and South Korea have all played a part.

References

Amin, A., 2002. Spatialities of globalisation. *Environment and Planning A*, 34(3), 385–400.

Barker, C., 1999. Television, globalization and cultural identities, Open University Press.

BBC, 2009. BBC – Science & Nature – Space – Exploration Timeline, available at: http://www.bbc.co.uk/science/space/exploration/missiontimeline/.

Bennett, W.L. et al., 2004. Managing the public sphere: Journalistic construction of the great globalization debate. *Journal of Communication*, 54(3), 437–455.

Branson, S.R., 2006. Screw it, Let's Do it: Lessons in Life, Virgin Books.

Brenner, N., 1999. Globalisation as reterritorialisation: the re-scaling of urban governance in the European Union. *Urban studies*, 36(3), 431.

Brocklebank, D., Spiller, J. & Tapsell, T., 2000. Institutional Aspects of a Global Navigation Satellite System. *The Journal of Navigation*, 53(02), 261–271.

Burrows, W.E. 1999. The Blue Ocean, Penguin Randomhouse.

Castles, S. & Davidson, A., 2000. Citizenship and migration: globalization and the politics of belonging, Routledge.

Cerny, P.G., 1995. Globalization and other stories: the search for a new paradigm for international relations. *International Journal*, 51(4), 617–637.

CNNMoney.com, 2009. Business, financial, personal finance news, CNNMoney.com, available at: http://money.cnn.com/.

Dick, S.J., 2007. Assessing the impact of space on society. *Space Policy*, 23(1), 29–32.

Ferguson, M. 2007. The mythology about globalization. In D. McQuail, P. Golding, & E. de Bens (Eds), Communication theory and research. Sage.

Fisk, L.A., 2008. The impact of space on society: Past, present and future. *Space Policy*, 24(4), 175–180.

Florida, R., 1996. Regional creative destruction: production organization, globalization, and the economic transformation of the Midwest. *Economic Geography*, 72(3), 314–334.

Foust, J., 2007. Review: Rocketeers by Michael Belfiore. *The New Scientist*, 195(2617), 45.

Friedman, T.L., 1999. The Lexus and the Olive Tree: Understanding Globalization, Farrar, Straus and Giroux.

Friedman, T.L., 2005. The World Is Flat: A Brief History of the Twenty-first Century 1° ed., Farrar, Straus and Giroux.

Glisby, M. & Holden, N., 2005. Applying knowledge management concepts to the supply chain: How a Danish firm achieved a remarkable breakthrough in Japan. *The Academy of Management Executive*, 19(2), 85–89.

Goodhart, M., 2001. Democracy, Globalization, and the Problem of the State. *Polity*, 33(4), 527–546.

Hannerz, U. & Featherstone, M., 1990. Global culture: nationalism, globalization and modernity, (Vol. 2). Sage.

Harvey, D., 1991. The Condition of Postmodernity. Blackwell.

Jones, R.A., 2004. They came in peace for all mankind: popular culture as a reflection of public attitudes to space. *Space Policy*, 20(1), 45–48.

Kobrin, S.J., 1997. The architecture of globalization: State sovereignty in a networked global economy. *Governments, globalization, and international business*. In J.H. Dunning (Ed.), Governments, Globalization and International Business, Oxford University Press, London.

NASA, 2009. U.S. Human Spaceflight History, available at: http://www.jsc.nasa.gov/history/hsf_history.htm.

Project, K., 2009. Kennedy 2 Lunar Exploration Project – K2LX, available at: http://www.kennedyproject.com/.

Robertson, P.R., 1992. Globalization: Social Theory and Global Culture, Sage Publications Ltd.

Sawamura, B. et al., 1992. Future manned systems advanced avionics study COTS for space. In IEEE/AIAA 11th Digital Avionics Systems Conference, 1992. Proceedings, 514–522.

Scholte, J.A., 2000. Globalization: a critical introduction, Palgrave Macmillan.

Scholte, J.A., 2005. Premature obituaries: a response to Justin Rosenberg. *International Politics*, 42(3), 390–399.

SpaceX 2016. Company profile, available at http://www.spacex.com/about.

Storper, M., 1995. The resurgence of regional economies, ten years later: the region as a nexus of untraded interdependencies. *European Urban and Regional Studies*, 2(3), 191.

Suzuki, K., 2007. Space and modernity: 50 years on. *Space Policy*, 23(3), 144–146.

Van Rooy, A., 2004. The global legitimacy game: civil society, globalization, and protest, Palgrave Macmillan.

2 Globalization and the pivotal role of the space industry

Introduction

In the opening chapter we have seen how the business of space itself has directly stemmed from globalization. In contrast in the first section of this chapter, we demonstrate that it has also facilitated and enabled some of the dynamics of globalization. We describe in the second section the fraying of globalization and its implications for the space sector while in the final section we offer some conclusions.

The pivotal role of the space industry in fostering globalization

A kind of global consciousness has emerged as a result of rapid transportation from one continent to another and of the growing capabilities enabled by information and communications technology. In what has been characterized as the "fifth phase of Globalization", which began several decades ago and continues today, global consciousness has increased, aided by space exploration (Robertson, 1992).

Globalization has been aided by the space industry since the industry's inception. Groundbreaking technological developments that have arisen out of the industry such as satellite based commodities have revolutionized weather prediction, television entertainment and navigational devices. Space has certainly been an influencing factor in "bringing the global local" (Castells, 1996). However, this relationship is not mutually exclusive. Without globalization it would not have been possible for the space industry to take off, so to speak. This is evident by looking at some of the fundamental driving forces behind the phenomenal process that is globalization. These are namely the increased expansion and technological improvements in transportation and communications networks; the liberalization of cross-border trade and resource movements; the development of services that support international business activities; the growing global consumer demand for products (space tourism, satellite television, GPS etc.); the increased global competition and collaboration; the changing political and economic situations.

Without the influence of the above forces, the space industry may not have evolved let alone reached the level of success attained today. Each of these driving forces is necessary to maintain the industry and also aid in the growth and expansion of the space industry. This symbiotic relationship also exists between globalization and the world of international business. The world has been suggested as "flat" in the sense that globalization has levelled the competitive playing fields between the developed and emerging countries (Friedman, 2005). The cross boundary connections between suppliers and markets for which globalization is renowned would not happen without international business and vice versa. Space, like international business survives on the fruits of globalization and to be without, would render global competition obsolete. This similarity is a crucial factor in determining whether space is the new frontier of international competition.

The importance of the space industry for the current process of globalization has been emphasized by Dudley-Flores and Gangale (2007). By taking an "astro-sociological approach" the authors claim that as an instrument of the Cold War, the satellite aided the end of it by speeding up the process of globalization across several broad categories of interactive phenomena: information technology, ecological effects, social movements and organizations, concern for equal rights, global recognition, the quest for breakthrough ideas and economic growth. These drivers were previously identified as the key patterns of interaction driving the globalization process (Peterson, 1972). But what does this mean for space today? Are we no longer interested in space? Have space activities lost their function as the symbol of statecraft and the glory of technological advancement? According to Suzuki (2007), to some extent, this is the case. Space activities can no longer be sustainable if we use them only for national prestige and as a marker of "progress". Some countries, such as China, South Korea and many developing nations, still cleave to the notion of progress and national prestige, just as many industrialized countries did in 1957. These so called 'late comers' are initiating their space programmes as the "old comers" did during the 1950s and 1960s. But for the "old comers" space activities need more justification than progress and national prestige. Space needs to serve society and its values. The social value of space lies in its ability to solve the dire problems of society and to help provide the infrastructure for the solutions. Thus, environmental monitoring, disaster management, support for navigation, long-distance communication and enhancing security have become prioritized objectives for space activities. "Progress" is not just the progress of technology but also the progress of humanity. In other words, according to Suzuki (2007) space is no longer an end in itself, but a tool to achieve social objectives.

This is the rationale for the space activities of the 21st century. During the 20th century, we invested in space technology because it was at an infant stage and it needed to be boosted by enthusiasm. Dreams and visions helped people support a significant amount of investment. However, 21st-century space activity must be quite different from what it used to be, and must align with the new social values.

According to Suzuki (2007) we must also be aware that the social values of the 21st century are not just environmental and humanitarian, but also include efficiency of investment or, in other words, "value for money". In today's world, the financing of space activity is quite different from that of 1957. Private actors are beginning to replace the traditional roles of states and national space agencies. As a result, space is adapting to these new social values of the efficiency of investment. It is not the state that looks after people's dreams but the market and private capital. Investment in space, therefore, needs to be more responsive to social needs because it needs to return benefits to taxpayers. Today, not all taxpayers appreciate the "progress" and "dream" aspects of space flight, but almost all taxpayers benefit from a better environment and safe navigation. Thus, it is imperative that space activities adjust to the values of the 21st century, including "value for money". Those who are keen to go into space and believe in "progress" cannot depend on state-sponsored space activity. After all, many of the latest technologies and progressive ideas have been realized through market interactions. Space is becoming one of them.

Information technology

The computer has been also heralded as the landmark invention of the advanced industrial way of life (Peterson, 1972). But, it is the satellite and all that it could do in earth's orbit that provided much impetus behind computer technology. Computers were necessary to the guidance of the rockets that were the satellites' delivery systems; they were needed to track satellites and they were needed to process the large amounts of data that came from them. The computer and the satellite are the heart and soul of Information Technology (IT). According to Dudley-Flores and Gangale (2007), amongst the factors that drive the globalization process, IT is the most seminal because it increases the frequency of human interactions at an exponential rate. The speed of social change is itself partly a function of the speed and ease of these interactions. Rapid exchange and processing of information contribute to the global erosion of the existing hierarchical structures. Hierarchical structures are the hallmark of tribalism, nationalistic movements, entrenched governmental bureaucracies and most corporations (Castells, 1996). As a result, this will lead to the kind of chaos that physicists and mathematicians refer to as the mathematical chaos that underpins a reordering of a system. In the end, the process of globalization itself ended the Cold War. The "winners" were those societies that had a more open stance toward globalization. The old fear of Mutually Assured Destruction that characterized the Cold War has given way to the uncertainty of the re-negotiation period. Non-state actors want to participate in the renegotiations. They are not a new historical phenomenon. Information technology and all the other things that drive the globalization process are breeding the new social forms that will make up the re-negotiating of global civil order. According to Dudley-Flores & Gangale (2007), this world order in the decades and centuries to come, will find itself inevitably extending off the planet.

Ecological effects

We are still in modern times. We are no longer in pursuit of progress and dreams of a high-tech, science fiction life, but we still use space technology to solve problems on earth and improve our quality of life within limited financial resources. According to Suzuki (2007), the modernity we are living in now is different from the modernity of 1957. Nevertheless, we must not forget that this new modernity (or "high modernity") was only made possible by those who contributed to the translation of the "dream" technology into reality. Without these achievements, we would not be able to enjoy our present quality of life and appreciate the importance of the environment.

Onoda (2008) describes how the development of remote sensing technology for instance was greatly spurred by wartime needs and the international settings of the Cold War, and thus historically it is associated with concerns over national security and sovereignty. Nevertheless, the technology also allowed humans to view the entire earth, and has enabled global data gathering for environmental policy making.

Similarly, Dudley-Flores & Gangale (2007) note that there is an historic trail to collaboration amongst countries, extending to increasingly longer duration space missions. Mastering long-duration space exploration is a prerequisite to human permanency in space, which is nothing short of the expansion of the human ecology off the earth. Yet, on the verge of longer duration missions, as in a manned mission to Mars by the United States, conceptualized for the 1980s, events of American history intervened – namely at the end of the 1960s in the form of the decisions of the Nixon administration to cut space funding. In the meantime, the potential for global manmade destruction in the form of nuclear madness has been replaced with the decline side of oil, global warming and large-scale natural disasters in ever-increasing populated areas. Once again, humanity wonders if it will survive. The things that matter most now are the answers to these questions: how do we power this world system of increasingly advanced industrial societies without petroleum? How do we mitigate, adjust to, or solve for rising sea levels and other direct and indirect effects of global warming? How do we mitigate natural disasters that occur in parts of the world becoming ever more populated?

How does "globalized space" help answer those questions? According to Dudley-Flores & Gangale (2007), this is the significance of the inquiry into the globalization of space. If space exploration can play a large role in the answers to these questions, it will be able to get out of first gear and lead to the expansion of the human ecology on this world and in places off the earth.

Social movements and organizations

Whether we are speaking of more established social movements and organizations or emerging ones, none of these would be able to meet their goals today without information and communications technologies developed by the space industry. High-tech industries have spurred trends in networking and cooperative organization. A "spin-off" of the environmental movement is an understanding of how ecosystems are organized and these are turned to for models for the human ecology. Dudley-Flores & Gangale (2007) speak of the "organic" growth of non-state actor organizations. And, as most commentators on globalization have remarked (Castells, 1996; Vallaster, 2005), much about the social formations of our modern world is characterized by "network" structures diffused from both the biological world and the worlds of broadcasting and the World Wide Web.

It is possible to argue that the power-shift from the nation-states towards regional/global political or economic institutions and the lack of or weak democratic control over these "higher" levels of governance, has prompted civil society organizations – and more specifically social movement organizations – to organize themselves beyond the nation-states in order to critically question the legitimacy and policies of international economic and political actors (Cammaerts, 2005). According to Cammaerts (2005), transnational civil organizations allow citizens to link up with a community of interest and action beyond their own nation-state. As such, transnational civil society could be perceived as resulting from "globalization from below", an attempt to counterbalance the globalizing economic, political and cultural spheres that increasingly escape the sovereignty of the nation-states. It is within this complex political context that the use of ICTs by transnational social movements should be situated. Cammaerts' study (2005) of the different usages of interactive communication technologies by social movements has identified three main categories of use. Firstly, social movements use ICTs to organize themselves and to interact with their members, sympathizers and core staff. Secondly, use relates to mobilization when ICTs are used to lobby within formal politics or to foster social change through online as well as offline direct actions. Thirdly, there is the potential of strengthening the public sphere through the mediation of political debate. Here the Internet is considered by many scholars as a potential means to extend the working of transnational social movements geographically, to organize internationally, to build global or regional coalitions with like-minded organizations, to mobilize beyond their own constituencies, to spread information on a global scale independently and thereby support the development of global or transnational public spheres.

Concern for equal rights

The number of issues requiring global solutions has also increased and became more prominent on the political agendas of citizens, civil society organizations and (some) governments. Examples of such issues are namely child labour, ecology, security, mobility, migration and human rights. With communication that permeates national boundaries, there is awareness among people throughout the world of each other's living conditions. While globetrotting journalists and early radio and television did plenty toward this end, satellite broadcasting and the Internet have brought a hard reality, a sense of urgency and a next-door-neighbourliness that Marshall McLuhan called in the sixties "the global village" (McLuhan & Powers, 1992). According to Dudley-Flores & Gangale (2007) the global village has never been so real as it is now. The atrocities of those nationalities that battled in the Balkans were like atrocities against your own neighbours. This breeds a concern for equal rights that does not require the nicety of abstract thought to comprehend. It comes from a concrete level of seeing something as it happens with one's own eyes.

Global recognition

Global recognition was once reserved for nation-states and rare others. It is now being extended to the individual. According to Dudley-Flores & Gangale (2007), while modern communication and transportation have made available the teachings and technologies of the world's cultures to nearly everyone, customers not only will shop and compare, but most importantly they will compare notes. It is a mathematical inevitability that deeper global understanding in all its many facets will emerge. The quest for breakthrough ideas is not in danger of being abandoned and individuals, corporations and nation-states will be empowered as a result (Friedman, 2005).

According to Cammaerts (2005), this change reflects the shifting notion of citizenship. The citizenship notion has also evolved considerably since the Greek city-states or the formation and consolidation of the Westphalian nation-states. Although citizenship is theoretically, but also empirically, still very much linked to and conceptualized within the "boundaries" of the modernist nation-state, the increased globalization of the world economy and revolutionary innovations in communication, transport and mobility; ecological and demographic pressures; as well as ethnic and nationalistic forces have considerably undermined the sovereignty and legitimacy of that nation-state, the core of the bounded notions of citizenship. These social, economic and political transformations would suggest it is fair to conceive of citizenship as more complex and diverse than a classic understanding linked to rights and nationality. In political theory, this is exemplified by the emergence of several concepts of citizenship that could be called unbounded and go beyond the nation-state. Examples of these are: ecological citizenship, net.citizenship, transnational citizenship, cosmopolitan citizenship or denationalized citizenship.

The quest for breakthrough ideas

According to Dudley-Flores & Gangale (2007), the infrastructure that has spread from the satellite and the computer is "the Gutenberg Press of our time". And, it was all made possible by the human exploration of space that results in its allure becoming more glorified and more embedded into popular culture through its use. An emblematic example of this is the recent initiative promoted by the Canadian astronaut Chris Hadfield who radically changed the way people in space communicated with the public in a series of viral tweets, Facebook posts and videos when he was aboard the International Space Station in 2013. What made the astronaut's tweets and videos so compelling is that they looked at space from the average person's perspective – those videos of Hadfield brushing his teeth, going to sleep and cutting his hair generated massive interest as these are things that everyone can understand and can relate to across the world, not just in Canada. After numerous Twitter and Facebook posts, the capper was a video of Chris performing David Bowie's Space Oddity in near-zero gravity. The song turned out to be a viral hit, garnering millions of views on YouTube. The very same technology that spun off from the sector is now serving to broaden its popular appreciation and legitimacy. Moreover, the same technology can be credited for recording the steps of our modern civilization.

According to an article on the future of our civilization, Shapiro (2009) claims that a process is well underway in which the scientific, technical and cultural information vital to our society is stored in digital form within a limited number of computer facilities. This practice is vulnerable to a variety of catastrophes that would destroy our knowledge base in addition to the losses they caused to population and structures. Shapiro (2009) believes however that the construction of a substantial lunar base as part of a programme to ensure the survival of human civilization on earth is a goal that would link and justify two main purposes. Firstly, he sees the need to preserve our cultural heritage. The past decades have seen such an explosion in the production of scientific data and cultural material that by necessity are being stored in digital form. Older materials are also being converted to digital form, allowing much of humanity access to a treasure of science and art that can readily be explored and utilized in innovative ways. However, this new storage medium is more fragile than paper, both because of its inherent nature and of its greater vulnerability to local disasters and global catastrophes. If our cultural heritage were substantially damaged or lost, our civilization could not function and humanity would be reduced to a barbaric state. A measure of protection could be using the moon for the purpose of preserving the scientific and cultural documents and objects that support our civilization. Secondly, the construction of a substantial lunar base as part of a programme to ensure the survival of human civilization on earth would also provide a transcendent purpose. A generation ago human beings walked on the Moon. The Apollo programme may have resulted as a by-product of competition between nations in the Cold War, but it produced media coverage and images that were inspirational. However, no further purpose emerged from that presence to stimulate the imagination of the public, and no further human expeditions beyond earth's orbit have been launched since that time. Several years ago President George Bush announced the Vision for Space Exploration, which involved a return of humans to the moon. More recently however, President Obama has revamped this vision to exclude the return of humans to the moon. Some emerging economies have also indicated an interest in lunar exploration. But the reasons provided have not really justified the expenses involved. In the absence of a transcendent purpose, the prospects for human expansion into space remain uncertain. Shapiro believes that a unique opportunity has arisen to link two worthy causes that have emerged (i.e. the need to preserve our cultural heritage and to plan a strategy for the survival of the human race) in the recent past; each of which might flounder if allowed to proceed separately.

According to Dudley-Flores & Gangale (2007), another breakthrough idea coming from the space industry is nanotechnology. It could, virtually overnight, change technology as we know it. Nanotechnology techniques can construct materials and alter the structure of matter at a molecular level. Nanotechnology is the logical extension of the miniaturization effort that began in the early days of space exploration.

Extra-globalization and the creation of a solar system economy

What about economic growth and the global economy as we know it in the present? This is usually the phenomenon that most people associate with globalization. It emerges from of all these categories of interactive phenomena. Only an interdependent global economy could provide the capital mass or the financial avenues to bankroll the application of breakthrough ideas, truly effective global organizations, the enhancement of each individual, the assessment of the environmental degradation and climatic shift of a whole planet and repair it and the extension of human ecology to other venues (Dudley-Flores & Gangale, 2007).

When pockets of people begin living sustainably off the earth, an extra-globalization process begins to occur. If globalization implies the increasing interconnectedness of earthly societies while also influencing space endeavors, then extra-globalization is the extension of these intertwined phenomena to those sustaining themselves indefinitely off the earth and the dialectic set up among them and the earth.

Let us look forward to a distant time when low transportation costs make the extraction of primary resources from celestial bodies economically feasible. In the past, colonization led to exploitative relationships, in which colonial powers took advantage of cheap, unskilled labour in the colonies to extract raw materials. These residual trade relationships have persisted into the 21st century. Wallerstein (1980) refers to the industrial core of the capitalist world-system, the semi-periphery of lesser-industrialized states and the underdeveloped periphery. However, space settlements will be high-tech by their very nature, and will be populated by highly educated, highly skilled workforces. Thus, once settlements are able to provide for their own subsistence, they will be able to turn to high value-added productive activities, many of which will be competitive with terrestrial products elsewhere in the solar system due to gravitational advantage (Dudley-Flores & Gangale, 2007).

Should settlements develop on the moon and Mars and even elsewhere, the most credible use of celestial resources is for either local use or for use elsewhere

Table 2.1 Characterizing globalization and the business of space

Friedman's arguments characterizing Globalization	The Business of Space
Collaboration	1975: the Apollo-Soyuz Test Project saw the collaboration of the US and the USSR
	1986: the MIR Space Station hosted astronauts of several nationality
	1998: the ISS saw the collaboration of US, Russia, Canada and Japan
Many Superpowers	Originally: USA vs. USSR
	Today: Europe, India, China, Japan, Iran, Brazil and Canada
Supermarkets	Space tourism and travel
	Mining of Resources
	Manufacturing opportunities
	Satellite technology
Super-empowered individuals	2004: Rutan
	Ansari Prizes

in space. In the absence of commercial revenue from direct trade with earth, interplanetary trade not involving earth directly would necessarily involve government contracts to private companies to provide goods and services to government-owned operations. Earth is the source of investment capital for outer space, and the accumulation of hard currency in outer space will require the creation and exchange of something that is of value to earth. It is such productive activities that must form the basis of a largely commercial, non-governmental, solar system economy.

As commercial interplanetary trade develops, interesting avenues of speculation arise. Adam Smith (1776) explained how two countries could profit in trading with each other by using their absolute advantages over each other in producing different commodities. In particular if all the planets could specialize in producing the commodity in which they enjoy absolute advantage, all planets would profit from trade. Each is buying a cheaper commodity from the other than it could produce. Productivity would increase on all the planets.

Drawing on our discussion from Chapter 1, Table 2.1 summarizes Friedman's arguments characterizing globalization and the main changes that took place throughout the evolution of the business of space.

The fraying of globalization

As globalization and the space industry are so closely intertwined, their fate is often tightly coupled. In particular, some trends characterizing the reversal of globalization are also noticeable in the space industry.

As the space sector has become more globalized, the risks inherent in glo-balization are also of concern for this sector. Goldin and Mariathasan's theory of the "Butterfly Defect" (2014) is not only applicable to globalization but also to the global space sector. With the growing integration of more nations and subsectors the overall system becomes more complex and as the result the actions of certain actors can initiate major shocks to the entire system. There is therefore a high level of systemic risk (Goldin & Mariathasan, 2014). The risks can develop unseen until their effects are manifest. According to Goldin and Mariathasan (2014), the increased number of connections within and between the various sectors and the increasing significance of individual nodes in these systems can lead to the propagation and amplification of effects. Such charac-teristics are not only found in the global economy but can also be applied to the global space sector.

Another threat according to Lal (2015) is to the hitherto major space nations like the US who face a loss of power due to the development of emerging space nations as major space players. This also increases rivalry between the different countries and makes it harder for non-wealthy countries to keep up with other nations in the global competitive market. For example despite the significant degree of international collaboration that has obtained in the space sector, there are tensions between the US and Russia that extend to space related matters with the quest by the US to free itself from dependency on Russian manufactured engines for some of its space launches. Likewise there is a remarkable lack of col-laboration between the US and China with the US refusing to allow the transfer of space technology or any sort of cooperation to take place. Nonetheless, the ESA continues its space related cooperation with China.

The stance of over 150 UN member states is another threat to commercial-ization prospects in space. Despite their usage of developed nations' technol-ogy and institutions, non-spacefaring nations stand against national and private appropriation and militarization of space. These nations advocate for the semi-appropriation or de facto appropriation theory, where space is free from owner-ship and open to all as commonly-held property. Outer space currently remains close to earth, ripe for development and exploitation by commercial interests. Therefore, some have suggested the creation of an international, non-partisan space committee defined by the Space Preservation Treaty as an overseer or otherwise policing force of proper space conduct, which would could inhibit exploitation of space resources. Further complications arise with current laws in place, though the language of many of these laws does not explicitly deny the prospects of private corporates. The Outer Space Treaty of 1967 states that celestial objects are not subject to national appropriation, but also has found that technology aiding military reconnaissance complies with space law so long as military actions constitute peaceful activity. Additionally, the definition of appropriation has hit a wall because the limits of outer space have yet to be defined since the issue first arose in 1958 despite the work of the Committee on the Peaceful Uses of Outer Space to address this issue. Finally, this law and many other laws on space do address and restrict the appropriation of space by national governments, but private corporations and institutions with an interest in commercializing space are not taken into account. No corpus of law exists regarding the entrance of private interests in outer space, and the Outer Space Treaty makes no mention of said intended commercialization. The rapid development of space technology is of a nature outside of the provisions laid out in the Outer Space Treaty. With the lack of action so far, the knowledge that machinery has already been placed by corporations on the International Space Station to extract materials weighs upon the non-spacefaring countries of the world, for it seems that steps are already being taken to secure the interests of particular corporations that are affiliated with developed governments. The potential issues that would arise regarding property ownership of the extracted materials or of new research have not materialized to date and have failed to stir up animosity among developed nations, private corporates and non-spacefaring nations, though the issue may become more pronounced if these acts became widespread.

The legal and regulatory framework determines the rules according to which space actors operate. During the 1960s and 1970s, a set of international treaties and principles was enacted establishing the peaceful uses and non-appropriation of outer space. Based on this regime, governments are liable under international space law whenever a space object is launched from their territory, even if it is by a private entity. This international regime is therefore complemented by national space laws, to mitigate the risks for governments involved in space activities with an appropriate national licensing structure that regulates institutional and private space activities taking place on their soil. Since the 1980s, the rapid progression of commercial space activities that followed the privatization of international telecommunications organizations, such as Intelsat and Eutelsat, has spurred the swift development of national laws and regulations worldwide. A diversity of governments are developing space laws, not only long-established space-faring nations, but also countries with limited space activities wishing to either attract new investments from abroad, or to cater to the needs of their own fledging space industry (e.g. supporting development of small satellite missions). The enactment of a national legal and regulatory regime for space activities can be an important component when trying to develop a competitive space industry. The most important piece of legislation that has been issued so far is probably the Space Act of 2015 approved by the United States, which includes a range of legislative changes intended to boost the US space industry. The most significant part are measures allowing US citizens to engage in the commercial exploration and exploitation of "space resources", with examples including includes water and minerals. The right to exploit resources covers anything in space that is not alive — so if a commercial exploration team discovers microbial life, they cannot exploit it for profit. For the purposes of this bill a "citizen of the United States" is defined as "(A) an individual who is a citizen of the United States", "(B) an entity organized or existing under the laws of the United States or a State" or "an entity organized or existing under the laws of a foreign country if the controlling interest (as defined by the Secretary of Transportation) is held by an individual or entity described in subclause (A) or (B) of this clause". That means not only individuals but also corporations, including those that are not wholly US owned, qualify as US citizens for the purpose of mineral exploitation in space. For example, Richard Branson is a British citizen, but he is also an investor in Planetary Resources, a self-described "asteroid mining company" that has been heavily involved in lobbying in favour of the Space Act. As a result, he is likely to be one of the first British people to profit from US commercial asteroid mining. Although opening space up to commercial resource exploitation could fuel technological development in a new space race, the Space Act 2015 is very controversial. The United States, like Britain, France and Russia, is a signatory of the 1967 Outer Space Treaty, which reads: "Outer space, including the moon and other celestial bodies, is not subject to national appropriation by claim of sovereignty, by means of use or occupation, or by any other means." Handing out the right to exploit space to your citizens sounds very much like a claim of sovereignty, despite the Space Act's direct statement that "the United States does not thereby assert sovereignty or sovereign or exclusive rights or jurisdiction over, or the ownership of, any celestial body."

In addition, it will become more and more difficult for governments to supervise and manage the use of space with more satellites being launched from many different facilities across different countries and without any general regulations for the usage and behaviour in space. At the moment there are no mandatory guidelines (Lal, 2015). Not only does the higher number of satellites threatens space and its economy but also the fact that "hundreds of thousands of objects bigger than 1 cm and several million objects smaller than this" (Lal, 2015) will be in space too. This not only poses the question of how to deal with the debris and its cost but also the loss of electromagnetic spectrums and its effects on rapid data transmission. An additional problem is caused by the pollution due to the increased number of launches (Lal, 2015).

Another issue is represented by the militarization of the sector. Today, the countries which own a military programme are the following: France (Helios 1B and Helios 2A), United Kingdom (Skynet), Italy (Cosmo and Skymed), China (Fanhui Shi Weixing), India (Risat 1 and Risat 2), Israel (Ofek) and Japan. Over 50% of the global space budget is devoted to the military area, of which 90% was accounted for by the US in 2010. While the European space budget is around USD 1 billion, the budget for the US is USD 25 billion. In fact, the treaty, ratified in 1967 by the US, the USSR, the United Kingdom and France, forbids the launch of any kind of arming in the orbit of the earth and in space. However, since this is not respected at all, if the arming in space keeps increasing without any form of control and regulation, one could consider that it would represent an important threat for the space sector from a safety point of view. Furthermore, the arming of the space sector is not the only phenomenon that could represent a potential threat for the sector. The recent appearance of new competitors within the sector is also potentially worrying from a global point of view, due to the politic instability and the lack of transparency of those nations such as China, North Korea and Iran.

Regarding the military debate, the exact definition of "peaceful activity" as deemed safe or acceptable by the treaty has also yet to be defined. With the current language of the treaty, essentially the military could do most things except for placing nuclear weapons into orbit or on celestial bodies. Unfortunately for countries without major militaries, the boundary of outer space, like everything else, has also failed to be clearly defined with respect to distance from earth's surface or atmosphere, so under the current law intercontinental missiles are legal depending on the size of the orbit. Finally, more recent advancements in warfare such as laser weaponry are also not addressed in any treaties and consequently could legally be employed by a military force in outer space without breaking international law. Again, the threats posed to the sector depends on the agent – national or private – but current treaties insufficiently address or account for developments in technology. Therefore, discomfort with the vagueness of laws or policing efforts could spur greater backlash.

Conclusion

In the opening chapter we addressed the evolution of the global space sector by outlining its most recent dynamics. We focused, in particular, on the dichotomy that exists between space and globalization. We introduced the main theoretical foundations by defining the concept of space from a globalization perspective, and the distinctive dynamics of de-territorialization and re-territorialization. We reviewed the origins of the sector from its early developments to the most recent dynamics of the business of space. Within this context, the emergence of the business of space is one of the direct consequences of globalization.

In this chapter we focused on the opposite trend by which the emergence of the space sector has also in turn facilitated and enabled some of the dynamics of globalization ultimately leading to the fraying of globalization. In the light of the evidence that we have provided in the chapter, the relationship between the space sector and globalization emerges as a very complex one – while the discovery and the use and the exploitation of the sector appear as a direct consequence of globalization, the space sector has also enabled globalization and has been significantly affected by it as the recent fraying of globalization seems to indicate. In sum the relationship between globalization and the business of space appears as a two-way process – on the one hand, the business of space stems as a direct result from globalization; on the other hand, the industry plays a pivotal role in shaping the recent dynamics affecting globalization.

References

Cammaerts, B., 2005. ICT-usage among transnational social movements in the networked society – to organise, to mobilise and to debate. Available at http://eprints.lse.ac.uk/3278/

Castells, M., 1996. The Rise of the Network Society, Blackwell Publishers Inc.

Dudley-Flores, M. & Gangale, T., 2007. The globalization of space – the astrosociological approach. AIAA Space 2007 Meeting Papers on Disc, AIAA-2007-6076, Reston, Virginia.

Friedman, T.L., 2005. The World Is Flat: A Brief History of the Twenty-first Century 1° ed., Farrar, Straus and Giroux.

Goldin, I., & Mariathasan, M. 2014. The butterfly defect: How globalization creates systemic risks, and what to do about it. Princeton University Press.

Lal, R. 2015. The nexus approach in managing water, soil and waste under changing climate and growing demands on natural resources. In M. Kurian and R. Ardakanian (Eds) Governing the Nexus: Water, Soil, Waste Change, 39–61. Dordrecht, Holland: Springer.

McLuhan, M. & Powers, B.R., 1992. The Global Village: Transformations in World Life and Media in the 21st Century, Communication and Society, Oxford University Press, USA.

Onoda, M., 2008. Satellite observation of greenhouse gases: Monitoring the climate change regime. *Space Policy*, 24(4), 190–198.

Peterson, R.B., 1972. A Cross-Cultural Perspective of Supervisory Values: Reply. *Academy of Management Journal*, 15(3), 369–370.

Robertson, P.R., 1992. Globalization: Social Theory and Global Culture, Sage Publications Ltd.

Shapiro, R., 2009. A new rationale for returning to the Moon? Protecting civilization with a sanctuary. *Space Policy*, 25(1), 1–5.

Smith, A., 1776. An inquiry into the nature and causes of the wealth of nations. London: George Routledge and Sons.

Suzuki, K., 2007. Space and modernity: 50 years on. *Space Policy*, 23(3), 144–146.

Vallaster, C., 2005. Cultural Diversity and Its Impact on Social Interactive Processes: Implications from an Empirical Study. *International Journal of Cross Cultural Management*, 5(2), 139.

Wallerstein, I., 1980. The Modern World-System I: Capitalist Agriculture and the Origins of the European World-Economy in the Sixteenth Century, Academic Press.

3 Industry analysis I

The upstream segment

Introduction

We have so far described the evolution of space related activities from the Cold War era to the globalization era. Much of 20th century space activities were dominated by Cold War considerations. Space activities reflected the superpower rivalries and represented one more source of competition between the US and the Soviet Union. The globalization era has been reflected in the evolution of space related activities. Competition in space has been increasingly accompanied by cooperation reflecting the collaborative imperative of globalization. Just as previously state controlled activities in many spheres have been privatized, so have space related activities entered the private realm. Increasingly space related activities have become the business of space as entrepreneurs and other private entities not only undertake activities previously undertaken by governments and its agencies, but also start to venture into previously unexplored and unexploited opportunities in space. These developments are consistent with the dialectic of de- territorialization and re-territorialization. More obviously, the establishment of permanently manned space stations in outer space and the vision of establishing lunar and Martian colonies are also consistent with the dialectic of de-territorialization and re-territorialization. As space activities continue their evolution from Space Race to the business of space, the globalization perspective provides us with a useful means of framing this evolution and with an enhanced understanding of the dynamics of the business of space.

Industry definition

Once we have defined the evolution of the sector within the context of globalization, we were then presented with the task of having to define the space industry. It became apparent that many articles and experts who analyze the "space industry" do not in fact manage to define the industry. The term is used so widely, and so loosely, that one wonders if the term has any real meaning. "The usual problem with the phrase 'space industry' is that it is too inclusive: it encompasses any number of companies for whom space may not necessarily be at the core of their business, in an effort to make the industry look as large, and thus as prominent, as possible" (Foust, 2003).

During our research, an investigation into what the space industry entails uncovered the reasoning behind this inclusiveness. Many of the support activities that would be involved in an aspect of the "space industry", such as wireless communication, allow for industry analysts to show greater benefits and rewards from the industry as a whole. As we all know every industry has a collection of organizations, each serving the needs of particular groups or market niches. Wireless communications can therefore be placed in an outright industry of its own.

In broad terms, the OECD Global Forum on Space Economics defines the space economy as all public and private actors involved in developing and providing space-enabled products and services. It comprises a long value-added chain, starting with research and development actors and manufacturers of space hardware (e.g. launch vehicles, satellites, ground stations) and ending with the providers of space-enabled products (e.g. navigation equipment, satellite phones) and services (e.g. satellite-based meteorological services or direct-to-home video services) to final users (OECD, 2014).

Thus, the space economy is larger than the traditional space sector (e.g. rockets and launchers); and it involves more and more new services and product providers (e.g. geographic information systems developers, navigation equipment sellers) who are using space systems' capacities to create new products and services. Hence, it must be noted that when we refer to the space industry, we are in fact referring to the overall economic activities in relation to space.

Estimates of the size of the space economy vary considerably, due to the lack of internationally comparable data. Worldwide, institutional budgets were around USD 64.4 billion in 2009 and an estimated USD 65.3 billion in 2010 for OECD countries, with the bulk of funding in G7 and BRIC countries. All G20 countries have space programmes. Five countries have invested more than USD 2 billion in 2010 (United States, China, Japan, France and the Russian Federation), with the United States leading the way at more than USD 43 billion. The data indicate that the underlying trend in the space economy is one of growth (OECD, 2014). And this remains true, despite the cyclical nature of commercial space activities (e.g. regular replacement of telecommunication satellite fleets).

Figure 3.1 provides a simplified view of the space economy; a public or private actor may be involved simultaneously in several space activities (e.g. being a manufacturer, as well as an operator and service provider).

Governments play a key role in the space economy as investors, owners, operators, regulators and customers for much of space infrastructure. As in the case of other large infrastructure systems (e.g. water, energy), government involvement is indispensable to sustain the overall space economy and to deal with strategic implications of such complex systems. In the case of space, infrastructure can be used for both civilian and military applications as space technologies are by nature dual use, and military developments often pave the way for the development of civil and commercial applications (i.e. today's rockets are derived from missiles).

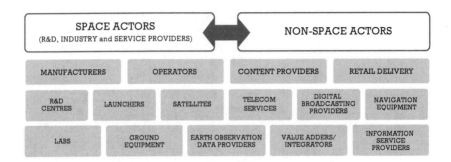

Figure 3.1 Overview of the space economy
Source: OECD, 2007.

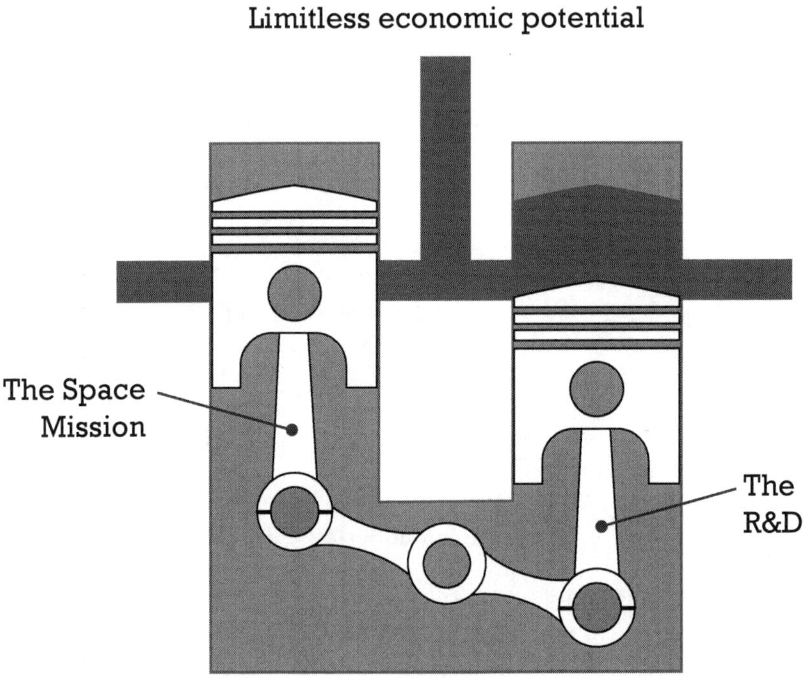

Limitless economic potential

The Space
Mission

The
R&D

Figure 3.2 The space industry and its core components

In particular, we refer to the space industry as the relationship between the space mission and the R&D sector, which, through its scientific explorations, gives rise to limitless economic potential. Figure 3.2 illustrates this process.

The first component of the definition, the space mission, refers to the phenomenon of the wondrous endeavour to conquer the unknown that has always been with man but which today is embodied by the move to be in the outer reaches of the heavens. That mission is sponsored by national governments and private corporations respectively and serves a number of areas such as the military and telecommunications. The second component, the R&D sector, is the intellectual transformer of all of the efforts of the space mission. It provides the knowledge drawn from the collected data and produces new techniques, understandings and technological devices. The relationship between the space mission and the R&D is one of mutual complementarity. So the industry is actually a dynamic industry that functions like the pistons in an engine where one feature, the space mission, propels the research and development sector and that feature in its turn informs, enhances and accelerates the space mission to higher levels of achievement.

Today, the space industry is still largely dominated by states. Figure 3.3 below provides the breakdown of the space budget by selected countries as a share of GDP in 2008 and in 2013 according to the latest available data.

Space budgets refer to the amounts that governments have indicated they will provide to public sector agencies or organizations to achieve space-related goals (e.g. space exploration, better communications, security). For example for OECD countries, the space budgets may serve both civilian and military objectives. However, significant portions of military-related space budgets may not be revealed in published figures.

In most countries, institutional space budgets fund a large range of activities in space research, development and applications in both civilian and defence domains. Budgets are usually spread across several government agencies (including defence), which makes them sometimes difficult to track in national accounts. The estimates provided here should therefore be considered as conservative. Although OECD economies account for the largest space budget globally in 2013, an increasing part of global space activities takes place outside of OECD. When comparing OECD and BRIC economies' space budgets in 2008 and 2013 (using USD purchasing power parities or PPPs), budgets from OECD countries have remained resilient to the economic crisis, with only a slight decrease overall. A number of European Union countries (EU15) have seen their national budgets augment in the period, while BRIC's budgets have shown a strong increase. The Russian space budget for instance rose 144% between 2008 and 2013, taking into account inflation. When national space budgets are converted from USD current value to USD PPP, China, India and the Russian Federation are among the top-four investors in space in 2013. Still using PPP to allow better international comparison; the United States has the highest space budget per capita, representing some USD 120 PPP per habitant, followed by the Russian Federation, France, Luxembourg, Japan, Belgium, Germany and Norway (OECD, 2014). In current US dollars, five countries had budgets above USD 2 billion in 2013, with the highest budget in the United States (USD 39 billion), covering the space activities of NASA, NOAA, USGS as well as other selected governmental defense organizations. China had the second-biggest space budget, estimated at around USD 6 billion (based on the intensity of its programmes and trends in its official defence budget), followed by the Russian Federation (USD 5.3 billion), Japan (USD 3.6 billion) and France (USD

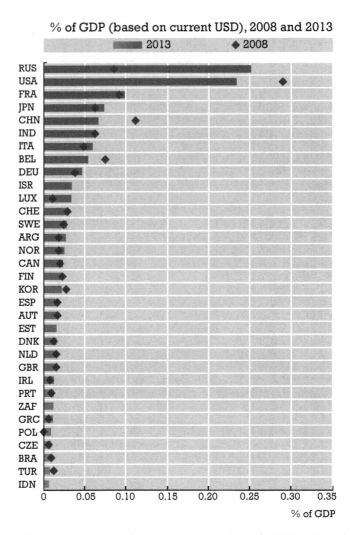

Figure 3.3 The space budget by selected countries as a share of GDP in 2008 and in 2013
Source: OECD, 2014.

2.7 billion). When looking at space budgets' shares in GDP, the percentages remain relatively modest. Only three countries' space budgets represent more than 0.1% of GDP (Russian Federation, United States and France).

Current state of the upstream segment

NASA's immediate goals focus on taking major steps to pave the way to Mars. Table 3.1 displays the space science line items and their associated budgets in millions of dollars for 2016. Over USD 5 billion is devoted to furthering space science, looking out to the universe and future destinations as well as looking back toward earth to further our understanding of our own planet. This fundamental piece of NASA research is a vital component to our knowledge of the universe. Another nearly USD 5 billion of the 2016 budget is devoted to space exploration, including the development of vital systems for future programs as well as supporting commercial space flight and transportation to the ISS. Space operations to support existing activities primarily in the ISS take up another USD 4 billion in the budget. NASA has specific goals in the short term to build on past successes and progress to the next level in the major mission to Mars.

By contrast, institutional programmes over time are more stable in Europe as shown in Figure 3.4. In most countries, institutional space budgets fund a large range of activities in space research, development and applications in both civilian and defence domains. Budgets are usually spread across several government agencies (including defence), which makes them sometimes difficult to track in national accounts.

The international balance of power has changed significantly in the past two decades. The disintegration of the Soviet Union, the economic rise of a number of Asian countries and the ever growing transfers of technologies, facilitated by the rise of the information society, have all contributed to this new international landscape. In 2011, it is characterized by two main features: an ever larger group of countries with satellite capabilities and the emergence of Brazil, India and China, alongside the Russian Federation (i.e. the BRIC countries), as exporters of space technologies. Space-faring countries have moved from being a small

Table 3.1 NASA space budget allocation for 2016

	FY2016
Science	$5,288.6
Earth Science	$1,947.3
Planetary Science	$1,361.2
Astrophysics	$709.1
	$620.0
Heliophysics	$651.0
Aeronautics	$571.4
Space Technology	$724.8
Exploration	$4,505.9
Exploration Systems Development	$2,862.9
Commercial Spaceflight	$1,243.8
Exploration Research and Development	$399.2
Space Operations	$4,003.7
International Space Station	$3,105.6
Space and Flight Support (SFS)	$898.1

Source: Adapted from NASA, 2017.

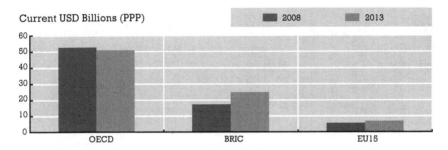

Figure 3.4 OECD, BRICs and EU-15 space budget 2008–2013
Source: OECD, 2014.

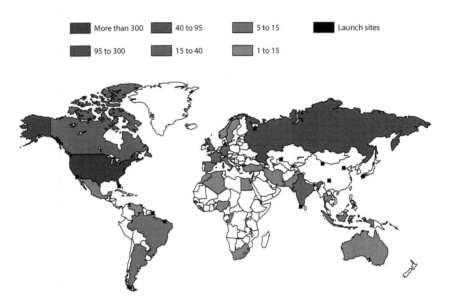

Figure 3.5 Countries with operational satellites in orbit in 2010
Source: OECD, 2011.

exclusive club relying on strong defence and aerospace industries, to a larger group of advanced and smaller developing countries with very diverse capabilities. As of early 2011, more than 50 countries have launched satellites as depicted in Figure 3.5 (OECD, 2011). As of 2017, 11 countries have so far demonstrated independent orbital launch capabilities (the Russian Federation, the United States, France, Japan, China, the United Kingdom, India, Israel, Ukraine, Iraq and North Korea).

We can also differentiate the space sector between a supply and a demand side. The supply side can be determined as "embracing all public and private actors involved in providing space-enabled products and services" (OECD, 2007).

Those actors belong to a value-added chain consisting of the upstream and the downstream segment. The upstream segment comprises the manufacturers of space hardware and the suppliers of launch services. The downstream segment includes the operators of satellites and the suppliers of space-enabled products and services. Space agencies play a decisive role in both segments because they conduct upstream and downstream research and development and from time to time act as operators of space systems (OECD, 2007).

The demand side includes two major elements: the institutional market and the commercial market. The institutional market obtains space assets for causes that range from manned space flight and scientific investigation to fundamental public services and supporting R&D (OECD, 2007).

The commercial market refers to private or semi-private firms supplying space-based services or space-enabled products to final customers or other firms. There are three major parts of the commercial market: telecommunications (mobile and fixed services), Earth Observation (EO) and Location-Based Services (LBS). The progress of the commercial market is dependent on the development of the institutional market, e.g. the commercial launcher/satellite market would almost certainly not exist in the absence of an institutional demand (Nelson & Winter, 1982; OECD, 2007).

The launch industry

Eleven countries currently have an autonomous capability to launch satellites into orbit. These are the Russian Federation, the United States, France, Japan, China, the United Kingdom, India, Israel, Ukraine, Iraq and North Korea. Many more countries have the capability to design and build satellites but are unable to launch them, instead relying on foreign launch services. This list does not consider those numerous countries, but only lists those capable of launching satellites indigenously.

The international space launch industry plays a pivotal role in enabling commercial and non-commercial actors to engage in civilian and military space activities (Table 3.2).

Only 11 countries in the world have the technology and facilities to carry out an orbital space launch, or to maintain a fleet of operational launchers. Since 1994, more than 1,300 successful launches have been carried out, with the Russian Federation and the United States accounting for almost 75% of all launches. The launch industry is subject to strong yearly variations (due to the low number of launches per year, satellite life and replacement cycles, etc.). After a drop in the early 2000s, launch numbers are back at 1990s levels, mostly due to increased activity in the Russian Federation and in China, which now has the same number of yearly launches as the United States.

In 2013, 78 successful launches were carried out as displayed in Figure 3.6: 31 Russian launches, 19 US, 14 Chinese and seven European while India and Japan had three launches each, and Korea's launch vehicle Naro-1 successfully placed STSAT-2C in orbit. There were three failed launches: one Russian,

Table 3.2 Total commercial and non-commercial launch events (2014)

Country/Region	Commercial Launches	Non-Commercial Launches	Launches
United States	11	12	23
Russia	4	28	32
Europe	6	5	11
China	0	16	16
Japan	0	4	4
India	1	3	4
Israel	0	1	1
Multinational	1	0	1
Total	**23**	**69**	**92**

Source: Federal Aviation Administration Compendium, 2015.

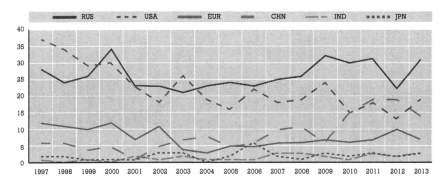

Figure 3.6 Number of successful space launches for selected countries 1997–2013

Source: OECD, 2014.

one Chinese and one commercial launch (Sea Launch). As most institutional satellites are placed into orbit by national launchers, the market open to international competition is relatively small. It was about USD 2 billion in 2013, a 20% decrease compared to 2012. As of spring 2014, there were six companies able to commercially launch satellites to geostationary (GEO) orbit, which is the most profitable orbit, home to large commercial communications satellites. They include the European company Arianespace (the current market leader, with the Ariane 5 launcher), the Russian Federation's International Launch Services (Proton launcher), the United States' Lockheed Martin (Atlas V) and Boeing (Delta launchers), China Great Wall (Long March launchers) and Sea Launch, an international consortium (Norway, Russian Federation, Ukraine and United States). Other companies can launch satellites in lower orbits, most notably SpaceX (US), which carried out its first commercial launch in December 2013 with its Falcon

9. India's Polar Satellite Launch Vehicle (PSLV) has a long track record. India is also developing and has successfully tested a heavy-lift cryogenic engine for its Geosynchronous Satellite Launch Vehicle (GSLV) with the ambition of entering the commercial GEO launch market. Launch demand in the next ten years is expected to remain robust, with stable or increasing demand from institutional and commercial actors driven primarily by growth in emerging economies.

Launch providers from the United States, Russia, Europe, China, Japan, India, Israel and one multinational provider conducted a total of 92 launches in 2014, 23 of which were commercial (see Table 3.2). This is higher than the previous five-year average of 79 total launches and 22 commercial launches per year. The worldwide orbital commercial launches in 2014, by country were the following: the United States conducted 23 launches in 2014, four more launches than in 2013. Eleven of the 23 launches were commercial, five more than in 2013. Russia had the highest number of total launches (32) in 2014, same as in 2013. It performed four commercial launches, down from 12 in 2013. Russia experienced one failure of a Proton M launch vehicle while attempting to launch the Express AM4R GEO communications satellite for the Russian Satellite Communications Company (RSCC). Europe conducted 11 launches in 2014, six of which were commercial, rebounding from the low number of seven launches in 2013, including four commercial ones. China had 16 orbital launches, all non-commercial, one launch more than in 2013. This is the second year in a row with no commercial launch activity in China. India had four successful launches, including one commercial launch in 2014, compared to three non-commercial launches in 2013. Israel successfully launched its Shavit vehicle carrying Ofeq 10 reconnaissance satellite, a non-commercial launch. It was the first orbital launch in Israel since 2010. Japan performed a total of four non-commercial launches in 2014, up one launch from 2013. The multinational Sea Launch Zenit 3SL launch vehicle performed one successful launch in 2014. In 2013, there was one failed commercial launch attempt by Sea Launch. There were ten commercial launches of GEO satellites in 2014, one launch less than in 2013. This year continued the downward trend in commercial launches to GEO with the new lowest number since 2007.

Estimated revenues from the 23 commercial launch events in 2014 amounted to approximately USD 2.36 billion (Figure 3.7). These revenues are nearly a half billion dollars higher than in 2013 while consistent with commercial launch revenue in 2009, 2010, and 2012.

The following are 2014 revenues by country. Commercial launch revenues in the United States amounted to USD 1.1 billion, the highest since 1998. Estimated commercial launch revenue for 2013 was USD 339.5 million. Russian commercial launch revenues were approximately USD 218 million, 30% of the previous year's USD 759 million. The delay caused by a civil government Proton failure in May resulted in only two commercial Proton launches in 2014. The other two Russian commercial launches this year were performed by the low-cost Dnepr vehicle. European commercial launch revenues were approximately USD920 million, a 30% increase from 2013. Just as in 2013, China did not perform any commercial launches in 2014. It earned an estimated total of USD

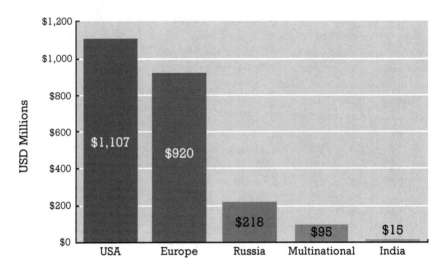

Figure 3.7 Commercial launch revenues by country (2014)

Source: Federal Aviation Administration Compendium, 2015.

90 million for two commercial launches in 2012. Multinational (Sea Launch) revenues from the single 2014 launch were estimated at USD 95 million, on a par with the 2013 results. India's revenues were estimated at USD 15 million in 2014.

Payments for launch services are typically spread over one to two years before the launch, however revenue is counted in the year a customer's payload launches. Launch revenues are attributed to the country or region where the primary vehicle manufacturer is based. These revenues are assessed based on commercial launch price estimates for each launch vehicle using publically available information.

Satellite manufacturing

According to the Satellite Industry Association Report (2016), satellite manufacturing revenues, reflecting the value of satellites launched in 2015, grew by 4% worldwide to USD 16.6 billion (Figure 3.8). There were orders for 17 commercial GEO satellites with 11 orders won by US manufacturers for a domestic market share of 65%, up from 57% in 2014.

In particular, as depicted in Figure 3.9, 202 satellites were launched in 2015, about the same as in 2014; 108 CubeSats launched and were mostly for commercial earth observation.

As depicted in Figure 3.10, communications satellites represented 42% of total revenues, military surveillance satellites accounted for 36% of 2015 revenues, compared to 38% in 2014. CubeSats represent less than 1% of total value.

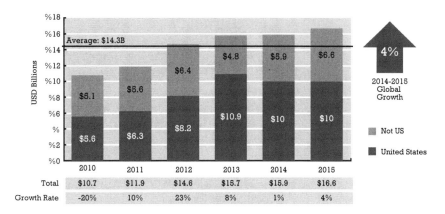

Figure 3.8 World satellite manufacturing revenues in billions of dollars (2010–2015)
Source: SIA Report, 2016.

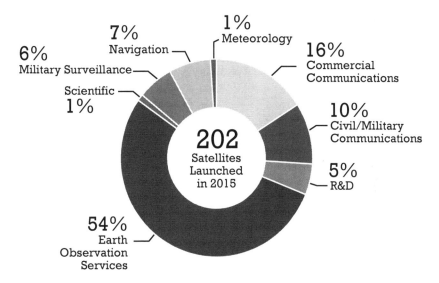

Figure 3.9 Distribution of satellites launched by mission type
Source: Satellite Industry Association: State of the Satellite Industry Report, 2017.

The US satellite manufacturing revenues stayed flat, with commercial sector slightly higher and government sector slightly lower. Within this context, 73% of US revenues were from US government contracts. Excluding CubeSats, US firms built 32% of satellites launched in 2015 and earned 60% of global satellite manufacturing revenues (Figure 3.11), a decrease from 63% in 2014. Including CubeSats, US firms built about 64% of satellites launched in 2015 and earned 60% of revenues. 89 of the 119 US-built satellites launched in 2015 were CubeSats.

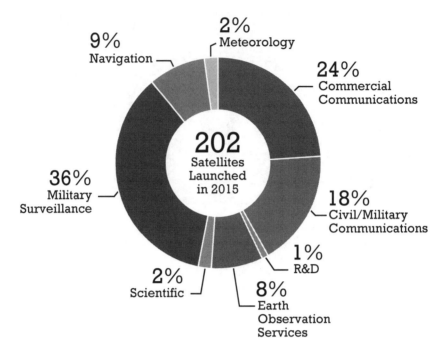

Figure 3.10 Distribution of value of satellites launched by mission type

Source: Satellite Industry Association: State of the Satellite Industry Report, 2017.

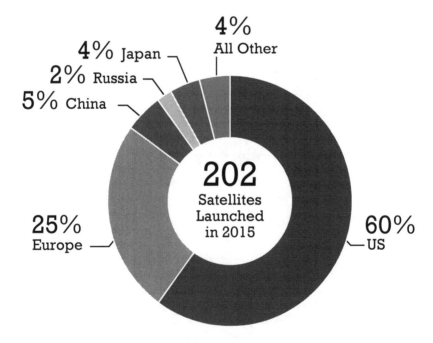

Figure 3.11 Value of spacecraft launched by country/region of manufacturer (2015)

Source: SIA Report, 2016.

Satellite producers compete on price and on the quality of the offerings and features provided. Thus the barriers to enter this market are presumably lower than for the launchers market and some companies can survive by concentrating on niche markets. As well as the launcher manufacturers, satellite producers have encountered hard times in recent years, leading to a consolidation of satellite operators. In particular, the significant advancement in terms of the stability and capacity of spacecraft has led to a sharp decline in the demand for additional satellites.

Satellite propulsion methods

In terms of innovation, according to many industry actors, the market for commercial satellites will be divided by 2020 between satellites with conventional chemical propulsion and satellites with electric hybrid propulsion (OECD, 2014). In 2012, two relatively new satellite telecommunications operators (Mexico's Satmex, bought by France's Eutelsat since then, and Hong Kong's Asia Broadcast Satellite) bought four commercial fully electric satellites, developed by Boeing Space and Intelligence Systems. The first two satellites were launched in late 2013. Electric propulsion technologies are classified into three categories: electrothermal, electrostatic and Plasma. These are types of propulsion that have been under study for more than 30 years in several countries, particularly the United States, France and the Russian Federation to save mass on interplanetary probes. On a satellite, the propulsion system aims to ensure the transfer of the satellite from its injection orbit to its final orbit. Once the satellite has reached its position, the propulsion system is necessary to modify the orbital moves induced by natural disturbances, and correct the orientation of the satellite when needed. Satellites often carry several propulsion systems, using solid propellant for transfer manoeuvres, and using electric thrusters for more precise control of orbit and orientation. The main constraint for electric thrusters is that the thrust force is less powerful, compared to chemical engines, so it takes more time to move a satellite or an interplanetary probe. The main advantage of electric propulsion used for commercial satellites is that due to the relatively lower weight of the satellite an operator can embark more marketable capacity, in place of the fuel the satellite would have needed if it used a classic chemical propulsion system. Since the satellite's mass to be launched is also smaller, it reduces the launch costs. Several space manufacturers are now offering or planning to offer all-electric satellites or hybrid solutions for satellite operators. However, the market is still nascent, as despite the lower costs, an important constraint from using fully electric propulsion for operators is the length of time it takes to reach the satellite's final operating orbit before being able to start commercial operations.

Small satellites

Small satellites have become very attractive in the past five years, due to their lower development costs and shorter production lead times. There is still a natural trade-off to be made between a satellite's size and its functionality, since the smaller a satellite is, the fewer useful instruments it can carry, and the shorter its lifetime will be since it carries less fuel. However advances in both miniaturization as well as improved satellite integration technologies have dramatically diminished the scope of that trade-off (OECD, 2014). Small satellites are also becoming much more affordable. Commercial off the shelf (COTS) components and consumer electronics are now commonly used to build small satellites at the lower end of the cost range. Several commercial companies fabricate structures for a large variety of small satellite missions, and it is even possible to buy online most of the components and subsystems to build a nano-satellite in-house. The main cost barrier remains the access to space, although significant progress may occur in that domain. There are different types of satellites, mainly sub-categorized by their mass as depicted in the Table 3.3 below.

Cubesats are very popular in universities as technology demonstrators. They are less than 20 years old, with their standardization realized in 1999 by academics at CalPoly and Stanford University in California. The use of small satellites by universities can help students put into practice much faster their engineering and scientific competences, and small satellites can be launched when excess capacity is available on diverse rockets. As of spring 2014, some 200 Cubesats have been launched. Twenty-six countries have developed Cubesats so far, with the United States launching over half of the satellites, followed by Europe, Japan, Canada and several South American countries. Some experts see this as an evolution similar to computers, i.e. large mainframe computers of the 1970s have evolved into networks of small computers connected via the Internet. India, for example, has recently launched 104 satellites from a single rocket, breaking a world record and thus ramping up the space race. This evolution is also leading to new commercial ventures. The firm Skybox Imaging that launched in 2013 its first satellite (SkySat-1) of a planned constellation of 24 small satellites, is focusing on making cheap high-resolution satellite imagery available, with continuous refreshed data. As a potential indicator of commercial interests linked to these small satellites' developments, Google acquired in spring 2014 the Skybox firm for some USD 500 million.

Table 3.3 Types of small satellites

Type of spacecraft	Mass
Mini satellite	100–180Kg
Microsatellite	10–100Kg
Nanosatellite (Cubesat)	1–10Kg
Femto and picosatellite	Less than 1Kg

Source: OECD, 2014.

Resources

The mining and utilization of the abundant resources in existence on the moon and Near-Earth Asteroids (NEAs) could potentially harvest trillion dollar industries in the future. The exploitation of the available resources presents multiple opportunities for financial reward. However as one might expect, there are great barriers to overcome before the potential of space in terms of resource commercialization can be realized. These barriers are legal, scientific, mechanical and financial in nature and all impede progress and evolution of the space resource industries.

Space resources that attract commercial attention can be basically classified into the following:

1   **Water**
2   **Solar energy**
3   **Metals: Ferrous, precious and strategic**
4   **Fusion reactor fuels**

The exploitation of each resource presents unique combinations of opportunities and threats and these are at various evolutionary stages in their development. Their utilization also varies; some resources are to be used in space, others are material commercially destined to return to earth or to be used as a source of energy supply to earth.

1. Water is an extremely versatile resource with the ability to provide for propellants for rocket engines as well as being an essential life sustaining material. Experts say that the hydrogen found in ice could be used to make fuel for space exploration and oxygen in water could provide air to explorers and even colonies. To haul the weight of water up through the earth's gravity well is extremely costly and if water could be accessed in space it has the potential to revolutionize both the mechanical and human aspects of space exploration and commercialization. Subsequently this resource could assume a lucrative position of economic importance within the era of space commercialization and billions of dollars have been spent in search of this precious commodity in space. The European Space Agency's Infrared Space Observatory (ISO) detected water vapour and confirmed visual observations of water in space between the years of 1995 and 1998. NASA's Lunar Prospector spacecraft orbited the moon in the years 1998 and 1999 and Alan Binder, Lunar Prospector's principle investigator, reported that the investigation had found small expanses of lunar surface that is believed to hold water-ice crystals mixed in with surface materials. The Lunar Prospector's intentional crash land on the moon uncovered evidence of hydrogen and possible surface water: "there could be vast quantities of it – as much as 200 million tons of ice crystals buried 18 inches (45centimeters) or so beneath the Moon's dusty surface. Thawed, that would be vast enough to fill a lake about 2 to 3 miles (3 to 5 kilometres) wide by 32 feet (10 meters) deep" (Space.com, 2009). Chemically broken down into hydrogen and oxygen, water could provide fuel for rockets or electrical generators, along with breathable air, this classifies its application as In-Situ Resource Utilization (ISRU). Gerald Sanders, Chief of the Propulsion and Fluid Systems Branch at NASA's Johnson Space Centre, describes ISRU as the stepping-stone for space development. If humans ever enter space at a mass level, for extended periods of time, for either commercial or touristic purposes, space resources could become a necessity to sustain life. With the evolution of the space tourism industry there is in turn greater strategic and economic interest in establishing ISRU by NASA and other programmes. The increasing interest in this space resource is therefore intensifying with the development of space tourism.

2. Energy consumption has been on a constant increase for many decades and has brought with it severe environmental consequences capturing the world media's attention as we try to find solutions to this global problem. The Organisation for Economic Co-operation and Development (OECD) is a unique forum where the governments of 30 democracies work together to address the economic, social and environmental challenges of globalization. The International Energy Agency (IEA) is an autonomous body, established in November 1974 within the framework of the OECD, with the aim of implementing an international energy programme. The IEA produces an annual report, the World Energy Outlook (WEO), and the latest report details how the trends in energy demand, imports, coal use and greenhouse gas emissions predicted up to 2030 have continued to worsen year by year. WEO identifies the emerging giants of the world economy, namely China and India, as transformers of the global energy system.

> The consequences for China, India, the OECD and the rest of the world of unfettering growth in global energy demand are alarming. If governments around the world today stick with current policies the world's energy needs would be well over 50% higher in 2030 than today. China and India together account for 45% of the increase in demand.
>
> (Agency, 2008)

There is a global challenge to shift to a more secure, lower-carbon energy system, without damaging economic and social development at large. The WEO 2007 states "to achieve a much bigger reduction in emissions would require immediate policy action and technological transformation on an unprecedented scale". The potential of developing a system in outer space to harness clean energy from the sun and then beam it back to earth is without question a feat of "technological transformation on an unprecedented scale". At present, solar energy as a renewable and clean source of energy is being selected as an energy choice for more and more people. The use of solar energy in multiple forms is spreading and has been aided by technological advancements. However there are problems inherent with the use of solar power as we collect it today since the energy is diffused, intermittent and unreliable in many parts of the world. The concept of collecting solar energy in space and transmitting it to earth as microwaves avoids these problems as it is more intense (with the sun shining 24 hours a day) and the energy collected can be delivered almost anywhere. The Space Solar Power (SSP) concept as it is known, is the work of Peter Glaser and was first proposed in 1968 and is still considered to be a very promising source of renewable energy. Despite its benefits, it remains in the research phase of development. The potential size of this market is predicted to be USD 100 billion by 2020 and the European Space Agency, the Japanese Space Agency and the private Space Island Group are all working together to commercialize this new source of energy (SPACE.com, 2009).

3. Metals: Ferrous, precious and strategic. Cobalt, gold, iron, magnesium, nickel, platinum and silver are all raw metals that are becoming increasingly rare here on earth but can be found abundant in their raw forms in space. The 3,000 approximately Near Earth Asteroids (NEAs), 750 of which are easier to reach than the moon, contain invaluable quantities of these metals. "The NEA Amun, about two kilometres in diameter, contains far more metal that the total amount used by the human race since the beginning of the Bronze Age. Its Earth- surface market value is tens of trillions of dollars, larger than the annual gross global product of Earth" (Fukushima, 2008). If extracted the different metals could be utilized for different uses in space or on earth. Some metals would provide radiation shielding for explorers and colonists, other ferrous metals could be employed in the building of space structures and scientific samples or precious and strategic metals could be transported to earth (Fukushima, 2008). At present mining specialists and space engineers are working on developing methods of extraction of these resources. Planetary Resources and Deep Space Industries are two private firms that are planning to engage in asteroid mining for the exploitation of metals.

4. Fusion reactor fuels. Helium-3 is a potential energy source in fusion power reactors. It is predicted that the Moon has about a million tons of this light helium isotope. "Recovering a single tonne of helium-3 requires perfect extraction and recovery of all the gas from 100 million tonnes of regolith a seemingly implausible amount. Nonetheless, the energy content of the recovered helium-3 is so large that the process may still make economic sense" (Fukushima, 2008). CNNmoney.com predicts that the value of one ton of helium-3 could be worth USD 7 billion and that by 2018 the helium-3 mining industry on the moon alone could be valued at USD 250bn. There is great interest in this fuel source from a number of governments and privately owned bodies and it is anticipated to be actively mined within the next two decades (CNNMoney.com, 2009).

Military sector

As the number of countries with space programmes continues to rise, so do government space budgets for military and civilian applications. However, significant portions of military-related space budgets may not be revealed in published figures. Looking at public budgets related to space poses several methodological challenges. First, when they are available publicly in some detail, budgets may not necessarily match current expenditures. Second, published budgets may not reveal certain confidential segments of space programmes (e.g. for military purposes). Third, some expenditure may be classified under other areas of government expenditure, e.g. telecommunications or R&D, and not under "space". Finally, up-to-data data were not available for all OECD member countries (although they were available for all major space participants).

By considering the global military budget of selected countries in 2015 as reported by Deloitte in 2017, global defence spending, inclusive of armed forces personnel, was estimated to be USD 1,760 billion (Deloitte, 2017). According to Deloitte's report, the US remained the largest defence-spending nation, representing 34% of the total global military spend of USD 1,760 billion in 2015. Many Middle Eastern and African countries spend a greater percentage of their GDP on military expenditures, with Oman, South Sudan and Saudi Arabia being the top three. With USD 85.4 billion in military expenditure in 2015, Saudi Arabia was also the fourth largest defence spender globally. In terms of affordability, the nominal amount spent on defence does not necessarily equate to the importance, requirements or priority of defence. Countries such as the Kingdom of Saudi Arabia spend a significant amount of their national economy on defence because they have national wealth created by their oil industry and security requirements based on their location in the Middle East and historical precedent. Israel spends a significant amount of its national wealth on defence for good reason – their homeland has experienced major military conflict six times since their founding in 1948. India, Brazil, South Korea and others are increasing their defence spending rapidly due to either their wealth creating affordability and/or significant military threats to their national security.

The report also addresses the issues of affordability and importance of defence by comparing military expenditures with gross domestic product (GDP) for selected countries in 2010 (Deloitte, 2017). Within this context, Kingdom of Saudi Arabia spends the highest percentage of its GDP on military expenditures at 10.1%, followed by Israel at 6.4%, and then the US, Russia and South Korea. The global average GDP spent on defence is 2.7% – which is a bit overstated considering the US raises the average significantly with a large portion of total expenditures.

We have a more detailed picture of the space budget in the US (Deloitte, 2017), where the budget allocated to defence and military purposes has been stable from 2008 to 2017. The report also illustrates the trend of the US Department of Defense (DoD) budgets from fiscal year 2008 through to 2017, showing a 5-year decline from 2010 to 2015, with an increase of USD 20.0 billion in 2016 and USD 9.0 billion in 2017, inclusive of Overseas Contingency Operations (OCO) funding.

Space exploration sector

Space exploration is the physical exploration of outer-earth objects, via robotic probes and human missions. More broadly, it also includes the scientific

Table 3.4 Popular extraplanetary destinations

	Asteroids and comets	Venus	Mars	Moon
Total number of missions[1]	29	45	46	116
Success rate	85%	55.5%	43.4%	50.8%
Successful orbiters	2	10	10	36
Successful landers/rovers	2/–	9/–	6/4	9/3
Successful crewed landing	–	–	–	6
En route Missions	3	–	2	–
Operational	3	–	5	5
Planned (funded) missions	4	1	3	6
Comments	ESA's Rosetta Mission reached the target comet and put a lander on the comet (November 2014)	Venera 3 (former USSR) was the first spacecraft to reach the surface of another planet in 1966	NASA's Mariner 9 made the 1st successful Mars orbit, while the USSR's Mars 3 made the first landing the same year.	This is the only extra-terrestrial body visited by astronauts (last flight in 1972)

Adapted from: OECD, 2014.
1. Includes flyby missions.

disciplines (e.g. astronomy, solar physics, astrophysics, planetary sciences), technologies and policies applied to space endeavours. Countries with space programmes are increasingly investing in "down-to-earth" space applications (e.g. telecommunications, earth observation) for strategic and economic reasons. Nevertheless, space exploration remains a key driver for investments in innovative R&D and sciences, and it constitutes an intensive activity for major space agencies.

Space exploration is probably the most visible face of space activities and constitutes an inherent mission of space agencies worldwide. Its achievements generate enthusiasm among the public and wide media interest, as shown by race to the moon, Mars exploration by robots or the probe landing on Titan. Space sciences and planetary missions have developed markedly over the years. To this purpose, Table 3.4 displays the most popular extra-planetary destinations.

Space exploration is a key driver for investments in innovation and science, and it constitutes an intensive activity for space agencies and industry. Space sciences and planetary missions have developed markedly over the years, with new actors joining in, although no country can today launch a major exploration mission alone. Another factor for co-operation is the need for deep space monitoring systems, based on international arrays of giant radio antennas installed in different countries, to keep communication links with interplanetary spacecraft missions. Out of the over 900 satellites orbiting the earth, a dozen are dedicated to space sciences, including large international space telescopes, and scientific missions searching for earth-like planets outside the solar system. Robotic spacecraft have been sent to all of the planets in the solar system. One of the more emblematic destinations for future missions is the planet Mars. Reaching Mars remains a challenge, as nearly two-thirds of all spacecraft destined for Mars have failed without completing their missions. Missions to Mars can be launched every two years or so due to the alignment of earth and Mars in their orbits around the sun that allows spacecraft to travel between the two planets with the least amount of energy, and the voyage can take up to six months. Although scientific missions and joint space exploration strategic planning remain the remit of the public sector, new private actors aim to become engaged in innovative space exploration activities.

Manned space flight sector

In the case of human spaceflight, several definitions for "astronaut" co-exist. The International Aeronautic Federation (IAF) calls anyone who has flown at an altitude of 100 kilometers an "astronaut". The US Air Force set the limit at 50 miles altitude (80.45 km), while other organizations consider that a person must have reached orbital velocity and remained in orbit (above 200 km) to be considered an "astronaut". The IAF definition has been used here as it was used by the OECD (OECD, 2014).

In addition to robotic exploration, the development of a human presence in space has been a recurring theme since the 1950s for both political and prestige-related reasons. More countries than ever are investing in indigenous human spaceflight capabilities, usually in collaboration, by providing scientific experiments and equipment to larger missions through a variety of means: suborbital flights and orbital spaceflight missions (currently only available via flights to the International Space Station (ISS) or the Chinese Tiangong-1 test-bed space station). The year 2014 marked the 16th anniversary of the ISS, with six astronauts continuously on-board since 2008. The countries involved in this partnership include the United States, Canada, Japan, the Russian Federation and participating ESA country members (Belgium, Denmark, France, Germany, Italy, Netherlands, Norway, Spain, Sweden, Switzerland and the United Kingdom). Since the end of the space shuttle missions in 2011, the only way for crews to reach the station has been by using the Russian Soyuz capsules. Other means are available to deliver cargo and crew supplies to the station: the Russian Progress (several flights a year), the European Automated Transfer Vehicle (the fifth to be launched in 2014), the Japanese H-II Transfer Vehicle (also the fifth to be launched in 2014) and commercial US capsules, SpaceX's dragon and Orbital's Cygnus. SpaceX and Orbital were awarded resupply contracts worth USD 1.6 and 1.9 billion respectively until 2015. As of May 2017, SpaceX has successfully executed nine of its twelve planned cargo missions to the ISS. Orbital Sciences Corporation's Cygnus capsule made its first delivery in January 2014. Following the retirement of the space shuttle fleet, commercial firms were selected by NASA to develop new spacecraft capable of carrying astronauts to the ISS by 2017–18. These are SpaceX, Boeing, Sierra Nevada and Blue Origin. In parallel, NASA is working on the development of a new heavy-lift launcher with a capsule dubbed Orion, capable of carrying astronauts beyond the earth's orbit, with long-term missions to asteroids and Mars. China has also started building a 30-ton space station, to be completed in the 2016–23 timeframe. In the meantime, the operational Chinese Tiangong-1 space station serves as a technology testbed, visited in June 2013 by Taikonauts for two weeks, China's longest manned space mission to date. Launched unmanned on 29 September 2011, it is the first operational component of the Tiangong programme, which aims to place a larger, modular station into orbit by 2023. Tiangong-1 was initially projected to be deorbited in 2013, to be replaced over the following decade by the larger Tiangong-2 and Tiangong-3 modules, but as of June 2017 it was still aloft, though in a decaying orbit. On 21 March 2016, after two years of extended lifespan, the Space Engineering Office announced that Tiangong-1 had officially ended its service. Tiangong-2 was launched in September 2016. Table 3.5 displays some selected human space-flights while Table 3.6 provides human-flight capabilities for selected countries.

The shift from government to commercial space transportation for cargo and ultimately crews of astronauts to low-earth orbit will be highly dependent on the performance of firms over the next five years. In parallel to these initiatives, space tourism activities are being developed particularly in North America and Europe, with zero-gravity/ parabolic flights, sub-orbital flights and orbital space travel offered to private consumers.

Table 3.5 Selected human space-flights statistics

Countries with autonomous capability to launch humans into space	2^1
Number of nationalities who have flown in space	+40
Number of launches with humans on-board	+270
Persons who have flown into orbit	+530
Operational and inhabited space stations since the 1960s	10^2
Professional astronauts living in orbit (the international Space Station is continuosly inhabited since 2003)	6
Number of paying orbital spaceflight participants ("space tourism")	7
Persons who have flown over the 100 km altitude threshold (including suborbital flights)	484
Astronauts who walked on the Moon (1969–1972)	12

Source: OECD, 2014.
1. China, Russian Federation; 2. 7 Russian, 1 American, 1 Chinese, 1 international.

Table 3.6 Human space-flights capabilities for selected countries

		Orbital capabilities			*Human-rated launchers capalbilities*		
		1990–2009	*2010–2019*	*After 2020*	*1990–2009*	*2010–2019*	*After 2020*
Government	**EUR**	Spacelab module on shuttle	ISS	ISS	None	None	None
	CHN	None	Tiangong-1 space station	Tiangong-2 space station	Long March	Long March	Long March
	RUS	Mir	ISS	ISS	Soyuz	Soyuz	Soyuz/ Angara
	USA	Space shuttle	ISS	ISS	Space shuttle	None[1]	Commercial/ governmental launchers

Source: OECD, 2014.
1. Since 2011.

Conclusion

After providing a definition of the space industry, this chapter has outlined the main dynamics affecting the upstream segment of the sector by focusing on satellites launch and manufacturing, the pursuit of resources, the undisputed role of the military sector as well as the manned space flight sector. The next chapters provide an overview of the downstream activities derived from the upstream segment, namely the products or services that are produced or provided by the space sector.

References

Agency, I.E., 2008. World Energy Outlook 2008. Available at: http://www.worldenergyout look.org/2008.asp.

CNNMoney.com, 2009. Business, financial, personal finance news. Available at: http:// money.cnn.com/.

Deloitte, 2017. 2017 Global aerospace and defense sector outlook. Growth prospects remain upbeat. Available at: https://www2.deloitte.com/content/dam/Deloitte/global/Docu ments/Manufacturing/2017-global-ad-outlook-january.pdf.

Federal Aviation Administration, 2015. The Annual Compendium of Commercial Space Transportation: 2014. Available at: https://www.faa.gov/about/office_org/headquarters_ offices/ast/media/2016_Compendium.pdf.

Foust, J., 2003. The Space Review: What is the "space industry"? Available at: http://www. thespacereview.com/article/34/1.

Fukushima, M., 2008. Legal analysis of the International Space Station (ISS) programme using the concept of "legalisation". *Space Policy*, 24(1), 33–41.

NASA, 2009. U.S. Human Spaceflight History. Available at: http://www.jsc.nasa.gov/ history/hsf_history.htm.

Nelson, R.R. & Winter, S.G., 1982. An evolutionary theory of economic change, Harvard University Press.

OECD, 2004. Space 2030: Exploring the Future of Space Applications. Available at: http:// www.oecd.org/document/18/0,3343,en_2649_34815_34726866_1_1_1_1,00.html.

OECD, 2007. The Space Economy at a Glance.

OECD, 2011. The Space Economy at a Glance.

OECD, 2014. The Space Economy at a Glance.

Satellite Industry Association, 2016. State of the Satellite Industry Report.

Space.com, 2009. SPACE.com: Astronomy and Science News and Information, Astronomy Features, Astronomy Pictures. Available at: http://www.space.com/scienceastronomy/.

4   Industry analysis II

The downstream segment

Introduction

The previous chapter provided a definition of the space industry and outlined the main dynamics affecting the upstream segment of the sector comprising satellite launch and manufacturing, resources, the undisputed role of the military sector as well as the manned space flight sector. This chapter provides an exhaustive overview of the activities derived from the upstream segment, namely the products or services that are produced or provided by the space sector. These are namely satellite communication services, satellite earth observation, satellite weather and climate monitoring, global positioning and navigating services as well as space tourism.

The current state of the downstream segment

Space-related services use a specific satellite capacity, such as bandwidth or imagery, as inputs to provide a more global service to business, government or retail consumers. Those services are as diverse as space applications themselves. The services are traditionally divided into three large application domains: telecommunications, earth observation (also known as remote sensing) and navigation. Value chains often involve public agencies as investors and final users. As such, public authorities remain significant customers even in well-established commercial markets, such as telecommunications.

Space-related services revenues are not easy to gauge nationally and internationally, but worldwide estimates indicate that they accounted for some USD 127.4 billion in 2015 (Figure 4.1).

Satellite communication services

Satellite services are a growing part of the global communications infrastructure. Through unique capabilities, such as the ability to offer point-to-multipoint communications distribution with small receivers, to effectively blanket service regions and provide a flexible architecture in hard to reach places, satellite services constitute an important complement to terrestrial telecommunications

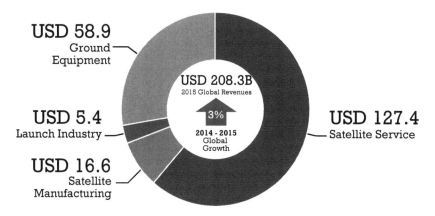

USD 58.9
Ground
Equipment

USD 208.3B
2015 Global Revenues

USD 5.4
Launch Industry

3%
2014 - 2015
Global
Growth

USD 127.4
Satellite Service

USD 16.6
Satellite
Manufacturing

Figure 4.1 World satellite industry revenues for services and others
Source: Satellite Industry Association: State of the Satellite Industry Report, 2017.

services. Satellite networks have been the backbone of the intercontinental telephone network from the 1960s to the 1980s. Although fibre cables have supplanted their uses on routes with the highest traffic volumes, satellite communications remain a highly profitable business. It branches out traditionally between providers of fixed satellite services (i.e. leasing capacity on geostationary-orbiting satellites for video, voice and data traffic) and providers of mobile satellite services (i.e. data services for mobile users, such as ships at sea and aeronautical markets). This distinction is increasingly losing its relevance, as operators are increasingly entering each other's markets. Another closely-linked ecosystem assembles the providers of satellite ground segment equipment and very small aperture terminals (VSATs), which provide communication receivers and full network solutions to public agencies (including defence) and private companies in banking, retail, oil and gas, rural communities.

According to the latest OECD report (2014), the top 25 actors in the fixed satellite services generated revenues of around USD 12 billion in 2013, a 29% increase as compared to 2008, with more than 300 commercial satellites in geostationary orbit. The top five actors (Intelsat and SES in Luxembourg, Eutelsat in France, Telesat in Canada, Sky Perfect Jsat in Japan) have some 4,600 employees and represent around 70% of the revenues, a continuing declining share as compared to 2008 (76.5% of revenues), as competition has grown and national satellite operators have set up business. On top of the fixed satellite services operators selling capacity, large media groups are providing the content and actual satellite broadcasting, broadband and telephone services to every-day consumers. Although it remains challenging to disassemble the revenues streams, some estimates point to a market of around USD 92 billion in 2013 for these satellite broadcasting services (SIA, 2016). Mobile satellite

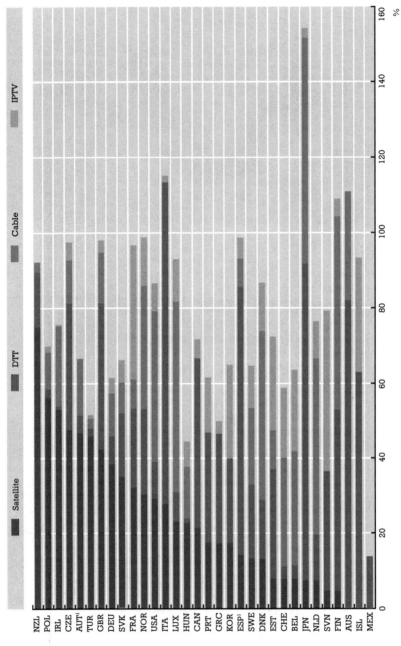

Figure 4.2 Penetration of satellite TV by country

Source: OECD, 2014.

operators have traditionally provided communications to the narrower but profitable aeronautical and maritime markets. In 2013, their revenues are estimated at around USD 2.6 billion, with three actors leading the market (Inmarsat in the United Kingdom, Iridium in the United States, Thuraya in the United Arab Emirates). Satellite radio is also a market segment representing more than USD 1 billion. Finally, the VSATs and ground equipment providers represent more than USD 7 billion in revenues, with most actors developing vigorous international subsidiaries networks (e.g. Hughes Network Systems, ViaSat Inc., iDirect in the United States, Advantech Satnet in Canada, Gilat Satellite Networks in Israel, Thales in France). In this context, satellite television remains the most profitable space business. Direct-to-home satellite television broadcast is almost universally available in OECD economies via one or more services, where the signal is received by satellite dishes and set-top boxes. As displayed in Figure 4.2, countries' uptake of satellite services varies widely, in New Zealand and Poland 50% of television households use satellite, but less than 10% in Belgium and Finland. Finally, broadband via satellite is becoming more common and cheaper, although it still remains a small market, representing only 0.2% of wireless broadband subscriptions by access technology in OECD economies in 2012 (OECD, 2014).

Satellite earth observation

Satellite earth observation (EO) systems are playing an increasingly important role in the global economy. They provide unique capabilities in close association with ground-based sensors to generate the data and information needed to manage and monitor natural resources, land-use and to better understand and cope with major societal issues (pollution, impacts of climate change). There are currently about 120 operational civil earth observation satellites in orbit (not including weather satellites), and around 40 military satellites. Out of these, more than 50 civilian missions are dedicated to gathering multipurpose land imagery. The United States, China, India, Europe and France lead the number of ongoing satellite missions. In terms of specific scientific instruments onboard satellites, the United States, China and France have the most instruments flying (on their national missions and in joint satellite missions). As of late 2013, more than 100 civilian missions are planned or are under consideration until 2030 to monitor land-use and oceans. However, the total number of EO satellites could double by 2021 to more than 300, according to different analyses, as an increasing number of countries are interested in possessing their own remote sensing satellites (e.g. Malaysia, Myanmar, Pakistan). One major earth observation initiative concerns the International Charter: Space and Major Disasters, which provides satellite imagery free of charge for disaster response purposes around the world. Initiated in 2000 by the European and French space agencies (ESA and CNES), twelve other organizations joined the Charter and agreed to provide data from their earth observation systems (from Argentina, Brazil, Canada, China, Germany, India, Japan, Korea, Russia,

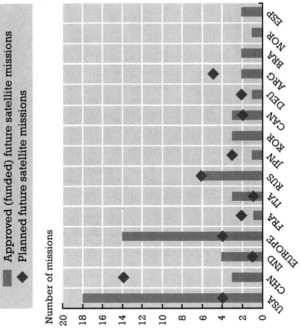

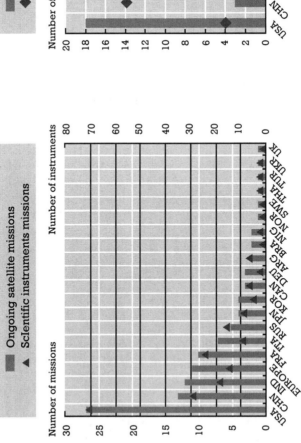

Figure 4.3 Selected ongoing and planned institutional earth observation missions by civilian agencies

Source: OECD, 2014.

United Kingdom and the United States). This co-ordination mechanism has been activated over 400 times in the past 15 years, providing imagery and maps to disaster-affected countries. The commercialization of earth observation data remains a niche area, with relatively few commercial satellite operators (e.g. Airbus' Spot Image, DigitalGlobe, MDA Geospatial Inc.). Their revenues are mainly derived from institutional customers. It is estimated that the security and military sectors account for about two-thirds of the commercial market. One example is the "Enhanced View" contract between DigitalGlobe and the US National Geospatial Agency, which accounted for 60% of the company's revenues in 2012 or about USD 250 million. Overall, the commercial satellite earth observation represents a market valued at some USD 1.5 billion in 2013, a doubling of revenues compared to 2008 (Satellite Industry Association, 2014). The share of satellite data sales to private actors is slowly increasing though. Finally, several new private initiatives are developing constellations with smaller, low-cost satellites, which may have strong impacts on the earth observation sector over the next decade.

As depicted in Figure 4.3, according to the latest OECD report (2014) the US is still the country with the largest number of EO missions, followed by China, India, Europe and France. The US is also the country with the largest number of approved future satellite missions, followed by Europe and Russia. We are on the edge of an exciting new era for earth observation and anyone can be part of it. For example, there is large scale satellite data from Copernicus, the largest single Earth observation programme in the world, probably also the most ambitious to date. Copernicus data is produced by satellite missions called the "Sentinels", aiming to autonomously and accurately provide global coverage of the earth. Each mission (composed of at least two satellites) has different sensors on-board and capabilities. Sentinel-1 (all weather radar mission) and Sentinel-2 (high-resolution optical mission) have six and five day repeat cycles at the equator, respectively. These satellites (along with Sentinel-3 and the upcoming missions 4, 5, 5P and 6) provide together a comprehensive picture of earth's health with unprecedented wealth of measurements both in quality and quantity, opening the floor to more extensive research and paving the way to new fields of research. All data is freely available and free of charge.

For many years, global earth observation services were offered by small number of operators. These were typically founded and financed by the space industry with the objective of providing high-resolution imagery. They would mostly rely on medium to large satellites with on-board data processing and advanced, custom-designed payloads. Governments were the primary customers. Recently, new competitors and new partnerships have recently emerged. These actors are now founded and financed by IT/analytics/tech sector to provide web-accessible, frequently updated imagery. They rely on smaller satellites, with lower costs of manufacture, launch and operation, supplemented with sophisticated ground-based data analytics. The main customer base is developing. Some of the new players include Planet Labs that acquired BlackBridge satellites and data library; UrtheCast purchased Deimos satellites and data; DigitalGlobe recently entered a joint venture with Saudi Arabia-based TAQNIA for a small constellation. In the sector, investments are mostly driven by interest in business intelligence products from satellite imagery. According to the latest data from the Satellite Industry Association (2016), 2015 was a record-setting year with investment in start-up space ventures of USD 2.3 billion, where several firms received venture capital investment in 2015. These were mainly BlackSky Global, GeoOptics, Hera, OmniEarth, Planet Labs, Satellogic, Spire Global.

Satellite weather and climate monitoring

Meteorology was the first scientific discipline to use space capabilities in the 1960s, and today satellites provide observations of the state of the atmosphere and ocean surface for the preparation of weather analyses, forecasts, advisories and warnings, for climate monitoring and environmental activities. Three quarters of the data used in numerical weather prediction models depend on satellite measurements (e.g. in France, satellites provide 93% of data used in Météo-France's Arpège model). Three main types of satellites provide data: two families of weather satellites and selected environmental satellites. Weather satellites are operated by agencies in China, France, India, Japan, Korea, the Russian Federation, the United States and Eumetsat for Europe, with international co-ordination by the World Meteorological Organisation (WMO). Some eighteen geostationary weather satellites are positioned above the earth's equator, forming a ring located at around 36,000 km. Their positioning – i.e. American satellites over the West Atlantic, European satellites over the East Atlantic, European and Indian satellites over the Indian Ocean – allows global coverage thanks to international co-operation in weather data exchanges. They share this congested geostationary orbit with more than 300 commercial telecommunications satellites. They are complemented by seventeen polar-orbiting weather satellites circling the earth at a much lower altitude (around 850 km) in sun-synchronous orbit, which allows them to revisit a given spot on earth every day at the same hour, making between seven and sixteen orbits per day (i.e. "morning" or "afternoon" satellite). The United States, Europe, China and the Russian Federation are so far the only ones operating these essential polar-orbiting satellites, which allow a closer monitoring of the earth's atmosphere. In addition to these dedicated weather satellites, around 160 environmental satellite missions in low-earth orbit are currently measuring selected climate parameters. Around 30% of these are bilateral or multilateral missions, with different countries providing key instruments on-board satellites. The United States, the European Space Agency and France have established the most joint operations for environmental satellite missions (e.g. NASA is co-operating with Japan's Aerospace Exploration Agency on the Tropical Rainfall Measuring Mission (TRMM); ESA and NASA cooperate on the Solar and Heliospheric Observatory (SOHO), while the French CNES is co-operating with India on the Megha-Tropiques mission to study the water cycle). Paradoxically, although

Table 4.1 Geostationary weather satellites

Actors:	Satellites' orbital position:	East Pacific	West Atlantic	East Atlantic	Indian Ocean	West Major Pacific
United States (NOAA)		1 sat. (GOES-15)	2 sats (GOES-12, GOES-14²)			
Europe (Eumetsat)				3 sats (meteosat-9, -10 and -11²)	1 sat. (Meteosat-7)	
India (Indian Space Research Organisation)					4 sats [INSAT-3C, Kalpana-1 INSAT-3D, INSAT-3A]	
Russian Federation (RosHydroMet)					1 sat. (Electro-L N1')	
China (China Meteorological Admin.)					2 sats (Feng-Yun-2D, FY-2E)	1 sat. (FY-2F²)
Korea (Korea Meteo. Administration)						1 sat. (COMS-1)
Japan (Japan Meteorological Agency)						2 sats (Himawari-6 and -7)

Source: OECD, 2014.
1. As of June 2014, some instruments are malfunctioning ("Warning" mode).
2. The satellite is about to become operational ("commissioning" mode).

there have never been so many weather and environmental satellites in orbit, funding issues in several OECD countries threaten the sustainability of the provision of essential long-term data series on climate. Table 4.1 below provides an overview of the geostationary weather satellites position for selected OECD countries.

Global positioning and navigation services

Like time-keeping, the ability to locate one's position or the position of various objects accurately and reliably is a growing need in our modern economies, with wide-ranging implications for traffic management, security, the environment, the management of natural resources and the provision of personal services (civil and commercial). As of spring 2014, six regional and global constellations are under development, with the American Global Positioning System (GPS) constellation already fully functional. All these constellations are institutional programmes, with satellites and ground segment systems contracted to national or regional space industries, but under national authority. The only exception is the Galileo programme, which is managed by the European Union. Around 100 navigation satellites could be in orbit by 2020, with at least four different satellite navigation systems with global coverage (GPS, Galileo, Glonass, Beidou), transmitting signals on multiple frequencies. Many consumer electronics companies are providing devices and services using location-based data. In terms of revenue generation, value-adders involved in satellite positioning, navigation and timing are perfect illustrations of downstream markets, only linked to the space industry by the satellite signals and data they use in their consumer products (e.g. navigation devices in cars, precision faming tools). When examining top actors in location based services such as Trimble, Mitac International, Tom Tom and Garmin, their 2013 revenues represent some USD 8 billion. These actors and others involved in Personal Navigation Device (PND) markets are looking at diversification, as smartphones and tablets are impacting the sale of proprietary PNDs. Other actors involved include manufacturers of receivers, and antennas. Some 47 manufactures surveyed in 2013 captured more than 95% of the market, with 380 receivers available commercially (OECD, 2014). Although estimates vary, a market report published by the European GNSS Agency estimates that Global Navigation Satellite Systems (GNSS) is used around the globe, with 3.6 billion GNSS devices in use in 2014. By 2019, this is forecasted to increase to over 7 billion – for an average of one device per person on the planet. Smartphones continue to dominate (3.08 billion in 2014), being the most popular platform to access location-based services, followed by devices used for road applications (0.26 billion). Other devices may be less numerous, but billions of passengers, professionals, consumers and citizens worldwide benefit from their application in efficient and safe transport networks, in productive and sustainable agriculture, surveying, and critical infrastructures (European GNSS Agency, 2015). Table 4.2 below provides an overview of the main satellite navigation constellations for selected OECD countries.

Table 4.2 Satellite navigation constellations

United States	Operational since April 1995, the Global Positioning Satellite (GPS) system is composed of 27 satellites, providing a horizontal accuracy of minimum 3 meters, which can be further enhanced by ground- or space-based augmentation systems. An upgrade of the constellation is currently under way with GPS-III satellites under production.
Russian Federation	Some 29 Glonass satellites in orbit, with 24 operating to provide global coverage. Accuracy is comparable to that of GPS, and commercial use of Glonass is increasing. The Russian Government approved a work programme in March 2012, allocating RUB 326,5 billion (≈USD 11 billion) for the period 2012–2020. The complete constellation would consist of 30 satellites in orbit, including six in reserve.
Europe	As of spring 2014, Galileo has four satellites, with six more satellites scheduled for launch by late 2014, at which point early services could be made available to the public. Galileo could reach full operational capability with 30 satellites around 2020. In 2008, a governance framework was established for the Galileo programme. It provides for the deployment of the full operational capability of the constellation under a public procurement scheme, entirely financed out of the European Union budget. The European Union also operated a GPS augmentation system, EGNOS, with transponders on three satellites, to improve accuracy.
China	The Chinese global positioning system, dubbed Compass/Bei Dou, is currently covering the Asia-Pacific region, with a constellation consisting of 14 operational satellites, as of May 2014. The constellation could reach global coverage by 2020, with 35 satellites.
India	The two first satellites in India's seven-satellites constellation, Indian Regional Navigation Satellite System (IRNSS), were successfully launched in July 2013 and April 2014. India has furthermore launched two out of three satellites that will contribute to the GPS augmentation system GAGAN, the last launch scheduled in 2014.
Japan	The Japanese Quasi-Zenith Satellite System (QZSS) is a space-based GPS augmentation system, compatible with GPS, which will consist of four satellites. The first satellites, Michibiki, was launched in 2010 with the remaining three satellites to be launched in the 2015–2017 period.

Source: OECD, 2014.

Space tourism

In recent years, public space travel, better known as space tourism, has evolved from a fringe market struggling to be taken seriously to an emerging, competitive market in which a large number of companies are seeking to gain a foothold. While orbital space tourism has maintained a steady level of activity, suborbital space tourism has seen a high degree of company activity and public interest. That is due in large part to the $10 million Ansari X Prize, won in October 2004 by Scaled Composites' SpaceShipOne, and concomitant activity by companies such as Rocketplane Kistler,

Space Adventures, and Virgin Galactic, all of which are selling tickets for commercial suborbital flights scheduled to begin before the end of the decade.

Space travel providers

As a result of increased public interest in space travel, several companies dealing with related activities have appeared. They offer services such as immersive computer simulations, training programmes similar to those of the astronauts using original means and equipment, parabolic flights of certain models of aircraft that simulate the feeling of weightlessness (such as Ilyushin 76 MDK), or flying at high altitude with jet aircraft type MiG-31. Nevertheless, we live in a society based on and driven by experiences, in which people constantly want new adventures. Therefore, there is a growing demand for new experiences regarding the space-related sphere of activities (Bunghez, 2015). The challenges involved in sending people into earth orbit go far beyond other tourism activities on earth. Therefore, the testing of technologies and their subsequent implementation is quite slow, as the hazards in case of failure can lead to the bankruptcy of companies that offer this type of service.

Since the 1980s, many organizations have enquired into the possibilities for space tourism. Although there was a great interest in this futuristic form of travel, the huge costs necessary for the development of space tourism made it an unprofitable venture. There was no viable financial solution to using space as a tourist area. Even so, a number of important advances in this area in recent years has brought hope and has created expectations (Billings, 2006a). An important step in the development of space tourism was made on the 4 October 2004, when the Ansari X PRIZE competition awarded a USD 10 million prize for the first non-governmental organization that managed to launch a reusable spacecraft at an altitude of 100 km. The winning project, SpaceShipOne, is capable of carrying three people to 100 km above the earth's surface, twice within two weeks (AnsariXPrize, 2017). Following this success, the project was taken under the wing of Virgin Galactic. Virgin Galactic is a British commercial space company founded by Richard Branson whose aim is to develop the technology necessary to offer travel services in the form of suborbital flights. The company is made up of hundreds of dedicated and passionate professionals. The staff includes scientists, engineers and designers united in their vision to create something new and resilient that stands the test of time: the first commercial space tourism network. The partnership between Scaled Composites and Virgin Galactic led to the development of an improved prototype. The spaceship was officially unveiled to the public on 7 December 2009 at the Mojave Air and Space Port in California. The current improved model, SpaceShipTwo, can carry six tourists along with the two pilots. The prototype has been tested several times, but progress was slowed down by several accidents. Nonetheless, continuous efforts have been made and on 29 April 2013, after nearly three years of unpowered testing, the first one constructed successfully performed its first powered test flight. However, on

31 October 2014 during a test flight, VSS Enterprise, the first SpaceShipTwo craft, broke up in flight and crashed in the Mojave Desert. The second Space-ShipTwo spacecraft, VSS Unity, was unveiled on 19 February 2016 and it is currently undergoing flight testing.

Once the spacecraft is deployed for tourism, the flight will start early in the morning and will be conducted in two phases. At launch, the spacecraft will be attached to a carrier aircraft that will take it to an altitude of 15 km. Then, the shuttle will come off the plane and will start the rocket engine that will propel it to an altitude of 110 km. There, the passengers will experience a feeling of weightlessness for about five minutes and will enjoy a panorama of about 1,600 km in all directions. Thereafter, the vessel will enter earth's atmosphere where it will be slowed down until it reaches an altitude of about 18 km. From here, it will land at the company's spaceport. The whole trip will last for about two and a half hours, but the actual flight time is much shorter. There will be two pilots and six tourists on board the shuttle. Each tourist will be assigned a seat next to a window to be able to enjoy the view and have enough space to experience the five minutes of weightlessness (Papathanassis, 2011). The SpaceShipTwo cabin was designed to offer tourists a maximum of safety and comfort, being the only spacecraft ever created to optimize the passenger experience. There are twelve windows on the side and above the tourists, thus giving passengers a better view of the earth and the cosmic space. Before the actual flight, the tourists will be staying for three days at a location near the space terminal, where they will go through a series of short training procedures that include training in an acceleration simulator, several presentations related to safety and a basic medical examination. The price of these services was set at USD 200,000 per person with the price expected to decrease as operations expanded and with the expansion of providers of such services in the market. There were more than 65.000 applications for the 100 tickets available for the first flights. In December 2007, Virgin Galactic recorded 200 customers who had paid in advance and 95% of them successfully passed the physical tests. By 2011, the number of paying customers had reached 400 and by early 2013, 575. In April 2013, Virgin Galactic increased the suborbital trip price to USD 250,000, the motivation being related to infla-tion (Papathanassis, 2011). The estimated total cost of the SpaceShipTwo project in 2011 was somewhere around USD 400 million. Except for the rocket engine that has to be replenished with fuel and oxidant after each flight, SpaceShipTwo is a fully reusable spacecraft.

Similarly, SpaceX CEO Elon Musk announced in February 2017 that SpaceX will fly two space tourists around the moon in 2018 and they had already paid a significant deposit for their trip (CNN, 2017). The travellers will undergo fitness tests and begin training later this year. For takeoff, SpaceX will use the same launch pad near Cape Canaveral, Florida, that was used for the Apollo missions. No humans have traveled past low earth orbit since the final Apollo mission in 1972. The company does not expect this to be a one-time mission. SpaceX said that more people have expressed a strong interest in making the trip. The names of the first two travellers have not been released nor the ticket prices for the trip. However, they are likely paying millions for the adventure since space tourists have previously paid the Russia government upwards of USD 20 million for a trip to the International Space Station. NASA has paid Russia USD 80 million a seat to send astronauts to the space station. SpaceX has not revealed the price of the roughly week-long trip. SpaceX is putting forward an aggressive timeline for the mission, which will rely on a rocket and spacecraft that have not flown yet. The Falcon Heavy rocket is expected to make a test flight in the summer of 2017 and the Crew Dragon spacecraft, which will hold the two tourists, will complete a demo mission later in 2017.

Other emerging players are also establishing themselves as space travel providers. Amongst these Space Adventures, an US-based space tourism company founded in 1998 by Eric C. Anderson. As of 2017, offerings include zero gravity atmospheric flights, orbital spaceflights to the ISS and around the moon and other spaceflight-related experiences including cosmonaut training, spacewalk training and launch tours. Seven clients have participated in the orbital spaceflight programme with Space Adventures and seven have participated in training only.

Similarly, World View is pioneering a new frontier at the edge of space. As an active, full-service commercial launch provider, World View's technology is already opening up new realms of possibility for commercial customers. In particular, World View's disruptive Stratollite flight platform, a helium-inflated balloon with an attached passenger capsule that soars 20 miles above the earth's surface enables previously unthinkable applications at a fraction of the cost of existing technology. Stratollites serve a variety of mission functions – from short duration research flights to long-duration flights over specific areas of interest and serve a broad range of critical commercial needs and applications. In the near future, World View will leverage the development of its Stratollite technology to pioneer a different type of discovery private space exploration. World View is led by experts in high-altitude ballooning, veterans of human spaceflight, and a team of retired NASA Astronauts, with a flight platform that is rooted deeply in technologies that have been successfully and safely used for decades. On 13 June 2017 KFC revealed the first details of its collaboration with World View. The chicken restaurant chain, which has been teasing the "spaceflight" in television ads for months, revealed the first details of its "Zinger 1" mission. KFC will fly a Zinger sandwich aboard the maiden voyage of World View Enterprises' Stratollite high-altitude platform. The breaded chicken breast filet, lettuce and mayonnaise sandwich will be carried high into the stratosphere under a helium-filled balloon before landing back on earth.

Go Russia, an authorized sale agent for MIG fighter flights in Russia, offers flights in supersonic MiG-29 fighter jets that flies to 14 miles above the earth's surface (twice the height of any commercial flight). They offer flights on MiG-29 and MiG-31 from the government authorized military site in Nizhniy Novgorod.

Another important space travel provider is Blue Origin. It is an American privately funded aerospace manufacturer and spaceflight services company set up by Amazon.com founder Jeff Bezos with its headquarters in Kent, Washington. The company is developing technologies to enable private human access to space with the goal to dramatically lower costs and increase reliability. Blue Origin is employing an incremental approach from suborbital to orbital flight, with each developmental step building on its prior work. The company motto is "Gradatim Ferociter", Latin for "Step by Step, Ferociously". Blue Origin is developing a variety of technologies, with a focus on rocket-powered Vertical Takeoff and Vertical Landing (VTVL) vehicles for access to suborbital and orbital space. Initially focused on sub-orbital spaceflight, the company has built and flown a testbed of its New Shepard spacecraft design. The first developmental test flight of the New Shepard was April 29, 2015. The uncrewed vehicle flew to its planned test altitude of more than 93.5 km (307,000 ft). A second flight was performed on 23 November 2015. The vehicle went just beyond 100 km (330,000 ft) altitude reaching space for the first time, and both the space capsule and its rocket booster successfully achieved a soft landing. On 22 January 2016 Blue Origin re-flew the same New Shepard booster that launched and landed vertically in November 2015, demonstrating reuse. On 2 April and 19 June 2016, the same New Shepard booster flew for its third and fourth flights, each time exceeding 330,000 ft (100 km) in altitude, before returning for successful soft landings. The first crewed test flights are planned to take place in early 2018, with the start of commercial service shortly after.

Already some emerging players have decided to abandon any ambition of providing space flights. For example, XCOR was initially planning to offer space flights to the public but the plan has been dropped. The company was founded in Mojave, California in 1999 and in 2012 XCOR had presold 175 Lynx flights at USD 95,000 each. The Lynx was planned to be capable of carrying a pilot and a passenger or payload on sub-orbital spaceflights over 100 kilometres (62 miles). Between 20 and 50 test flights of Lynx were planned, along with numerous static engine firings on the ground. In May 2016, the company halted development of the Lynx spaceplane and pivoted company focus toward development its LOX/LH2 engine technology. Subsequently the company laid off a significant portion of its workforce and placed the development of the Lynx Spacecraft on indefinite hold to focus on development of a rocket engine.

Bigelow Aerospace also abandoned its ambition of offering space flights to focus on its core competences – providing modular habitats for space. The firm is an American space technology startup company, based in North Las Vegas, Nevada that manufactures and develops expandable space station modules. Bigelow Aerospace was founded by Robert Bigelow in 1998 and is funded in large part by the profit Bigelow earned through his ownership of the hotel chain Budget Suites of America. In 2004 Bigelow established and funded a USD 50 million prize, America's Space Prize, to stimulate development of manned vehicles. The prize expired without a winner in early 2010. In August 2009, Bigelow Aerospace announced the development of the Orion Lite spacecraft, intended to be a lower cost, and less capable version of the Orion spacecraft under development by NASA. Orion Lite was an unofficial name used in the media for a lightweight crew capsule proposed in collaboration with Lockheed Martin. It was to be based on the Orion spacecraft that Lockheed Martin was developing for NASA. It would be a lighter, less capable and cheaper version of the full Orion. The intention of designing Orion Lite would be to provide a stripped down version of the Orion that will be available for missions to the International Space Station earlier than the more capable Orion, which is designed for longer duration missions to the moon, Mars, Lagrange points, and near Earth asteroids. Bigelow began working with Lockheed Martin in 2004. Orion Lite's primary mission would be to transport crew to the International Space Station, or to private space stations such as the proposed Sundancer from Bigelow Aerospace. While Orion Lite would have the same exterior dimensions as the Orion, there would be no need for the deep space infrastructure present in the Orion configuration. As such, the Orion Lite will be able to support larger crews of around seven people as the result of greater habitable interior volume and the reduced weight of equipment needed to support an exclusively low-earth-orbit configuration. The proposed collaboration between Bigelow and Lockheed Martin on the Orion Lite spacecraft has ended. As for 2017, Bigelow seems to have abandoned any ambition in the field of space travel. The company's effort is now geared towards providing safe and low-cost commercial space platforms for low earth orbit, the moon and beyond.

Space travel demand

According to Bunghez (2015), research shows that people generally have the curiosity to travel to space. Nevertheless, this desire is expressed without fully acknowledging the costs and risks that space tourism entails. From the existing bookings, it is clear that enough people show interest and have the financial capacity to fulfill this dream. In this context, marketing research is essential for space tourism to better understand the consumer's behavior regarding such services. Since space tourism is technologically feasible, there is a wide range of variables to be analyzed from the point of view of entrepreneurs as well as that of potential consumers. For example, the relationship between customer demand and pricing and what would be considered as the most important set of characteristics of a space tourism experience that would determine the willingness of clients to pay that amount. Clearly, people focus their attention on the price of the travel. However, the safety aspect of that kind of an experience has also to be considered. Flying in space is still dangerous and all tourists must accept that they are subject to relatively high risks in terms of health. Dawson (2017) for instance in her book *The Politics and the Perils of Space Exploration* devotes an entire chapter to the dangers of longer orbital missions in the outer space. Amongst these, the long-term effects of microgravity on muscle atrophy as well as bone loss. Additionally, months in space are known to cause weakened immune systems and impaired vision. Dawson also mentions radiation as another possible danger, cardiovascular effects and "madness" that might occur if a human were left to experience long periods of microgravity and isolation on a long-term space mission. For shorter missions Bunghez (2015) mentions the stress placed on the body during takeoff, landing, the effects of exposure to the feeling of weightlessness and the fact that the whole journey is performed in a relatively small space are characteristics that can influence the health of even the most enduring people therefore requiring a set of basic medical examinations.

People around the world are already prepared for an adventure in space, despite its high price and physical risk. One emblematic example is the stunning number of applications received by Mars One. The Mars One organization has proposed to land the first humans on Mars and establish a permanent human colony there by 2035. The private spaceflight project is led by Dutch entrepreneur Bas Lansdorp, who announced the Mars One project in May 2012. Mars One's original concept included launching a robotic lander and orbiter as early as 2020 to be followed by a human crew of four in 2024 and one in 2026. Organizers plan for the crew to be selected from applicants to become the first permanent residents of Mars with no plan of returning to earth. The application period extended from 22 April 2013 to 31 August 2013. This first application consists of applicant's general information, a motivational letter, a résumé and a video. More than 200,000 people expressed interest, so Mars One plans to hold several other application periods in the future. By 9 September 2013, 4,227 applicants had paid their registration fee and submitted public videos in which they made their case for going to Mars in 2023.

One of the most comprehensive studies of the market is Futron's Space Tourism Market Study report, published in 2002 (Futron Corporation, 2002). That report provided a forecast for the demand for orbital and suborbital space tourism activities through 2021. The forecast was based on a comprehensive survey by Futron and polling firm Zogby International of individuals with the means to pay for such flights, which set it apart from many previous surveys that polled the public at large, often through self-selecting non-scientific means.

According to the report, space tourism should target initially rich and adventurous young people. They seem to form the most suitable target market due to their carefree rebellious approach and a willingness to accept a low level of comfort to be among the first passengers in space (Crouch, et al., 2008). Then to ensure sustainable profits, space travel providers should implement a skimming pricing strategy (Goehlich, 2005). This is a marketing strategy that at first introduces high prices for a new product in order to obtain the maximum profit possible. Thus, initially, the tickets for these space trips will be bought by very wealthy people with a considerable disposable income. Then the cost of the tickets will decrease over time, targeting an ever-growing market segment with each sequential drop in price. This pricing strategy will make every client pay the maximum amount they would be willing to pay. It is expected that the number of space travelers will grow somewhere to a million per year when the price of a ticket will be under USD 10,000 (Bunghez, 2015).

In terms of uptake of the service, when the market adopts a completely new technology services, it generally follows a model called the "S" curve (Furtron, 2002). According to this model, there is initial slow customer absorption until the market becomes familiar with the product, followed by a period of rapid adoption when the market fully engages in the purchase of the product, culminating in a slowdown, when the market reaches saturation. Since the original forecast was completed in 2002, there have been many major developments in the space tourism marketplace, principally in suborbital space tourism. Short of performing an entirely new study, in 2006 Futron decided to recalibrate the original results. To date this is the most recent comprehensive study on the likely evolution of the space industry (Futron Corporation, 2006).

The forecast of suborbital space tourism passenger demand from both the original study as well as the current revision are shown in Figure 4.4. Passenger demand is lower in the new forecast, with a projected demand of just over 13,000 passengers in the final year of the forecast, 2021, compared to over 15,000 passengers in the original study.

Both the original study and the revised forecast used a 40-year period to market maturity to define the Fisher-Pry S-curve used to project demand. Changing this value will affect the passenger demand forecast: a shorter period will increase demand, particularly in the out-years of the forecast.

Future scale of space tourism industry

The forecast of potential annual revenue from suborbital passenger services from the revised study is shown in Figure 4.5. The potential revenue in 2021 in the

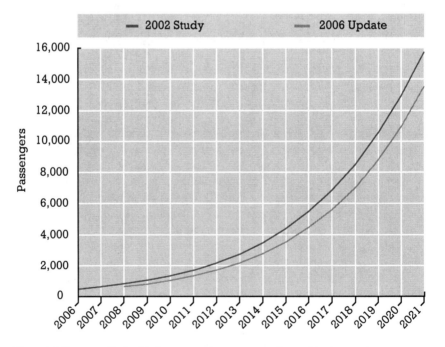

Figure 4.4 Forecast of suborbital space tourism passenger demand in thousands

Source: Futron Corporation, 2006.

revised forecast is USD 676 million, compared to USD 785 million in the original study. The difference in passenger demand causes the lower revenue figures in the revised forecast, although the impact of initial ticket prices actually produces higher revenues in some parts of the forecast period, reflecting the interaction of price changes and user demand.

As can be inferred from the figure, the economic potential of space tourism development is extraordinary and holds great potential. The expansion of this type of tourism will bring significant benefits, both economically and socially. The development of the space tourism sector would generate, in addition to indirect scientific and technological advances, a direct important economic component. This will lead on to an exponential growth of this sector. Because space tourism has the potential to become a new important branch of the tourist industry using advanced aerospace technology, the economic effects of this development will be significant for both these industries involved, as well as for the global economic progress and development of society as a whole. In particular research shows that implementing an effective strategy of informing the public and media regarding global economic benefits that would result from the development of commercial space travel is crucial for its uptake (Futron, 2006; Bunghez, 2015). It is expected that space tourism will become a significant economic generator. As launch costs decrease dramatically in the future, this will lead to a significant acceleration of the development of this industry. According to Collins (2002), in addition to its

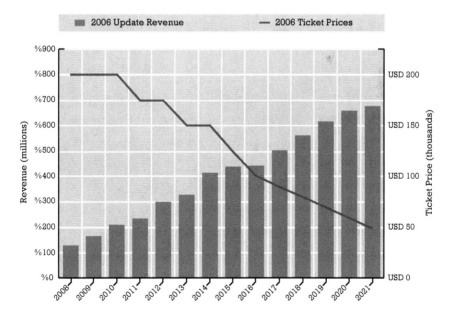

Figure 4.5 Revenue forecast for space tourism

Source: Futron Corporation, 2006.

economic value as a popular consumer service, making space travel available to the general public would have great social value. Thanks to its well-known inspirational and educational value it would seem highly desirable in comparison with many other "unnecessary" activities that are proliferating in rich countries, such as the use of recreational but often addictive drugs, gambling and pornography, to mention a few. In addition to the great popularity of the activity itself, there is enormous scope for provision of even more interesting experiences in space with the development of progressively more advanced hotels, orbiting sports centres, lunar hotels, and other facilities such as space ports. Spaceports are an emblematic example of how space in the future could further generate economic value and many ancillary activities can actually spur from the sector.

Although some critics have claimed that space tourism will be no more than a pastime of the very rich (Billings, 2006b), the basic scenario proposed by Collins (2002) is aimed firmly at serving the middle-class market, and leads to some 700,000 passengers paying a little more than USD 20,000 each for return flights to orbit. Further growth to reach 5 million passengers, would require an annual growth rate of some 16%, which is not unrealistic by comparison with growth rates seen in other popular services. This would give a scenario like that shown in Figure 4.6.

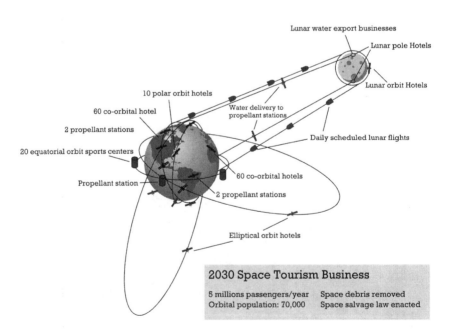

Figure 4.6 2030 Space Tourism Industry
Source: Collings, 2002.

On this scenario, 40 million people would have visited space by 2030, that is an estimated 2% of the middle class at that time. The cost to taxpayers to realize this scenario would be far less than the USD 750 billion that they would have to pay through 2030 for space agency activities on their existing budgets, since most of the investment would come from the private sector. Several million people would be directly and indirectly employed in related activities, and tens of thousands of people would work part-time in space as hotel staff. The low cost of access to space that would be brought about by such large-scale space tourism would also lead to other forms of economic development in space which are not possible at present high launch costs. By bringing costs down and providing services for which there is a large consumer demand, space tourism uniquely offers the promise of realizing these long-term possibilities.

Conclusion

This chapter has provided an overview of the downstream activities derived from space infrastructures, mostly in the form of services that are provided by the space sector. As well as generating revenues, the delivery of space services generates indirect benefits such as the positive externalities stemming from the industry and affecting society at large. The next two chapters are devoted to the analysis of the individual capabilities of selected countries that play a crucial role in the industry.

References

AnsariXPrize, 2017. Prize Progress. Available at: http://ansari.xprize.org/.

Billings, L., 2006a. How shall we live in space? Culture, law and ethics in spacefaring society. *Space Policy*, 22(4), 249–255.

Billings, L., 2006b. Exploration for the masses? Or joyrides for the ultra-rich? Prospects for space tourism. *Space Policy*, 22(4), 162–164.

Bunghez, C. L., 2015. Space Tourism Market Analysis. Current Situation and Future Trends. *International Conference on Marketing and Business Development Journal*, I(1/2015), 97–103.

CNN, 2017. Available at: http://money.cnn.com/2017/02/27/technology/spacex-moon-tourism/.

Collins, P., 2002. Meeting the needs of the new millennium: passenger space travel and world economic growth. *Space Policyi*, 18 (1), 183–197.

Crouch, G. I., Devinney, T. M., Louviere, J. J. & Islam, T., 2008. Modelling consumer choice behaviour in space tourism. *Tourism Management*, 30(3), 441–454.

Dawson, L., 2017. The Politics and Perils of Space Exploration, Springer.

European GNSS Agency, 2015. Available at: https://www.gsa.europa.eu/system/files/reports/GNSS-Market-Report-2015-issue4_0.pdf.

Futron Corporation, 2004. Space Tourism Market Study – Orbital Space Travel & Destinations with Suborbital Space Travel.

Futron Corporation, 2006. Suborbital Space Tourism Demand Revisited. Available at: https://www.rymdturism.se/images/pdf/Futron-Suborbital-Space-Tourism-Demand-Revisited-Aug-2006.pdf.

Goehlich, R. A., 2005. A ticket pricing strategy for an oligopolistic space tourism market. *Space Policy*, 21, 293–306.

OECD, 2014. The Space Economy at a Glance. Available at: http://www.keepeek.com/ Digital-Asset-Management/oecd/economics/the-space-economy-at-a-glance-2014_9789264217294-en#.WleREqjiZPY.

Papathanassis, A., 2011. The long tail of tourism. Gabler.

Satellite Industry Association, 2016. State of the Satellite Industry Report. Available at: http:// www.sia.org/wp-content/uploads/2016/06/SSIR16-Pdf-Copy-for-Website-Compressed. pdf.

Section II
The national players

5   The USA space programme

Introduction

The United States is the leading nation with respect to championing the development of the commercial space sector. In this chapter we explore the history of the US space programme and then we discuss how NASA has gradually moved towards higher involvement with commercial space, following government policy that has been fostering this direction. We begin by outlining how the space race has spurred investment in space technology. We then discuss NASA's creation, and its ethos and organization, before noting environmental and regulatory changes that have resulted in increased bureaucracy and inertia. We note how the "faster, better, cheaper" approach tried to shake up the agency with mixed results. Funding and policy uncertainty, combined with critiques of NASA's performance were the backdrop for the emergence of commercial space. We note how NASA has developed its own capabilities over time as a state actor in collaborating with commercial space more effectively; and how commercial space is changing the shape of the industry from a hierarchical one dominated by NASA, to a network one where NASA is an orchestrator and influencer.

The space race spurs investment in space technology

The space race between the United States and the USSR for supremacy in space took place between 1955 and 1972, in the context of the ongoing Cold War between the two nations (Beggs, 1984). The space race had both ideological and military overtones. The basic technology of space launch rockets was derived from intercontinental ballistic missile rockets developed by Nazi Germany in the Second World War. The allies (United States, the USSR and the United Kingdom) all captured parts of the German rocket technology, plans, data and engineering personnel. The United States arguably captured the leading members of the German engineering body, including Wernher von Braun, the technical director of the German ballistic missile program.

In the context of the Cold War, both the US and USSR announced in 1955, four days apart (the former on 29 July and the latter on 2 August), that they would launch artificial satellites in space in the near future. This was the symbolic start to the space race. In October 1957 the USSR surprised the US by successfully launching the satellite Sputnik 1, which conveyed the first signals to earth from orbit. The United States then tried to accelerate its own satellite launch, which was attempted on 6 December of the same year at Cape Canaveral with Project Vanguard. This was a televised failure, which further sparked controversy and concern in the United States regarding the USSR's assumed supremacy in space-faring technology. This concern was further intensified in April 1961, when the USSR launched the first human in space, Cosmonaut Yuri Gagarin, who also achieved the first manned orbital flight. In May 1961, the United States launched Astronaut Alan Shepard in space in spacecraft Freedom 7. Even though he did not achieve orbit, he was the first person in space to manually control their spacecraft.

After Yuri Gagarin's flight to space, public concern in the US prompted President Kennedy to seriously consider the United States' investments in space-related activities and to focus these efforts in a way that would display American superiority in space. On 25 May 1961, President Kennedy made a speech to Congress where he argued that the United States should "commit itself to achieving the goal, before this decade is out, of landing a man on the Moon and returning him safely to the Earth". Kennedy delivered a further speech on 12 September 1962 at Rice University in Houston, to over 35,000 American citizens that served to win popular support for the United States' space effort.

Given the immense cost of a space programme and the cost and technological synergies that could result from collaboration, President Kennedy had proposed on 20 September 1963, during his speech at the United Nations General Assembly that the United States and the USSR could work together on their space activities. Soviet Premier Khrushchev initially did not agree to this suggestion. By the time Khrushchev had the time to reconsider, President Kennedy had been assassinated on 22 November 1963 and collaboration between the two nations was delayed until 1972.

Both the United States and the USSR continued their space activities in earnest, despite occasional setbacks and fatal accidents on both sides. Important milestones were accomplished by both nations, as shown in Table 5.1 below.

The space race reached its climax when the United States' Apollo 11 mission landed on the moon on 20 July 1969. The crew consisted of Commander Neil Armstrong, Command Module Pilot Michael Collins, and Lunar Module Pilot Edwin "Buzz" Aldrin. When Armstrong took the first steps on the moon, and uttered the words "That's one small step for man, one giant leap for mankind", it was a global event watched by over 700 million people. The United States accomplished five more lunar landings with Apollo 12, 14, 15, 16 and 17, between 1969 and 1972.

After the United States' moon landings, the USSR focused on launching orbital space stations, launching the Salyut 1 laboratory in April 1971. The Salyut programme consisted of four crewed scientific space stations and two crewed military reconnaissance stations. The United States launched Skylab in May 1973, followed by three manned missions to Skylab.

Table 5.1 The space race

Date	Milestone
1955 (29 July and 2 August)	The US announces that it would launch artificial satellites in space, followed by similar announcement 4 days later by the USSR. The Space race is sparked.
1957 (4 October)	USSR launches first artificial satellite (Sputnik 1) that conveys signals from space
1957 (3 November)	USSR places first animal in orbit, Laika the dog, on Sputnik 2
1958 (31 January)	US launches its first satellite, Explorer 1, that detects the Van Allen radiation belts
1959 (2 January)	USSR launches the first lunar spacecraft (Luna 1), that detects solar wind
1959 (17 February)	US launches the first weather satellite (Vanguard 2)
1959 (7 August)	US satellite Explorer 6 takes the first photo of the earth from space
1959 (14 September)	USSR satellite Luna 2 makes the first impact into a celestial body, the Moon
1960 (19 August)	USSR craft Sputnik 5 brings back the first alive animals and plants from space
1961 (12 April)	USSR Cosmonaut Yuri Gagarin achieves the first human spaceflight and first manned orbital flight on the Vostok 1 craft
1961 (5 May)	US Astronaut Alan Shepard achieves first spaceflight manually controlled by a pilot on the Freedom 7 craft
1963 (16 June)	Valentina Tereshkova becomes the first woman and first civilian in space on USSR craft Vostok 6
1965 (18 March)	First spacewalk by Cosmonaut Alexey Leonov on the USSR Voskhod 2 craft
1966 (3 February)	USSR craft Luna 9 achieves first soft landing on a celestial body (the Moon) and takes the first photos from the Moon
1966 (16 March)	US craft Gemini 8 achieves the first docking with another spacecraft
1968 (21 December)	First manned flight to, and orbit of, the Moon by US craft Apollo 8
1969 (20 July)	First humans walk on the Moon, and first launch from a celestial body (the Moon) is achieved, with the US' Apollo 11 craft
1970 (15 December)	USSR craft Venera 7 achieves first soft landing on Venus and sends first signals from Venus
1971 (14 November)	US craft Mariner 9 is first craft to orbit Mars
1971 (2 December)	USSR craft Mars 3 makes the first soft landing on Mars and sends first signals from Mars
1972 (17 July)	USSR Soyuz and US Apollo crafts dock together, and their crews carry joint experiments and exchange gifts. Space race symbolically ends

Beginning in 1969, there was an easing of political tensions between the United States and the USSR, known as détente. In this context, in May 1972, US President Richard Nixon and Soviet Premier Leonid Brezhnev decided that the two nations would collaborate on a joint mission, the docking of an Apollo and a Soyuz crafts. This took place on 17 July 1972. The American and Soviet crews conducted joint experiments, visited each other's crafts and exchanged gifts. This collaboration marked the symbolic end to the space race.

NASA's creation and organizational setup

NASA was instituted by the US Congress as a legal entity in 1958 with the mandate of accomplishing "the preservation of the role of the United States as a leader in aeronautical and space science and technology" (National Aeronautics Space Act, 1958, Sec102, c5). NASA was initially mainly constituted through the pre-existing research centres of the National Advisory Committee for Aeronautics (NACA), created in 1915 to help expedite the development of US aeronautical technology after the onset of the First World War (NASA History Program Office, 2015). On 1 October 1958, five NACA facilities officially made up NASA. At its founding NASA had 8,240 staff, 8,000 of which came from NACA, and an annual budget of USD 100m (Portee, 1998). NACA's culture emphasized a can-do, problem-solving attitude, applied experimentation in well-run laboratories with a focus on aeronautics, and worked with contractors as needed, to supply required infrastructure such as parts of large wind tunnels or other simulators (Bugos & Boyd, 2008).

In July 1960 the Army Ballistic Missile Agency in Alabama, which included German rocket scientists who had moved to the US after the Second World War, formally became a part of NASA and was renamed the George C Marshall Space Flight Center. In May 1961 President Kennedy issued the challenge of "landing a man on the moon and returning him safely to earth" before the decade was out. Later that year, in September, newly appointed NASA Administrator James Webb announced that the Manned Spacecraft Center in Houston (renamed as the Lyndon B Johnson Space Center in 1973), would be the centre responsible for human space flight. The John F Kennedy Space Center was then founded in 1962 in Florida, as a primary launch facility, managed by German engineers from the Marshall Space Flight Center.

Each centre developed a particular culture through its history. Employees of Langley laboratory for example took pride in Langley's intellectual prowess in terms of technology. The Ames laboratory was a spin-off of the Langley laboratory and displayed a strong engineering hands-on approach. The rocket scientists at the Army Ballistic Missile Agency embodied a highly technocratic culture with particular emphasis on detail, proceeding incrementally and being in control of all stages of a project from technical research and planning to actual fabrication of equipment. In contrast to the in-house culture at Langley Center and the ABMA (later Marshall Center), the Manned Spacecraft Center (later Johnson Space Center) relied to a larger extent on contractors' assistance for a significant part of its activities (McCurdy, 1993; 2010). Each centre was dedicated to exploration in its own domain, within a largely decentralized corporate design. Reliance on technical competencies that were found within the organization was a founding principle. The centres had a robust sense of autonomy, engendering a "not invented here" attitude and a sense of technical superiority that was part of the political narrative at the time. At the time, accomplishing technological breakthroughs that would aid space exploration and achieving the geopolitical goals of the US was instrumental.

NASA had to still fulfill the core function of aeronautics research that was its NACA legacy while embarking on the human exploration of space. Langley, Ames and Lewis were centres dedicated to ongoing aeronautics research, providing services and knowledge to the aeronautics industry, while the newer centres were focused on exploration of space. The Centres' different histories, cultures, spatial separation across the country, decentralization and high degrees of autonomy facilitated the agency's ability to simultaneously employ existing resources and infrastructure to support the growing aeronautics industry while taking the risks required to achieve the goal of landing a man on the moon by the end of the decade. The loose coupling across the centres enabled organizational adaptability as the demands of the environment and mission imperatives changed (Beggs, 1984). NASA maintained the spatial separation of centres when it added the Goddard Research Center and Jet Propulsion Laboratory.

However, there was some duplication of resources and research efforts across centres, which challenged efficiency. According to Levine (1992: 199), "From its very inception, NASA was not a unified whole . . . Glennan, the first NASA administrator, saw as one of his main tasks the integration of these diverse units into one organization. But that integration never took place", leading to overlap of responsibilities and poor coordination. According to the Space Foundation (2012: 17) report, "while the centers can and do cooperate on specific matters, anything that challenges a center's autonomy, independence, or turf is met with immediate and stubborn resistance".

Shared norms and mission lead to outperformance

Despite differences in culture across NASA's centres, there were from the early years several common norms which derived from their laboratory, applied research-oriented history, as well as the professional cultures of scientists and engineers: "a commitment to research, testing and verification; to in-house technical capability; to hands-on activity; to the acceptance of risk and failure; to open communications; to a belief that NASA was staffed with exceptional people; to attention to detail; and to a 'frontiers of flight' mentality" (McCurdy, 1989: 302).

In the early years NASA was able to develop and maintain its technical capability by practicing and prioritizing in-house technical work and a hands-on work environment for its engineers which had originated with NACA and AMBA. Hands-on work helped to maintain in-house technical capabilities, a pride in NASA's own competencies, the ability to keep engineers up to date and the potential to attract exceptional employees (McCurdy, 2010). The emphasis on extensively testing hardware before sending it into space was an important operating principle of each of the centres, a shared value that became stronger when human space flight begun. This also shaped the relationship with contractors in terms of "contractor penetration" by NASA personnel to ensure that these norms were adopted (McCurdy, 1993: 117).

The precipitating event triggering higher degrees of cooperation among the dispersed units was the shared desire "to go to the moon, plus the competition and the deadline that was imposed by the knowledge that the Russians were trying to do the same . . . When project Apollo came along in 1961, it transformed the requirements that were placed on these research laboratories" (McCurdy, 2013). President Kennedy's vision of going to the moon and returning safely before the decade was out, was a super-ordinate goal that precipitated a period of intense focus and collaboration at NASA, and enabled the Apollo programme that accomplished manned missions to the moon.

Expanded regulation and organizational inertia

After its founding in 1958 and during the Apollo era (1961–1972), NASA enjoyed a great degree of autonomy in terms of determining its own operating procedures and policies, for example in terms of recruitment and remuneration. NASA enjoyed a reputation as a high-end, frontier-pushing scientific organization, able to attract young employees from top tier universities. The average age of employees in the control room during the moon landing in 1969 was 26 (Teitel, 2012). Under NASA's first Administrator, Keith Glennan (who led NASA from October 1958 to January 1961) Congress had allowed NASA to fill over 700 positions that were not subject to federal pay scales, affording the organization flexibility to compete with industry for the brightest, most capable employees (Levine, 1982).

The Ethics in Government Act of 1978, introduced after the Watergate scandal, had the noble intent of creating more transparency and limiting lobbying power. Public officials had to disclose financial and employment history, and public agencies were hampered in their ability to employ people who have worked in industry due to possible conflicts of interest. The Federal Civil Service Agency reversed NASA's rights to pay salaries to specialists that were not subject to Federal Payment Regulation thereby limiting NASA's recruitment flexibility (Levine, 1982).

Employee turnover rates at NASA reduced and new hires decreased, leading to a steadily aging demographic within the agency. Between 1960 and 1968, turnover rates ranged between 10% and 15%, whereas between 1969 and 1990 they ranged between 5% and 10% (McCurdy, 1993). Employee turnover rates have been on a downward trend, with the turnover of non-retiree employees falling to 1.7% in 2013 (Heracleous & Gonzalez, 2014; NASA, 2014). Further, the average age of NASA employees has been on the rise. In 1993, 45–59 year-old employees made up 38% of NASA's workforce; by 2013 this figure was 57%.

In 1993, 20–34 year-old employees made up 32% of NASA's workforce. By 2013, this figure decreased to 15%.

Meanwhile, more structured management approaches were implemented. Given the administrative requirements of the Apollo programme, the government ushered in large systems engineering principles imported from the military. These were authorized by headquarters (level A) and employed by programme offices (level B) to coordinate projects across subunits (level C). Hierarchy and formalization, inspired by military roots, increased. Progressive budget restrictions following Apollo led NASA to expand contracting out to organizations that could perform tasks or develop technology more efficiently, and less hands-on work was conducted internally (McCurdy, 1989). This shift towards private industry also provided seed capabilities to grow the commercial space community. As more contract funding and expertise was distributed to the contractor community it provided opportunity for new aerospace companies to emerge and leverage this engineering input.

Concurrently general federal regulations grew, imposing higher administrative demands on NASA in terms of the introduction of expanded accounting standards, occupational health and safety and environmental protection laws, and over 60 new procurement laws between 1965 and 1991. US Congress staff grew 300% in the first 30 years of NASA's existence, which increased the demands on government agencies in their efforts to engage with US Congress (McCurdy, 1993). Tragic accidents such as the fire on board of Apollo 1 in 1967 and the Challenger disaster in 1986 heavily increased political oversight.

NASA was not immune to the growth of state administrative regulations and the need for detailed reporting led to corresponding growth in all of the government agencies including NASA's own dedicated administrative resource. Up till 1956, around 2% of NASA's employees were working in the agency's headquarters. By 1990, this figure had risen to almost 9%. Further, while around 5% of NASA employees were professional administrators in 1961 working in all of NASA's units, this figure had risen to over 18% by 1991 (McCurdy, 1993).

Process management tools such as ISO and Six Sigma have been implemented at NASA. Benner & Tushman (2003) note that the standardization and efficiency orientation of such tools have a variation decreasing effect; they streamline processes but at the same increase inertia and decrease adaptability. Researchers have associated inertia with a company's age and size, higher levels of which tend to foster bureaucracy (Han et al., 2001) unless there is a strong market orientated culture to act as an effective countervailing force. Tushman and O'Reilly (1996: 18) associate firms that have grown in size and age with structural and cultural inertia, the "organizational equivalent of high cholesterol". The burgeoning of regulatory demands on NASA, and the corresponding internal increase in administrative resource, coupled with lower flexibility in terms of human resource decisions and a low turnover in the workforce, were factors that together contributed to an increase in structural and cultural inertia at NASA.

The faster, better, cheaper approach brings mixed results

Responding to stakeholder concerns about NASA's high costs, Daniel Goldin, NASA administrator from 1992 to 2001, introduced the "faster, better, cheaper" (FBC) approach which aimed to continue bold exploration but at significantly lower cost (Lambright, 2007; Spear, 1998). Historically, NASA processes have been influenced by the systems management approach brought in from the Air Force during the Apollo era. Systems management combined both decentralization, leaving individual centres the freedom to carry out technical hands-on activity and extensive testing, with centralization through the employment of highly detailed procedures by central project managers to track the progress of large projects with the ultimate aim of tracking performance and reliability (McCurdy, 2001). The focus on testing and reliability reduced the likelihood of failure, but at the same time downplayed cost consciousness (Augustine, 2009; McCurdy, 1992). In order to achieve maximum reliability, and influenced by NASA's technocratic culture, engineers incorporated redundancy for multiple scenarios, tested parts relentlessly and built in various sensors and safety features, resulting in skyrocketing costs and stretching of schedules (McCurdy, 2001).

Goldin's FBC approach involved focus on smaller missions, incorporation of advanced technology, reduction of headquarter management and decentralization to centres, a higher emphasis on teamwork and co-location, reduction of agency headcount and less emphasis on detailed documentation. When Goldin arrived at NASA he announced that multi-year contracts that did not meet certain criteria would be cancelled, something unprecedented. He noted that this led to increased competition for NASA contracts by both established and entrepreneurial companies, and to reduced costs (Goldin, 2002). It also created "the appearance of chaos, but it wasn't chaos. It was the unleashing of competition. And it was the competition of ideas that allowed us to triple the number of craft we were building, cut the average cost of building each spacecraft by two-thirds, and cut the cycle time by 40%" (Goldin, 2002: 24).

Nevertheless, FBC programmes as a whole met with a 37% failure rate, significantly above previous norms. There were two main reasons for these higher failure rates. First, linear increases in project complexity entailed exponential increases of required project costs to effectively address this complexity (Bearden, 2003; Sarsfield, 1998). FBC however involved cost and schedule reduction at a faster rate than that which complexity could be reduced, leading to higher failure rates. Second, there was incongruence between the FBC streamlined way of doing things and the established large systems management approach. This large systems approach involved hands-on extensive testing and documentation and continued significant outsourcing to contractors who were not entirely on board with the FBC approach. The inertia of existing processes led to inadequate coordination between different teams and centres involved in projects (McCurdy, 2001).

For example, for the Climate Orbiter project carried out under the FBC approach, the Jet Propulsion Laboratory cooperated with the private corporation

Lockheed Martin Astronautics. The project, which aimed to launch a probe to Mars, failed due to the fact that JPL used the metric system for their calculations whereas Lockheed Martin used English imperial measurements. The Climate Orbiter cost USD 326.6m to develop and simply disappeared behind Mars (NASA, 2013). It would be fair to say that the FBC approach left a mixed legacy within NASA (Lambright, 2007; McCurdy, 2013).

Funding and policy uncertainty

NASA's budget accounted for 4.5% of the federal budget in 1969, the year of the moon landing, having risen steeply to that percentage from a base of around 0.1% in 1958, the year of NASA's founding. The dramatic rise in funding in NASA's initial years had a significant impact on NASA's cultural attitude towards cost control. The goal of human spaceflight in the 1960s was primarily geopolitical (National Research Council, 2012). Given the Cold War context that triggered the space race, the belief developed within NASA that the US government would spend any amount needed to establish US leadership in space. Accomplishing the goals mattered much more than doing so efficiently (Hall, 2003; McCurdy, 2001). After the manned moon landings (1969–1972), many politicians were not convinced about the need to continue spending large amounts on spaceflight, which led to gradual reductions in NASA's budget (McCurdy, 2001). By 2017 NASA's share of the federal budget had progressively dropped to 0.4%, while stretch goals such as a manned flight to Mars were being planned (Amadeo, 2017).

In order to receive funding for large projects, project managers often indicated overly optimistic cost projections when applying for funding (National Research Council, 2012). Year after year NASA received cuts to its budget necessitating it to re-plan programmes and reduce capabilities from the original design, that resulted in impacting the total life cycle cost. For example, individual launch costs of the space shuttle were estimated at USD 450 million but then cost USD 1.3 billion per flight (Pinchefsky, 2012).

Over the years, there has been some ambivalence in how stakeholders view NASA. According to a 1961 Gallup poll, 52% of Americans believed that NASA would reach the moon before the decade was over, but 58% felt that Congress was spending too much money for this endeavor (McCurdy, 2001). A 2009 Gallup poll indicated that 58% of respondents agreed that NASA had created enough benefits for the US and is worth its costs, 13% believed that NASA was doing an excellent job, and 45% thought it was doing a good job (Gallup, 2009). When the National Research Council conducted an independent assessment of NASA's strategic direction and agency management, it reported that NASA's strategic planning process was influenced to a greater extent by outside forces than internally (National Research Council, 2012), consistent with NASA's external source of funding. NASA programmes and direction are influenced by its stakeholders: the public, congress and the president.

NASA is expected to accurately forecast, for projects that take years or decades to develop, how much cost it will incur in a specific year. Yet, the appropriation of funds by Congress occurs on an annual basis. Hence, there is a temporal incongruence between NASA's programme development and US Congress funding mechanisms. McCurdy argues that this "encourages bureaucrats to spend money they do not need or waste time waiting for appropriations they have not received" (McCurdy, 2001: 96) and may lead to "maintaining people on the payroll without giving them the money to build something" (McCurdy, 2013). The annual budget-driven approach creates planning uncertainty and often results in NASA having to stretch project schedules to accommodate the changes and the re-planning that increases fixed and indirect costs (National Research Council, 2012).

Further, uncertainty is exacerbated with the tenure of the president of the United States being four years and the tenure of US Congress officials being two years (House of Representatives) or six years (Senate). Political (and thus financial) support of space endeavor might shift with a new president. A prime example of political uncertainty was exemplified by the cancellation of the Constellation programme (that had been initiated in 2004 to provide capabilities to return to the moon and in time to accomplish manned missions to Mars), by President Obama in 2011, in favor of shifting more resources to commercial industry to provide such capabilities.

Critiques of NASA

Reports of independent inquiries after the Challenger and Columbia disasters were critical of several organizational aspects of NASA, including its risk management and safety processes. More recent reports continue to be critical. The National Research Council (2012) report for example found that there is no national consensus on NASA's strategic goals and objectives, without which NASA cannot be expected to have a clear long-term plan and implement it effectively. NASA's strategic plan was described as vague, lacking prioritization and clarity, and its vision and mission statements were described as generic rather than unique. Secondly, the report contended that there is not sufficient integration across the different NASA field centres, which compromises the accomplishment of agency-wide goals and objectives. Thirdly, that significant constraints imposed by legislation and regulation, such as rules regarding variations in workforce and uses of infrastructure impede NASA's flexibility in accomplishing its goals. Fourth, that there is a significant mismatch between the programmes NASA has set out to carry out, and the budget available (see also Augustine et al., 2009).

Published in the same year, the Space Foundation (2012: 1) report noted that there are "frequent redirection and constantly shifting priorities at NASA, mixed signals from Congress and the administration, organizational conflicts, and the lack of a singular purpose, resulting in a space agency without a clear, stable direction". The report made several strategic and tactical recommendations, including the development of a clear purpose for NASA, more stable funding and the appointment of NASA administrators with a fixed term of five years that would be unaffected by changes in presidency and "arbitrary changes in the direction of the agency" (2012: 2) that a new administration can bring. Observers believe that the lack of clarity in terms of a national space strategy continues. Pace (2014: 2) for example notes that "there is no clear U.S. plan or intent for human space exploration beyond the International Space Station, as there is no longer any real funding or any defined architecture for such endeavors." He advocates a return to the moon as a catalyst for a variety of international collaborations, and commercial and research activities.

Pelton (2006, 2010) considers programmes such as the Space Shuttle, the International Space Station and Constellation to have been failures, and criticizes NASA's organizational loss of focus. He suggests a revitalization plan for NASA that includes restructuring, rightsizing, focusing on applications of space research to earth challenges and expanding public-private partnerships. His prompting to enlarge the role of the commercial sector is based on the view that "commercial organizations are, on balance, better managed, more agile, more innovative, and more market responsive than government agencies" (2010: 78).

Resource constraints and the promise of commercial space

Part of the state's concern has been to spur innovation in the space sector, and to accomplish things more efficiently, given its own budgetary constraints. NASA has been criticised for a lack of efficiency, despite the fact that its budget has been decreasing over the years as a percentage of the federal budget. Chapman (2015: 13) for example has argued that "while it has had significant scientific and political successes in its more than half century history, NASA has not been immune to programmatic waste, duplication, inefficiency, and uncertain institutional purpose during this time period". Chapman (2015) discusses examples of inefficiency in terms of use of infrastructure and the development of programmes such as Constellation, James Webb Space Telescope and weather satellite management.

NASA used its own cost estimation methodology (NASA-Air Force Cost Model or NAFCOM) to estimate the development costs for the Falcon 9 rocket developed by SpaceX, if NASA was to develop the rocket itself, using its traditional development model (NASA, 2011). SpaceX has been using Falcon 9 as a launch vehicle for the Dragon spacecraft to provide supplies to the International Space Station since 2012. SpaceX plans to employ the Dragon spacecraft to also ferry astronauts to the space station in the near future. Using its traditional development model that assumes heavy involvement of the government in all stages, the costs were estimated as USD 4 billion. Then the model assumptions were changed to a more commercial approach where there is less involvement by the government and higher flexibility for the commercial partner, and the estimated costs were USD 1.7 billion. SpaceX has revealed that the development costs of the Falcon 9 (plus an earlier version, Falcon 1), were USD 390 million, one quarter of the NASA's lowest estimate. NASA concluded that:

> it is difficult to determine exactly why the actual cost was so dramatically lower than the NAFCOM predictions. It could be any number of factors associated with the non-traditional public-private partnership under which the Falcon 9 was developed (e.g., fewer NASA processes, reduced oversight, and less overhead), or other factors not directly tied to the development approach. NASA is continuing to refine this analysis to better understand the differences.
>
> (NASA, 2011: 40).

The traditional and the commercial space models (whose assumptions were used to estimate the two development cost figures) were juxtaposed as follows by NASA (2012: 4):

Table 5.2 Traditional vs commercial development approaches

Programme characteristic	Early space age approach	Commercial-oriented approach
Owner	NASA	Industry
Contract fee-type	Cost plus	Fixed price
Contract management	Prime contractor	Public-private partnership
Customer(s)	NASA	Government and non-government
Funding for capability demonstration	NASA procures capability	NASA provides investment via milestone payments
NASA's role in capability development	NASA defines "what" and "how"	NASA only defines "what" (industry defines "how")
Requirements definition	NASA defines detailed requirements	NASA defines top-level capabilities needed
Cost structure	NASA incurs total cost	NASA and industry cost share

Adapted from NASA 2012.

It is clear that the two models differ in significant ways, and that the growth of the commercial-oriented approach has created impetus for cultural change within NASA (Terrier, Heracleous & Gonzalez, 2017). For example, a change programme referred to as JSC2.0 has been launched at the Johnson Space Center in 2013 by the Director, Ellen Ochoa, who noted: "My concept of JSC 2.0 asks a fundamental question: If we were starting JSC today, how would we build a space center to reach our vision of leading a global enterprise in human space exploration that is sustainable, affordable and benefits humankind?" (Roundup, 2013: 2). This change programme was intended to enable more effective collaboration with partner organizations, as well as higher operational effectiveness and efficiency. The Director noted: "how would we collaborate? How would we be organized to most efficiently and effectively carry out our work? What tools and processes would we use? How can we be more nimble and adaptable to change, and stay that way in the future?" (Roundup, 2013: 2). Director Ochoa had previously noted the need for "paradigm change" at JSC towards a culture that is "reliable, progressive, innovation-centered and easy to work with" (Ochoa, 2012). Heracleous and Gonzalez (2014) suggested that given the substantial shifts in NASA's external and internal environment, the agency should be given more flexibility to manage its infrastructure and human resources based on market-based, competitive principles. They also suggested that NASA should become a real network organization, effectively integrated both internally across its own field centres, and externally with commercial organizations, research centres, universities or think-tanks that produce space-related knowledge.

NASA has more recently started experimenting with open innovation, posing innovation challenges online in open competitions, as a complement to internal innovation efforts (Gustetic et al., 2015). The possibility for task decomposition and the wide problem-solving capabilities (Lakhani, Lifshitz-Assaf & Tushman, 2013) make this a potentially effective exploration approach, at lower cost. Gustetic et al. (2015) note that open innovation approaches such as prizes, challenges and crowdsourcing can accomplish reduced costs for developing a particular technology as needed, bringing new perspectives to bear, and ultimately helping to create new markets and jobs as offerings are developed. They describe several open innovation challenges including a call for improvements to astronaut glove design, design of a lunar lander, non-invasive measurement of intracranial pressure and development of a material that is strong and light enough to support a tether that is 60,000 miles long. While not all challenges resulted in usable technologies, all had useful lessons. Particularly where more pure research is needed, open innovation can address only a particular part of NASA's total technological and operational challenges, making it a useful but not sufficient approach to innovation.

Emergence of the commercial space industry

Meanwhile, both the private sector and other nations have been investing in and developing space technologies, challenging NASA's historical dominance of and leadership in space exploration. Private space companies such as SpaceX and Blue Origin, even though they often license NASA technology, compete for NASA contracts and employ NASA scientists, can also undertake certain tasks (such as transporting cargo to the International Space Station) more efficiently than NASA and have commendable innovation goals. Hyper-ambitious and well-funded national space agencies such as China National Space Administration mean that NASA has real competition on space-faring competence.

Since its early days, NASA has been working with the commercial sector in terms of allocating contracts for the supply of specialized equipment and services. The Jet Propulsion Laboratory operated by the California Institute of Technology was a contractor facility before becoming part of NASA. NACA (the National Advisory Committee for Aeronautics), NASA's predecessor, allocated the contracts for the airframe (in 1955) and engines (in 1966) for the X-15, a hypersonic rocket-propelled aircraft to private companies. When NASA was formed in 1958 it continued the practice of working with the commercial sector.

Still, the involvement of the commercial sector was not seen as sufficient. Michael Griffin, NASA Administrator 2005–2009 noted in an interview conducted in 2007 that:

> We grew aviation policy in the United States with the thought in mind that we are a capitalistic nation rooted in doing things that cause free enterprise to succeed. So rather than trying to suppress it, we tried to sponsor it. In space we didn't do that. We emphatically didn't do that. We made it the province of government employees, which was not in itself bad, but we missed the other part.
>
> (Wright, Johnson & Dick, 2012: 22)

Beginning in 2006, NASA started the process for contracting out the construction and operation of Commercial Resupply Services vehicles, that would carry out unmanned resupply missions to the International Space Station. Then in 2010 NASA initiated the Commercial Crew Program, to contract out the creation and operation of spacecraft that could conduct manned missions to the International Space Station, to carry at least four astronauts, dock for 180 days and return them to earth. These two programmes provided seed funding, opportunity and impetus to commercial companies to enter the space industry.

The commercialization of space has been a long-standing policy of the federal government that has instituted corresponding legislation. The Commercial Space Launch Act (1984) noted that:

> private applications of space technology have achieved a significant level of commercial and economic activity, and offer the potential for growth in the future, particularly in the United States. . . . the development of commercial launch vehicles and associated services would enable the United States to retain its competitive position internationally, thereby contributing to the national interest and economic well-being of the United States. . . . the United States should encourage private sector launches and associated services.

This and subsequent acts have also exempted the commercial space sector from certain types of federal regulation, to ease its expansion.

The size of the global space industry in 2015 was almost USD 323 billion, and is expected to double over the following decade. The figure in 2014 was USD 329 billion, even though the appearance of decline was due to the strong US dollar rather than actual decline in activity. 39% of the 2015 spending was accounted for by commercial space products and services (such as telecommunications, broadcasting and earth observation), and 37% by commercial infrastructure and support industries (such as spacecraft manufacturing, launch services, space and ground equipment, and insurance). 14% was US government space budgets, including both civilian and military spending and 10% was spending by other governments (Space Foundation, 2016). These figures mean that governments account for less than a quarter of global spending on the space sector, compared to three quarters accounted for by commercial organizations.

The availability of expanded sources of financing is enabling new entrants to compete in the space sector (Canis, 2016). There were 80 new space ventures created in the US during the period 2000 to 2015. These received a total of USD 13.3 billion in funding during this period. Of this, USD 5.1 billion was debt financing, USD 2.9 billion was venture capital, USD 2.2 billion was the value of acquisitions and USD 1.8 billion was private equity. During the first five years total funding was USD 1.1 billion, with USD 6.1 billion 2006–2010 and USD 6.1 billion 2011–2015 (Tauri Group, 2016).

The development of small satellites is creating more cost-effective options for companies offering broadband, remote imaging and communication services (Canis, 2016). According to the United Nations Office for Outer Space Affairs, 7,677 objects have been launched into space since 1957 (UNOOSA, 2017). The Union of Concerned Scientists (UCS) notes that the total number of satellites that are currently operating is 1,459. Of these, 593 are US satellites, 135 are Russian, 192 are Chinese with the remainder belong to other nations. Of the 593 US satellites, 297 are commercial, 150 are military, 136 are government and 10 are civil (UCS, 2017).

NASA's capability development in collaborating with commercial space[1]

While the binary comparison between the old space age and new commercial models at NASA is useful, it also somewhat oversimplifies things. We can better understand NASA's new approach in terms of an evolution over time, that includes a transitional phase in which NASA honed its capabilities and learning to be able to advance to the network model. Further, NASA has been able to advance to the network model by developing particular organizational, cultural, relational and technological capabilities over time, so as to be able to work more effectively with commercial entities.

The traditional approach, the transition phase and the commercial development phase can each be exemplified by an archetypal project: Apollo, International Space Station, and the Commercial Resupply Program respectively.

The Apollo programme was initiated as a response to perceived Russian superiority in space and challenge of the US for long-term space leadership (Siddiqi, 2000). Substantial budgetary and organizational resources were allocated to the programme by the government with the focused objective accomplishing the challenge that President Kennedy posed in 1961: of getting a man on the moon and returning him safely to earth before the decade was out. In the Apollo programme, NASA's organizational capabilities included technological knowledge that allowed it to develop detailed engineering specifications; large systems integration imported from the military, and the ability to supervise contractors (Beggs, 1984). There was a cultural belief in technological superiority and exceptionalism (McCurdy, 1993). NASA's relationships with contractors were hierarchical, with NASA delivering specifications as Moses delivered the Ten Commandments. Technological capability development was agency-driven, with a unitary engineering architecture.

The International Space Station fostered and exhibited organizational capabilities of international collaboration and inter-governmental partnerships (DeLucas, 1996). Culturally, the sense of technological superiority was still there, but now accompanied with greater cost consciousness. Relationally, the sense of hierarchical pecking order was supplemented by a cluster of international governmental organizations, with NASA as the orchestrator and influencer. Technologically, NASA leveraged international public investments, distributed technical responsibility and worked on developing shared technical interfaces, standards and protocols (Kitmacher & Gerstenmaier, 2005). During this phase, NASA honed its learning of how to function in a cluster of partners rather than how to be the dominant party in a supplier/buyer relationship.

The Commercial Resupply Program was initiated to carry cargo to the International Space Station after the space shuttle was retired (Lambright, 2015) and formed a substantial impetus to further development of the commercial space sector, including SpaceX that won the contract to resupply the International Space Station (Lindenmoyer & Stone, 2010). In the Commercial Resupply Program, NASA's organizational capabilities were focused on specifying end goals and ongoing partnering (public-private partnerships). Culturally there was higher commercial awareness and cost consciousness, as well as openness to solutions created anywhere within the network. Relationally NASA was part of a network of clusters rather than a single cluster, and acted as a catalyst for industry technology development. Technologically NASA leverages industry investments and initiates open innovation programs. Table 5.3 below outlines the above discussion:

Table 5.3 Development of capabilities at NASA over time

Development approach	Traditional development	Transition phase	Commercial development
Project examples	Apollo	International Space Station (1993–present)	Commercial Resupply Program (2006–present)
Selected sources	Beggs (1984) Siddiqi (2000)	DeLucas (1996) Kitmacher et al (2005)	Lambright (2015) Lindenmoyer & Stone (2010)
Organizational capabilities	Engineering specifications, Contractor supervision, Large systems integration	International collaboration, Inter-governmental partnerships (public-public partnerships)	Specification of end goals, Ongoing partnering public-private partnerships)
Cultural attributes & capabilities	Technical superiority, Exceptionalism	Technical superiority, Increased cost consciousness	Commercial awareness, Cost consciousness, Openness to industry-sourced solutions
Relational capabilities	Hierarchy, Positional authority, NASA as Moses	Cluster, NASA as orchestrator, Exercise of influence	Network of clusters, NASA As catalyst for industry technology development
Technological capabilities	Agency driven investments, Unitary engineering architecture	Agency leverages international public investments, Distributed responsibility, Interfaces, common standards & protocols	Agency leverages industry investments, Initiates open innovation programs

In order to understand NASA's evolution in its relationship with commercial entities, from its traditional contracting model to its current network model, we need to view it as a learning process, where organizational, cultural, relational and technological capabilities were gradually honed towards that objective. Reaching this point is one step in the process of focusing resources on reaching Mars and deep space. NASA's Global Exploration Roadmap (Laurini & Gerstenmaier, 2014), particularly the end goal of accomplishing manned missions to Mars via progressively building on missions of increasing complexity, is predicated on dynamic capabilities that evolve over time as a result of learning from experience.

A shifting industry: from hierarchy to network

The space exploration industry has therefore been going through a structural shift from state dominance in earlier days towards commercial enterprise, lower barriers to entry, higher collaboration between state and commercial actors, and innovation in terms of its offerings. The traditional industry model was a hierarchical one, where commercial entities were suppliers to state agencies that conceived of, led and carried out missions. The industry has been morphing to a network model where collaboration across commercial as well as state entities is crucial and where commercial entities can launch their own missions both as partners and as competitors. Government space agencies are contracting out more aspects of low earth orbit missions, and are focusing their resources on the bigger prize of deep space exploration such as NASA's planned mission to Mars (Heracleous, 2015).

It should be acknowledged that the commercial space sector is standing on the shoulders of giants. Commercial space companies are drawing on technologies, infrastructure, human capital and accumulated experience of agencies such as NASA. Recent accidents suffered by SpaceX, Orbital Technologies and others reminded stakeholders that space-faring is difficult, dangerous and unpredictable.

Yet, there is still no substitute for the entrepreneurial spark, creative energy and ambition that drives commercial space companies and that will ultimately lead to a multitude of space-related offerings and services not yet conceived of (Brennan, 2013). Asteroid mining, space tourism, faster cross-continent earth transport, more efficient and expanded scientific, entertainment and military applications, and all sorts of services yet to emerge, will become possible and commercially viable. The first steps are being taken to make that possible.

Continued development of the US commercial space sector will be affected by issues such as regulation and growth constraints placed by export controls (Canis, 2016). In addition to NASA, there are several other agencies with commercial space interests and responsibilities, including FAA's Office of Commercial Space Transportation, Department of Commerce, Department of Defense, the Department of State and the Federal Communications Commission. Despite relevant legislation calling for some relief from regulation of the space sector compared to other industries, the multitude of agencies involved creates red tape for new entrants and established companies. Further, export controls currently limit the export of selected space technology since some items are regarded as dual-use in that they have possible military applications.

The shift in the space exploration industry from a tightly regulated domain with high barriers to entry and a select few competitors towards a more deregulated, easier to enter and hotly contested field will not only spur innovation, but is ultimately beneficial for humanity. This shift applies biological principles (variety, competition and performance as the most efficient ways to select winners and allocate resources) to an industry that is instrumental for the ultimate survival of the species (Brennan, 2017). Further, space exploration feeds the human spirit. Nothing has captured the imagination more than the original space race, when humans set foot on the moon. Spacefaring feeds that human urge to push frontiers, to break the mold, to go beyond what had previously seemed possible. It is partly for this reason that critiques and pessimism of the commercial viability of this industry miss the point. If we seek to justify space exploration with short-term return on investment calculations, we will never have the green light or the opportunity to go beyond earth.

The commercial space race is different from the US/Russia space race in the 1950s and 1960s, when the race was between two superpowers where the outcome would be a single winner and the goal was unitary (put a man on the moon). Rather, the commercial space race is a race of consortia that include both private entities and inputs from government agencies from more than one state, a race of ingenuity and persistence to conceive of and make a number of offerings commercially viable, a race to expand the human domain and presence beyond a single planet. In many ways this is the one that ultimately matters.

Note

1 The discussion in this section draws from Heracleous, L., Terrier, D. and Gonzalez, S., 2017, NASA's capability evolution towards commercial space, Working Paper.

References

Amadeo, K., 2017. NASA budget: Current funding and history. 22 March. Available at: https://www.thebalance.com/nasa-budget-current-funding-and-history-3306321.

Augustine, N. R. et al., 2009. Seeking a human spaceflight program worthy of a great nation. Washington, D.C.   •

Bearden, D.A., 2003. A complexity-based risk assessment of low-cost planetary missions: when is a mission too fast and too cheap? *Acta Astronautica,* 52, 371–379.

Beggs, J. M., 1984. Leadership: The NASA approach. *Long Range Planning,* 17(2), 12–24.

Benner, M. J. & Tushman, M. L., 2003. Exploitation, exploration, and process management: The productivity dilemma revisited. *Academy of Management Review,* 28, 238–256.

Brennan, L., 2013. Space exploration is a necessity for the human species. Letters to the Editor, *Financial Times,* 12 January. Available at: https://www.ft.com/content/77c64c9c-5671–11e2-aaaa-00144feab49a.

Brennan, L., 2017. What if we have reached the point of no return? Letters to the Editor, *Financial Times*, 15 July. Available at: https://www.ft.com/content/88497496-631d-11e7–8814–0ac7eb84e5f1.

Bugos, G. E. & Boyd, J. W., 2008. Accelerating entrepreneurial space: The case for an NACA-style organization. *Space Policy*, 24, 140–147.

Canis, B., 2016. Commercial space industry launches a new phase. Congressional Research Service, R44708. Available at: www.crs.gov.

Chapman, B., 2015. Waste and duplication in NASA programs: The need to enhance US space program efficiency. *Space Policy*, 31, 13–20.

Commercial Space Launch Act. 1984. Available at: https://www.gpo.gov/fdsys/pkg/STATUTE-98/pdf/STATUTE-98-Pg3055.pdf.

Core Magazine, 2016. NASA's new space race, 1 September. Available at: http://www.wbs.ac.uk/news/core-nasa-s-new-space-race/.

DeLucas, L. J., 1996 International space station. *Acta Astronautica*, 38(4–8), 613–619.

Gallup, 2009. Majority of Americans say space program costs justified. Available at: http://www.gallup.com/poll/121736/majority-americans-say-space-%20program-costs-justified.aspx.

Goldin, D., 2002. Leading ferociously (interview). *Harvard Business Review*, 22–25.

Gustetic, J. L., Crusan, J., Rader, S. & Ortega, S., 2015. Outcome-driven open innovation at NASA. *Space Policy*, 34, 11–17.

Hall, J. L., 2003. Columbia and Challenger: Organizational failure at NASA. *Space Policy*, 19, 239–247.

Heracleous, L., 2015. Why Jeff Bezos has entered the space race. Fortune, 30 November. Available at: http://fortune.com/2015/11/30/jeff-bezos-entered-space-race/.

Heracleous, L. & Gonzalez, S., 2014. Two modest proposals for propelling NASA forward. *Space Policy*, 30, 190–192.

Kitmacher, G. H., Gerstenmaier, W. H., Bartoe, J-D F, & Mustachio, N., 2005. *Acta Astronautica*, 57: 594–603.

Lakhani, K. R., Lifshitz-Assaf, H. & Tushman, M. L., 2013. Open innovation and organizational boundaries: Task decomposition, knowledge distribution and the locus of innovation. In Grandori, A. (Ed.) *Handbook of Economic Organization: Integrating Economic and Organization Theory*, Edward Elgar, 355–382.

Lambright, W. H., 2007. Leading change at NASA: The case of Dan Goldin. *Space Policy*, 23, 33–43.

Lambright, W. H., 2015. Launching commercial space: NASA, cargo, and policy innovation, *Space Policy*, 34, 23–31.

Laurini, K. C. & Gerstenmaier, W. H., 2014. The global exploration roadmap and its significance for NASA. *Space Policy*, 30, 149–155.

Levine, A. L., 1992. NASA's organizational structure: The price of decentralization. *Public Administration Review*, 52, 198–203.

Levine, A. S., 1982. Managing NASA in the Apollo era. Available at: http://history.nasa.gov/SP-4102/sp4102.htm.

Lindenmoyer, A. & Stone, D., 2010. Status of NASA's commercial cargo and crew transportation initiative. *Acta Astronautica*, 66, 788–791.

McCurdy, H. E., 1989. The decay of NASA's technical culture. *Space Policy*, 5, 301–310.

McCurdy, H. E., 1992. NASA's organizational culture. *Public Administration Review*, 52, 189–192.

McCurdy, H. E., 1993. *Inside NASA: high technology and organizational change in the U.S. space program*. Baltimore: Johns Hopkins University Press.

McCurdy, H. E., 2001. *Faster, better, cheaper: low-cost innovation in the U.S. space program.* Baltimore: Johns Hopkins University Press.

McCurdy, H. E., 2010. Inside NASA at 50. In Dick, S. J. (Ed.) NASA's first 50 years: Historical perspectives. NASA SP-2010–4704.

McCurdy, H. E., 2013. Learning from history: Low-cost project innovation in the U.S. National Aeronautics and Space Administration, *International Journal of Project Management*, 31, 705–711.

NASA, 2011. Commercial market assessment for crew and cargo systems. Available at: https://www.nasa.gov/sites/default/files/files/Section403%28b%29CommercialMarketAssessmentReportFinal.pdf.

NASA, 2012. Commercial spaceflight status briefing. September. Available at: https://www.nasa.gov/sites/default/files/files/CommercialStatus_September_508.pdf.

NASA, 2013. Mars Climate Orbiter Fact Sheet. Available at: http://mars.jpl.nasa.gov/msp98/orbiter/fact.html.

NASA, History Program Office. Available at: http://www.hq.nasa.gov/office/pao/History/SP-4406/chap1.html.

NASA, Workforce Information Cubes for NASA. Available at: https://wicn.nssc.nasa.gov/wicn_cubes.html.

National Aeronautics and Space Act of 1958 (Unamended). Available at: http://www.hq.nasa.gov/office/pao/History/spaceact.html.

National Research Council, 2012. *NASA's strategic direction and the need for a national consensus.* Washington DC: National Academies Press.

Ochoa, E., 2012. NASA Johnson Space Center: Leading Human Exploration. Presentation to the NASA Advisory Council, Commercial Space Committee, on 1 May 2012. Available at: https://www.nasa.gov/sites/default/files/files/Ochoa_NACCommercialSpaceMay2012_508.pdf.

Pace, S. 2014., American space strategy: Choose to steer, not drift. *Space Policy*, 30: 1–4.

Pelton, J. N., 2006. Revitalizing NASA? A five-point plan. *Space Policy*, 22, 221–225.

Pelton, J. N., 2010. A new space vision for NASA – and for space entrepreneurs too? *Space Policy*, 26, 78–80.

Pinchefsky, C., 2012. 5 horrifying facts you didn't know about the space shuttle. Available at: http://www.forbes.com/sites/carolpinchefsky/2012/04/18/5-horrifying-facts-you-didnt-know-about-the-space-shuttle/.

Portee, D. S. F., 1998. NASA's origins and the dawn of the space age. Monograph 10, NASA History Division. Available at: http://history.nasa.gov/monograph10/.

President's Commission on Implementation of United States Space Exploration Policy. 2004. *A journey to inspire, innovate, and discover.* Washington: U.S. Governmentt Printing Office.

Report of the Presidential Commission on the Space Shuttle Challenger Accident, 1986. Available at: http://history.nasa.gov/rogersrep/genindex.htm.

Roundup (internal publication), 2013. JSC Director. Spring, page 2. Available at: https://jscfeatures.jsc.nasa.gov/media/1_spring_2013.pdf.

Sarsfield, L., 1998. *The cosmos on a shoestring: Small spacecraft for space and earth science.* RAND, Critical Technologies Institute, Santa Monica, CA.

Siddiqi, A. A., 2000. *Challenge to Apollo: The Soviet Union and the space race.* NASA SP-2000–4408, NASA History Division, Office of Policy and Plans.

Space Foundation, 2012. Pioneering: Sustaining US leadership in space. Available at: www.spacefoundation.org.

Space Foundation, 2016. Ensuring U.S. leadership in space. Available at: www.spacefoundation.org.

Spear, T., 1998. NASA FBC task final report. Jet Propulsion Laboratory. Available at: http://mars.jpl.nasa.gov/msp98/misc/fbctask.pdf.

Tauri Group, 2016. *Start-up space: Rising investment in commercial space ventures*. Available at: https://brycetech.com/reports.html.

Teitel, A. S., 2012. Apollo's youthful glow. Available at: http://amyshirateitel.com/2012/08/11/apollos-youthful-glow/.

Terrier, D., Heracleous, L. & Gonzalez, S., 2017. Enabling paradigm change and agility at the Johnson Space Center: Interview with Chief Technology Officer, Douglas Terrier. Forthcoming, *Space Policy*, 39–40, 20–25.

Tushman, M. L., & O'Reilly, C., 1996. Ambidextrous organizations: Managing evolutionary and revolutionary change. *California Management Review*, 38, 8–30.

UCS, 2017. UCS satellite database. Available at: http://www.ucsusa.org/nuclear-weapons/space-weapons/satellite-database#.WP6Z_FPyuqB.

UNOOSA, 2017. Outer space objects index. Available at: http://www.unoosa.org/oosa/osoindex/search-ng.jspx?lf_id.

Wright, R., Johnson, S. & Dick, S. J., 2012. NASA at 50: Interviews with NASA's senior leadership. NASA SP-2012–4114. NASA History Program Office.

6   The main country players

Introduction

Today, the industry of space exploration and space technology is given considerable attention in many governmental policies across the globe and is also attracting considerable attention from the private sector. Nations such as the US, Russia, Japan, China, Brazil, Canada, as well as collaborative space agencies such as the ESA in Europe have formulated and published their visions for the future of the space industry. So too have an increasing number of private ventures such as Burt Rutan, Richard Branson, Elon Musk and others. While the previous chapter provides an analysis of the space sector in the US, this chapter primarily focuses on the other space nations starting from the more established players (i.e. Russia, ESA and Japan), the fast growing emerging economy players (i.e. China, India and Brazil), others players (i.e. Israel, Iran, Korea, Saudi Arabia and Pakistan) to the space service economy country players (i.e. Luxembourg and the Isle of Man).

Currently, much of the vision surrounding the next generation of space missions and technology is tied to the perceived "second race to the Moon" and beyond. This civilian theme is complemented by an ongoing discussion about the military facets of space activity, as well as the role of both current and emerging commercial enterprises in space access and exploration. Together, the civilian, military and commercial space sectors focus the broader space discourse around questions about the elements of space competitiveness, the relative competitive position of traditional space leaders and the role of emerging space powers such as China and India.

When we examine the literature published by the different bodies involved in this industry some common themes are easily identifiable. NASA's strategic plan, published in 2003, sums up these themes most succinctly with its maxim: "To improve life here, to extend life to there, to find life beyond". NASA, of course, pioneered mankind's entry into space along with the then Soviet Union in the third quarter of the 20th century. The world's two superpowers at the time were engaged in the "space race", some might argue, as a game of one-upmanship during a period when the dynamic between the two ideologies of Capitalism and Communism entailed direct competition to vanquish the other.

Today however, there is a shift towards collaboration between the nations of the world to advance our knowledge, and harness the potential benefits that space presents us. Vladimir Putin acknowledged that: "for the modern . . . world nations, cosmonautics now is not only the subject of national pride. Exploration and application of Earth-orbital space become serious resources of national development and real advancement of people's living standards" (Zak, 2008).

The space industry today has evolved from the romanticism of the 1960s and 1970s when putting a man on the moon captured the imagination of the world although it should be noted that until the change in strategy by the Obama administration NASA had credible intentions of returning, permanently, to the moon by 2020. Now, a multi-pronged approach to space exploration is attempting to address environmental issues, advance technology and industry, and cater for the next generation of holidaymakers – the space tourists.

A number of factors have contributed to the globalization of the space industry. Political changes in the 1990s and the end of the "space race" meant that almost all trading nations function with market-based economies and their trade policies have tended to encourage free markets between nations. The globalization of the space industry has been further encouraged by technical standardization between countries. Host governments actively seek to encourage global operators to base themselves in their countries (i.e. the US space infrastructure, Russian know-how, Brazilian lower launch costs). The national home base of an organization in the space industry plays an important role in creating advantage on a global scale. As elaborated in Porter's Diamond, the determinants of national comparative advantage stem from demand and factors conditions, firm strategy structure and rivalry and related and supporting industries. In countries like the US and Russia, experience in space technology and space infrastructure provided initial advantages that have been subsequently built upon to yield more advanced factors of competition. At the same time home demand conditions (American early adopters at the early stage of space industry segments' life cycles), technology transfer, related and supporting industries (American, Russian, Japanese technological supremacy) and domestic rivalry have also provided a basis upon which the characteristics of the advantage of an organization competing at the new frontier of international competition have been shaped. Yip (2003) cites decreasing costs, globalisation, scale economies and sourcing efficiencies as offering the potential for competitive advantage to some countries.

In the 21st century, space has been transformed from an object of wonder to an arena of geopolitical, economic and strategic consequence. To understand this arena, and the motivations informing the national and business actors operating within it, a structured framework is required. Leaders who seek to maximize their investments in space activity require a nuanced and rigorous analysis of its changing dynamics. Futron Corporation, a premier provider of decision management solutions, created its annual, independent and self-financed Space Competitiveness Index (SCI) for this express purpose. The Space Competitiveness Index is a decision management tool. It offers decision-makers an ongoing benchmark to continuously re-assess the competitive landscape of space activity – and to contemplate its meaning for their respective governments, enterprises and institutions in an organized way. Now in its seventh year, the SCI methodology has been annually updated and refined. The accumulated seven years of data and analysis contained in this report offer salient insight into the strengths, weaknesses, trends, recent developments and likely trajectories of 15 leading space-participant nations.

Futron's Space Competitiveness Index is a globally-focused analytic framework that defines, measures and ranks national competitiveness in the development, implementation and execution of space activity. By analyzing space-related government, human capital and economic drivers, the SCI framework assesses the ability of a country to undertake space activity, and evaluates its performance relative to peer nations, as well as the global space arena.

The SCI considers comparative space activities for fifteen leading space actors, offering a comprehensive overview of their recent, current, and planned future activities, their national capabilities and competitiveness dynamics, their government, human capital and industry attributes, and their relative strengths, weaknesses, opportunities, and threats (as depicted in Figure 6.1).

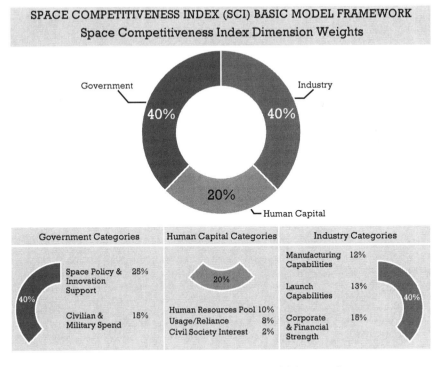

Figure 6.1 2014 Space Competitiveness Index – Basic model framework

Source: Futron Corporation, 2014.

These nations are compared across some 50 individual qualitative and quantitative metrics, each collected for all fifteen nations. These metrics are divided among three overarching competitiveness dimensions: government, human capital and industry. Futron evaluates these indicators using a proprietary data model whose assumptions are annually reviewed and refined. The resulting scores form the foundation of the index itself, which is then interpreted through a written analysis featuring country-by-country profiles of national space activities and competitiveness dynamics. The integrated result is an annual report, published by Futron Corporation each year since 2008: Futron's Space Competitiveness Index.

Since Futron's inaugural study in 2008, space globalization has only accelerated. Some countries with zero participation in space seven years ago now have space agencies; others with negligible space involvement have significantly increased the scope of their activities. Recognizing this change, in 2012, for the first time, Futron added five new emerging nations to its Space Competitiveness Index. These five nations are retained (Argentina, Australia, Iran, South Africa and Ukraine), and tracked alongside the original ten countries (USA, Europe, Russia, China, India, Canada, Japan, South Korea, Israel and Brazil), in the 2014 SCI. The fifteen leading space-participant nations in alphabetic order are: Argentina, Australia, Brazil, Canada, China, Europe (treated as a single actor), India, Iran, Israel, Japan, Russia, South Africa, South Korea, Ukraine and the United States.

One distinction of the SCI is its assessment of Europe as an integrated space actor. The activities that European countries undertake through individual space agencies such as ASI, CNES and DLR are significant. Nonetheless, recognizing that the whole is more than the sum of its parts, Europe has chosen to pool national resources for a multilateral space approach through ESA. While the SCI considers European national activities, our analytic focus is on Europe as an integrated space actor.

In 2014, Futron reviewed its foundational 2008–2013 studies to provide a fresh perspective, surveying multi-year trends to enhance discussion of national dynamics. Futron's 2014 SCI expands its country profiles, providing added data on space assets, infrastructure, budget and commercial sector revenues. In addition, the 2014 SCI continues to use an optimized written analysis structure, designed to accommodate the interests of both casual readers and executive decision-makers.

From the latest available report issued by the Futron Corporation (2014), highlights include that:

- China trailed the United States in orbital launches in 2013 for the first time in two years, yet continues to far outpace other emerging nations in the speed with which it achieves new space milestones. Yet its commercial space role lags behind, and is beginning to reduce its competitiveness.

- The United States remains the leader in space competitiveness, but is the only nation to decline for seven straight years. As other countries enhance their space capabilities while the US undergoes uncertain transitions, it should not view its unique space agenda-setting power as guaranteed.
- Argentina continues to adapt its satellite manufacturing sector for the international marketplace, exploring both commercial and government-to-government deals. It stands to benefit from increased investment in spacecraft subcomponents.
- Australia's space re-emergence continues, with the government reviewing national policy segment-by-segment, focusing on the uses of space to Australian society – although momentum may be stalling as Australia pivots from policy formulation to implementation. The Australian private sector is assuming a larger role, including non-traditional entrepreneurial start-ups.
- Brazil is re-examining its national space priorities, but also reducing its civil space funding. Its next space steps are a wide open question.
- Canada has experienced a small bounce in its space competitiveness, and retains a skilled space workforce, but ongoing implementation challenges threaten to offset these advantages.
- Europe's governance approach is organized enough to mobilize competing national priorities into collective action, yet flexible enough to fluidly accommodate new member states. How well it mediates the fateful question of Europe's next-generation launch vehicle will be an important test.
- India has raised its game, developing fully indigenous launch vehicles and a mission to Mars.
- Iran has made faster progress than any new space participant since the Cold War, but fairly or unfairly, questions about the tenor of its programme – civilian or military – impede collaboration.
- Israel has finally implemented civil space funding increases and published new policies, but lack of industry scale continues to limit its commercial space presence, despite a vibrant start-up sector.
- Japan continues to improve thanks to its thorough space policy reforms, and has enjoyed recent commercial progress. Its ability to increase its launch and mission frequency and assertively market its commercial benefits are important to its future competitiveness and regional leadership.
- Russia has surged, largely restoring its launch success rate (Figure 6.2), remaining vital to ISS resupply, weighing long-term independent space station plans, and developing its new Vostochny Cosmodrome. Yet its annexation of Crimea strains its relationships, and may stall its resurgence.
- South Africa continues to develop its space policy and human capital base, but its technology and industrial base remain negligible despite the important Square Kilometer Array (SKA) project.

ORBITAL LAUNCH AND SPACECRAFT MANUFACTURING TRENDS, 2004-2013

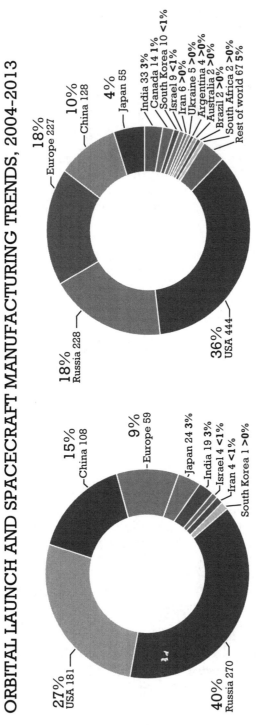

Total : 670 Successful Orbital Launches

Total : 1,236 Spacecraft Manufactured

Figure 6.2 2014 Space Competitiveness Index – Orbital launch and spacecraft manufacturing trends 2004–2013

Source: Futron Corporation, 2014.

- South Korea's KSLV success has helped bolster its credibility. The key now is to ensure this success does not go unnoticed, but instead builds upon it to pursue commercial space goals.
- Ukraine has advanced in competitiveness even while suffering turmoil domestically. Yet it struggles to commercialize its space industrial base, and overlooks key emerging markets.
- International collaboration is increasingly taking shape as a concerted competitiveness strategy.
- Four distinct space competitiveness tiers have emerged. The first tier of traditional space leaders is dynamic, but relatively stable. The second tier of Asian space powers is intensely competitive: each country could plausibly surpass its near-peers within a short period of time. The third and fourth tiers are highly diversified: nations with disparate activities can attain similar scores, but for different reasons. And throughout, small gaps in score results can lead to large gaps in rankings.
- A critical benefit of the SCI is the ability to track competitiveness trends over time, supported by statistical analysis as depicted in Table 6.1. Since introducing the SCI in 2008, Futron has identified notable movements among leading space-participant nations, now supported by seven years of tracking data, which are detailed in the 2014 edition of the report. For instance, of the fifteen countries analyzed, only the United States has shown seven straight years of competitiveness declines. By contrast, China, Japan, Russia and India have improved their own space competitiveness by 35%, 44%, 20% and 16%, respectively, over their own relative starting points from when Futron's benchmarking process began in 2008. The SCI also allows direct comparisons between individual nations. Table 6.1 offers a preview of relative competitiveness changes. Positive scores indicate competitiveness gains, while negative scores indicate competitiveness losses. For instance, Japan gained 0.14 basis points in overall space competitiveness relative to China, while Canada lost 2.31 basis points against Russia.

The long-established players

Russia

Apart from the United States, the Soviet Union was the only country in the world which pursued the entire spectrum of space research and applications, scientific, commercial and military. From the late 1960s onwards, the number of Soviet space launches by far surpassed the combined launch rate of all other countries in the world (Tarasenko, 1996a).

According to the Russian government, 173.2 billion rubles would be allocated for the Russian space activities in 2017. It included 92.46 billion for the Federal Space Program and 38.27 billion for the GLONASS constellation. The launch infrastructure was expected to receive 21 billion. Roskosmos, the Russian Federal Space Agency earmarked 2.2 billion for the nuclear-electric module (TEM) under

Table 6.1 2014 Space Competitiveness Index – Relative competitiveness changes by country, SCI 2013 to SCI 2014

Relative competitiveness changes by country, SCI 2013 to SCI 2014

	Argentina	Australia	Brazil	Canada	China	Europe	India	Iran	Israel	Japan	Russia	South Africa	South Korea	Ukraine	Usa	Average Change
Argentina	0.00		−0.30													
Australia		0.00										−1.02				−0.92
Brazil			0.00											−0.38		
Canada				0.00							−2.31					+0.66
China					0.00				−1.01							
Europe						0.00									+1.53	
India							0.00						−1.07			
Iran		+0.35						0.00								
Israel								+0.60	0.00							
Japan					+0.14					0.00						
Russia							+3.05				0.00					+2.98
South Africa		+0.92										0.00				
South Korea										+1.84			0.00			
Ukraine						−0.95								0.00		
Usa				−1.39											0.00	

Source: Futron Corporation, 2014.

the Prioritized Innovation Projects line item, which is a considerable increase from 1.6 billion initially projected by the Ministry of Finance (Russian Space Web, 2017).

The Soviet space programme began with ICBM development in the 1950s. The rocket and space programmes were considered to be an integral part of the Cold War rivalry with the United States. As such, a powerful rocket and space industry, versatile R&D facilities, and an extensive infrastructure to support both missile testing and space operations were put in place (see Figure 6.3).

Hundreds of enterprises with a cumulative workforce of more than 1 million people were estimated to have directly participated in the Soviet missile and space programmes (Tarasenko, 1996b). An important difference in the Soviet space programme compared to that of the US was that there was no clear separation of military and civilian space activities. However, the upheaval that accompanied the end of the USSR extended into its space activities. Ultimately the space programme including the various assets and enterprises of the former Soviet Union ended up largely under the control of Russia. Over the period from the collapse of the Soviet Union, there has been an increasing emphasis on the exploitation of Russia's extensive space capabilities, including some hitherto dedicated military systems, for various civil applications. Despite the disruption

Figure 6.3 Rocket test ranges and major rocket production facilities

Source: Tarasenko, 1996b.

caused by the breakup of the Soviet Union and the subsequent economic crisis, the decline in space activity as measured by the number of space launches was halted with the transfer of the space programme to Russia with the number of space launches returning to the level of the late 1980s.

The commitment of Russia to space can also be measured by the diversity of satellite constellations that are being kept functional with Russia keeping more than 20 operational satellite systems (Tarasenko, 1996b). At the end of 1992 the total constellation of operational Russian spacecraft consisted of about 140 satellites, more than the year before.

Tarasenko has classified Russian space systems according to the missions performed. This classification is presented in Figure 6.4 These systems can be subdivided into: space weapons; space surveillance and intelligence systems; support systems and scientific systems.

Focusing on navigation, two generations of satellite navigation systems are currently in use. First generation systems provide naval and trade vessels with the opportunity to determine their positions within one or two hours anywhere at the globe. The second-generation system (known as GLONASS in the West, but named Uragan by the Russian military) is similar to the US Navstar Global Positioning System. Operational deployment started in 1989 and has now resulted in a constellation of fifteen satellites making it a complete system.

In the early 2000s, during Vladimir Putin's presidency, the Russian economy started recovering, growing more each year than in all of the previous decade.

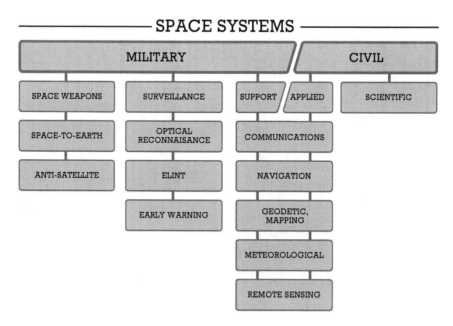

Figure 6.4 Classification of space systems by missions performed
Source: Tarasenko, 1996b.

The funding outlook for Russia's space programme started to look more favourable. In 2001, the development of the GLONASS satellite navigation system was made a government priority with the introduction of a new Federal Targeted Program (Moskvitch, 2010). The main contractor for GLONASS, NPO PM (later renamed ISS Reshetnev), thus received a boost in its finances. In total, 4.8 billion rubles was allocated for the space programme in 2001, of which 1.6 billion was earmarked for GLONASS. By 2004, Russia's space spending had grown to 12 billion rubles. In 2005, a new strategy for the development of the country's space programme, titled the Federal Space Plan 2006–2015, was approved. It stipulated the completion of the International Space Station, development of the Angara rocket family, introduction of a new manned spacecraft and completion of the GLONASS constellation, among others.

In the mid-2000s, funding of the space programme continued to improve substantially, amounting to 21.59 billion rubles in 2005 and rising to 23 billion rubles in 2006. In 2007, 24.4 billion rubles was spent on the civilian space programme, while the military space programme's budget was 11 billion rubles. The industry also continued to receive very substantial funds from exports and foreign partnerships.

Under Dmitry Medvedev's presidency, space technology was named as one of the key areas of the country's modernization programme. Spending increased to 82 billion rubles (USD 2.4 billion) in 2009. In 2011, the government is planning to spend 115 billion rubles (USD 3.8 billion) in the national space programsmes.

According to Dawson (2017), Russia has always excelled in rocket design and development, and their designs have been reliable and powerful in a variety of missions over the past several decades. Their launch systems are currently used regularly to travel to the ISS, carrying both US and Russian cargo. The RD-180 and the NK-33 rocket engines made in Russia have been part of the US–Russian partnership to transport cargo to the ISS. The RD-180 rockets are powerful and more efficiently designed that any American rocket engines. The other Russian rocket engine of note, the NK-33, was first built in the 1960s to take Russians to the moon. After the space race was over, some of these engines were mothballed in warehouses. In a similar deal as the RD-180s, dozens of NK-33s were sold in the 1990s to Aerojet General for a little over USD 1 million. The company also acquired a license to build the engines. The engine was used in the heavy lift Antares rocket, an expendable launch system developed by Orbital Sciences Corporation to launch spacecraft to low earth orbit and the ISS. Antares was launched for the first time in 2013 and had four successful launches until the fifth launch in October 2014, when the rocket failed catastrophically, destroying the vehicle and its payload. The explosion reinforces the idea that the United States cannot compete with the Russians in the development of reliable and powerful rocket engines and integration into a launch system.

Many military space systems have civil applications. For example, the same space launch services are used for civilian and military payloads. Communications, navigation and weather data are equally necessary for civilians and military operations. Soviet meteorological satellites and some navigation satellites have already been utilized by both military and civilian users. In recent years, in the face of resource constraints, there has been some relaxation of security restraints with the result that many proposals have been made to Western businesses by the Russian space industry. Among the assets made available for commercial use were Russia's extensive launch support infrastructure, the former Soviet system of strategic communications and earth observation satellites. There have been some examples of joint ventures between Russian and Western enterprises.

Europe

The importance of space to Europe's is defined within the Lisbon Strategy which aims to make "the Union the most advanced knowledge-based society in the world". In 2007, the European Union further extended its scope and diversity by enlarging the Union to 27 Member states and 500 million citizens. Naturally, this means adapting existing or creating new instruments and technologies, for successfully managing the Union.

Space technologies are particularly useful in this respect due to their capacity to collect and distribute information at any place for every citizen. The ways that space affects the lives of citizen's ranges from healthcare to transport systems. Yet most Europeans are not even aware of the fact that they are stemming from technologies derived from space. The need to reinforce Europe's capabilities in space is becoming ever more apparent as Europeans are increasingly relying on satellites for communication, navigation, monitoring the environment, developing innovative technology and increasing scientific knowledge as well as numerous other space-related technologies. Daily personal benefits include weather forecasting and satellite TV. In Europe 1,250 television programmes are broadcasted by satellite to 100 million homes. Given the importance of space activities to the standard of living of Europeans, space was accordingly included in the EU Constitutional Treaty.

The benefits that have emerged from leveraging space activities provide clear incentives for the European Space Agency (ESA) to be a competitive force in this sector. Numerous benefits for improving daily life, such as, environmental security, better telecommunications, the creation of new jobs and navigational assistance stem from space related activities and thus make space involvement an essential area for European countries to be investing in (Eurospace, 1995).

Until the 1960s space was originally driven by individual motives and endeavours nations. Overtime, it was recognized that a better collaborative effort was needed amongst the European countries that would benefit all. In 1964 the European Space Research Organization and the European Launcher Development Organization were created in an attempt to create a collaborative framework. In 1975 these two organizations combined to form what we now know today as the European Space Agency (ESA). Since then, ESA has been responsible for coordinating the collective efforts of the European member states in the space arena.

The European Commission (EC) and ESA share a common aim: to strengthen Europe and benefit its citizens. ESA is an intergovernmental organization with no formal organic link to the EC. However, in recent years the ties between the two institutions have been reinforced by the increasing role that space plays in strengthening Europe's political and economic role, and in supporting European policies. To facilitate relations between the two organizations, ESA set up a liaison office in Brussels, the site of the EC.

The overall structure of the European space industry comprises of three layers: the EU, intergovernmental organizations like that of ESA and the national space agencies. The total business of the European Space industry has a double nature: institutional and commercial (Eurospace, 1995). Space activities are gradually evolving from publically financed to commercial ventures. The emergence of the ESA allowed companies to foresee income streams long-term as a result of the industrial policy.

The commercialization process in Europe has been also driven by increased technical maturity in space technologies as well as the overall globalization of the space market. The private market represents around 30% of global space activities amounting to a turnover of 3 billion. The remainder constitutes institutional demand. Attention to the institutional sector has been low in the EU providing the US with a very strong competitive advantage. In order to maintain long-term sustainability and fully reap the benefits of the space sector, Europe needs to create a more robust institutional market fuelled by national security and defence. The US bases its market heavily on national security and defence, which is closed to foreign suppliers (Eurospace, 1995).

One of the most important strategic objectives of any economy like that of the EU is economic prosperity. In order to secure growth and job creation the Union must successfully facilitate the transformation of its society into a knowledge-based one. Space adds value to a knowledge-based society. Research provides access to advanced technologies and services, making Europe more competitive. European space activities employ 40,000 people. Indirect employment is estimated at 250,000. These numbers are increasing as space technologies develop. ESA aims to nurture SMEs in their early development. As they generally grow and develop after the initial assistance of capital, they thereby relieve ESA of some responsibility that can be shifted to the creation of other start-up companies. The ESA also underpins much of the risk associated with the space industry by returning most of each nation's budgetary contribution, in the form of industrial contracts, called geographic return. However, prosperity and growth cannot come without investment. As depicted in Figure 6.5, the annual ESA budget is currently 5.75 billion euros. ESA's activities fall into two categories – "mandatory" and "optional". Programmes carried out under the General Budget and the Space Science programme budget are "mandatory"; they include the agency's basic activities (studies on future projects, technology research, shared technical investments, information systems and training programmes).

ESA budget for 2017: 5.75 B€

ESA activities and programmes

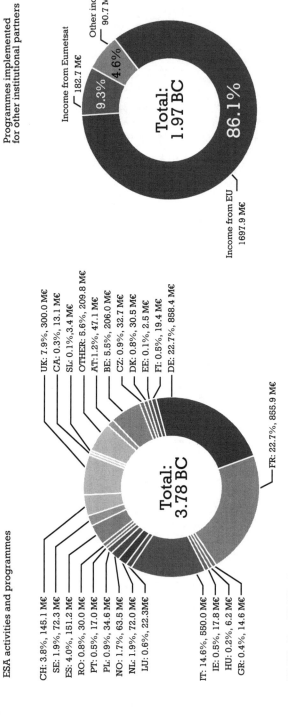

CH: 3.8%, 145.1 M€
SE: 1.9%, 72.3 M€
ES: 4.0%, 151.2 M€
RO: 0.8%, 30.0 M€
PT: 0.5%, 17.0 M€
PL: 0.9%, 34.6 M€
NO: 1.7%, 63.5 M€
NL: 1.9%, 72.0 M€
LU: 0.6%, 22.3M€

UK: 7.9%, 300.0 M€
CA: 0.3%, 13.1 M€
SI: 0.1%, 3.4 M€
OTHER: 5.6%, 209.8 M€
AT: 1.2%, 47.1 M€
BE: 5.5%, 206.0 M€
CZ: 0.9%, 32.7 M€
DK: 0.8%, 30.5 M€
EE: 0.1%, 2.5 M€
FI: 0.5%, 19.4 M€
DE: 22.7%, 858.4 M€

FR: 22.7%, 855.9 M€

IT: 14.6%, 550.0 M€
IE: 0.5%, 17.8 M€
HU: 0.2%, 6.2 M€
GR: 0.4%, 14.6 M€

Total: 3.78 BC

Programmes implemented
for other institutional partners

Income from Eumetsat
182.7 M€

Other income
90.7 M€

9.3%

4.6%

Total:
1.97 BC

86.1%

Income from EU
1697.9 M€

BC: Billion Euro   MC: Million Euro

Figure 6.5 ESA budget for 2017

Source: Adapted from European Space Agency, 2018 (http://www.esa.int/spaceinimages/Images/2017/01/ESA_budget_2017).

All Member States contribute to these programmes on a scale based on their Gross Domestic Product (GDP). The other programmes, known as "optional", are only of interest to some Member States, who are free to decide on their level of involvement.

Optional programmes cover areas such as earth observation, telecommunications, satellite navigation and space transportation. Similarly, the International Space Station and microgravity research are financed by optional contributions.

Japan

The Japanese equivalent of NASA is the Japan Aerospace Exploration Agency (JAXA). Japan's space development competitiveness has been ranked seventh in the world behind India and Canada. Its annual space budget of USD 2.5 billion is one fourteenth that of the United States and one half that of Europe. Japan launched its first mini two-stage rocket in 1957. This is regarded as the beginning of the Japanese space programme. Japan has two launch centers in Kyushu: one near Kagoshima and another on the southern island of Tanegashima (JAXA, 2010).

The Japanese space programme is helped by access to advanced technology produced at home and friendly relations with the United States but is restricted by tight budgets and limited popular support. The program has gotten a boost as result of competition from China and India, which have been making great advances in space even though they lack Japan's advanced technology (JAXA, 2010).

Two Japanese spacecraft swept up wind from Halley's Comet in the 1980s. In November 2005, a mini-robot vehicle sent to investigate the surface of an asteroid was lost in space for many years after it was released from a spacecraft only 55 meters from the asteroid only to be located again in 2010. The vehicle was only 10 centimeters long and weighed 600 grams. It was designed to sample rocks on the asteroid surface.

In October 2008, the Japan Origami Association announced that it had created a special paper airplane made with a special heat-resistant, glass-coated paper that its makers said would allow it to survive reentry into the atmosphere from space and float to earth. They makers hope to release the plane from the International Space Station.

Japan has very well developed rocket production facilities (JAXA, 2010). The Japanese-built H-2 rocket is 48 meters in height, weighs 260 tons and can carry a 2,200 kilogram payload into geostationary orbit. It had five successful launches before 1998 but was very expensive – costing Japan twice as much to launch per payload as Europe's Arian rockets – partly because of Japan's insistence of an "all-made-in-Japan" rocket. The M-5 is a three-stage solid-fuel rocket capable of lifting 1.8 tons into orbit at a height of 250 kilometers. Six were launched. All but one launch was successful but the rockets were scrapped because they were too expensive (each launch cost ¥7 billion). The H-2A is a 290-ton, 53 meter (172-foot) rocket first launched on 29 August 2001. Made with foreign parts that reduced its costs by half, it has boosters and two liquid-filled engines and has been used to launch commercial satellites and spy satellites. In the future it hoped that the H-2A will be used to launch an unmanned space shuttle. Three launches, two H-2s and an M-5, beginning in 1998, ended in failures, costing Japan eighteen launch contracts with two US satellite manufacturers. A launch failure of an H-2A in 2003 was described as "the world's most expensive firework's display". Japan had six successful launches in 2006, four with H-2A rockets. In December 2006, Japan successfully launched its heaviest satellite ever, the Kiku No. 8 test satellite. Weighing 5.8 tons, it was launched from an H-2A liquid fuel rocket with four solid-fuel boosters. The satellite was placed in geostationary orbit and uses two huge 18-meter-long antennae. There were some problems unfolding of the antennae. As of November 2009, there had been ten consecutive successful H-2A launches and fifteen successful launches overall. After the unsuccessful launch in 2003 the H-2A had eight straight successful launches. As of 2008, the success rate of the H2-A rocket is 93% (eleven of twelve launches), deemed good enough for commercial applications. In January 2010 IHI Corp decided to liquidate the GX rocket development programme after the government decided to opt out of the project a month earlier. The GX rocket project was scrapped because it consumed too much money and its prospects as a commercial satellite launcher seemed dim (JAXA, 2010).

As for satellites, the first Japanese satellite, the 24-kilogram Ohsumi, was launched in the 1960s. In March 2006, Japan successfully launched its first infrared satellite, the Astro-5 observation satellite, with an infrared telescope designed to search deep space for planets. It was launched from Uchinoura Space center on a three-stage, 30.8-meter-high, M-5 rocket. It was the third successful space launch in a month. Two previous satellites had been sent up on H-2A liquid fuel rockets. In September 2006, Japan successfully launched a solar observation satellite on an M-5 solid fuel rocket. The third solar observation satellite launched by Japan is equipped with telescopes capable of detecting optical wavelength, X-rays and extreme ultraviolet waves. In February 2008, Japan successfully launched a 2.7-ton satellite designed for high-speed Internet transmissions, on an H-2A rocket. The project was delayed and cost USD 500 million and many questioned its cost effectiveness, especially when considering that land-based Internet service has become much faster and efficient. Japan is well advanced with the setting up of its own version of a GPS. In January 2009, eight satellites were launched a board an H-2A rocket. The rocket and the satellites were all successfully launched, the satellites includes one that will observe lighting and carbon dioxide concentrations.

In March 2003, Japan launched its first two spy satellites from Tanegashima Island off of Kyushu. They were launched with a H2A rocket and placed in polar orbit at altitudes of 400 to 600 kilometers. One of their main purposes is to keep an eye on North Korea and its nuclear reactors and missiles. The satellites were made by a consortium of Japanese companies headed by Mitsubishi Electric and are part of a USD 2.1 billion public and private project (JAXA,

2010). After China successfully blew up a weather satellite in space in January 2007, Japan quietly overturned a law restricting its space programme from being put to use for military purposes. Japan has launched its own spy satellites because it does not want to rely on American satellites. Photos from American satellites are often expensive and delayed. Often times requests were turned down for security reasons. With their own satellites, Japan can get information whenever it wants. The launch of a second set of spy satellites in November 2003 was a failure. The satellites and rockets were destroyed because one of the two boosters failed to separate. In February 2007, Japan put its fourth spy satellite into orbit, giving its satellite system full global coverage and allowing the Japanese military to survey the entire globe: to photograph any point on earth at least once a day. Of the four satellites two have optical sensors and two have synthetic aperture radar. The optical satellites can discern objects as small as one meter on the ground. Each of these four satellites is designed to orbit the earth fifteen times and observe any location on earth at least once a day. Within a few years Japan hopes to have sixteen to 20 spy satellites orbiting the earth.

Japan had hoped to enter the commercial satellite business in the 1980s (JAXA, 2010). A lot of government money was pumped into rocket and satellite projects with that goal in mind. The current cost of lofting a satellite with an H-2A rocket is between ¥10 billion and ¥12 billion. Analysts say is necessary to reduce the cost to ¥8 billion to compete with Europe and the United States. In 2007 the H-2A rocket program was privatized and transferred from JAXA and the government to Mitsubishi Heavy Industries (MHI). In April 2007, MHI announced that it was in discussion with European competitors to work together to offer satellite-launching services. The satellite-launching market has been dominated by Russia, Europe and the United States. Japanese launches cost about 20% to 30% more than European ones and the launch period is limited to 190 days a year because of concerns about damaging fishing boats in the launch area. Japan aims to become more competitive in the satellite industry by developing mini satellites that will be considerably cheaper to launch because of their small size. The aim was to develop satellites with desired features that weigh between 100 kilograms and 300 kilograms rather than the standard three tons and launch them by 2011. Production and management of the H-2A shifted from JAXA to MHI on 1 April 2007. Flight 13, which launched the lunar orbiter SELENE, was the first H-IIA launched after this privatization (JAXA, 2017).

As for space exploration, several Japanese, including a woman, have gone on space shuttle missions. Some have brought along special spherical "noodles" that are easier to swallow in zero-gravity than conventional noodles. Japanese astronaut Soichi Noguchi was on the space shuttle Discovery flight in July 2005, the first shuttle flight in two and a half years. Noguchi participated in space walks in which repairs were made to tiles damaged during takeoff. In March 2008, Japanese astronaut Takao Doi went into space aboard the Space Shuttle Endeavor and became the first Japanese to participate in a docking procedure when the space shuttle docked with the ISS. Doi's primary mission was installing the four-meter-long experiment module for Japanese Kibo laboratory on to the ISS using the shuttle's robotic arm. In June 2008, on another space shuttle mission, the Kibo storage facility was installed on the experiment module. Japanese astronaut Akihiko Hoshide was responsible for operating the bolts to join the sections at the early and latter stages of the process. Daisuke Enomoto, a former executive with the troubled Internet company Livedoor, paid the USD 21 million space tourist fee to fly on a ten-day trip to the International Space Station aboard the Russian Soyuz capsule in September 2006 but was pulled from the three-person crew at the last minute and replaced with Dallas businesswoman Anousheh Ansari, reportedly because he had kidney stones. Space Adventures, the space tourism company that arranges trips into space said the cancellation of the flight due to medical reasons meant that Enomoto was not entitled to a refund of his USD 21 million. Enomoto sued Space Adventures, saying the company was well aware of kidney stones when he signed up for the trip and Ansari was given a place because she had invested in Space Adventures. Japanese astronaut Koichi Wakata was selected as the first Japanese astronaut to do an extended stay on the International Space Station. He was delivered to the space station by the space shuttle Discovery in March 2008 and stayed on the space station for three months. One of his first chores was operating the robotic arm, which he helped design, to check the Discovery for tile damage and install solar wind panels on the ISS. Other goals include cultivating cells that will develop into frog kidneys and monitoring how his body reacts to being weightless for extended periods of time. In December 2009, Japanese astronaut Soichi Noguchi arrived at the International Space Station for a six month stay during which time he was involved in scientific studies making use of the space environment, growing a space garden with mint, dandelions and other plants and engaging in the installation of the robotic arm on the Kibo laboratory. Noguchi's six months stay is the longest space trip among Japanese astronauts. Five months was the previous record. It was Noguchi' second trip in space. Because he is staying for such a long time he gets a private room in the ISS. Naoko Yamazaki was one of the astronauts aboard a space shuttle mission in 2010. She was Japan's eighth astronaut and first Japanese mother in space.

Kibo, which means "hope" in Japanese, is Japan's first manned space facility (JAXA, 2010). An attachment on the International Space Station, it has room for up to four astronauts to perform experiments for a long period of time. The project was launched in 1985 and endured delays, overruns and near cancellation under the Clinton administration to finally make it to the ISS in 2008, fifteen years behind the date it was originally supposed to attached to the space station. Among the experiments conducted on Kibo are ones controlling the crystallization process of silicon melting that can lead to the production of stable, homogeneous chip materials, which are known to be susceptible to liquid convection. The Kibo laboratory was completed in July 2009. Japan spent USD 7.6 billion on it.

In September 2009, Japan successfully launched the H-2 Transfer Vehicle (HTV), Japan's first unmanned spacecraft, aboard an H-2 rocket and maneuvered it so it docked with the ISS. Japan hoped the HTV would be the main supply vehicle for the ISS after the Space Shuttle is retired. The development of the HTV began in 1996. Perhaps its most remarkable feature is its ability to be manoeuvered to another spacecraft and dock with it using remote control. In its maiden voyage, it used the global positioning system to maneuver from five kilometers from the ISS to within 500 meters of it. From there it was carefully and gradually eased to the ISS by controllers on the ground. To prevent a crash the HTV could not proceed until it cleared several checks along the way. Crew members aboard the ISS had the power to stop the HTV if necessary. The ISS moves at 7.7 kilometers per second 350 kilometers above the earth. Successfully docking the HTV with it one JAXA official said "is as difficult as threading the eye of a needle via remote control." One of the HTV greatest attributes is that it is unmanned. If something happens to it there is no danger of loss of life and expensive safety systems and back systems used for astronauts do not have to be installed (JAXA, 2010).

In September 2007, Japan launched its first probe to the moon. The probe, the Kaguya lunar explorer, comprised of a main satellite and two subsatellites, took extraordinarily high definition pictures of the dark side of the moon and a full image of the earth from above the moon and scanned the surface with X-ray and infrared devices from about between 100 kilometers and 800 kilometers above the lunar surface. The probe was launched on H-2A rockets built by the private company, Mitsubishi Heavy Industries. The cost of the project was around USD 500 million. The launch of the Japanese moon probe came a week before China launched its own lunar probe and was seen as escalation of Asia's undeclared space race which also includes India who launched a lunar probe in April 2008. Japan has plans for a spacecraft to land on the moon in the 2010s and release a lunar rover similar to the ones used by the United States on Mars. One plan calls for a Japanese manned mission to the moon between 2025 and 2030. Japan has hopes of mining materials for fusion reactors on the moon and setting up an observatory there. Shimizu Corp., a large Japanese construction company, has a team researching the construction of a base on the moon. It has developed technology for manufacturing concrete on the lunar surface and building solar-powered satellite power plant. Japan is experimenting with prototypes of a reusable space capsule and a delta-wing space shuttle. Japanese scientists are working on a solar sail used to propel spaceships using sunlight. Akatsuki (which means "Dawn"), also known as the Venus Climate Orbiter (VCO) and Planet-C, is a space probe tasked to study the atmosphere of Venus. It was launched aboard an H-IIA 202 rocket on 20 May 2010, and failed to enter orbit around Venus on 6 December 2010. After the craft orbited the Sun for five years, engineers placed it into an alternative elliptical Venusian orbit on 7 December 2015 by firing its attitude control thrusters for 20 minutes. By using five different cameras, Akatsuki studies the stratification of the atmosphere, atmospheric dynamics as well as cloud physics. Japan and Russia have also discussed conducting joint missions to Mars that would involve sending a probe to one of the Martian moons to collect soil and bring it back to earth in what would be the first round trip journey to Mars or one its moons. A Japanese mission to put a satellite in orbit around Mars came close to succeeding but failed (JAXA, 2017).

Japan reacted to China's anti-satellite system by ending their previous ban on military activities in space (2008). Tokyo has increased its space efforts with a new launch vehicle and renewed efforts in space science and human spaceflight. This includes scientific research on its Kibo module on the International Space Station. Japan's H-II Transfer Vehicle spacecraft now provides the only non-US and non-Russian transport vehicle able to ferry supplies to the ISS. Japan also fears that China's space accomplishments might affect its own technological dominance. One of Japan's more ambitious space missions is the Hayabusa 2, launched in December 2014. The purpose is to put four landers on an asteroid by 2018 and return soil samples to Earth. Japan's lunar missions (Kayuga) explored the Moon's surface – its geography and composition (Dawson, 2017).

The fast growing emerging economy players

China

On 8 October 1956, the Central Committee of the Communist Party of China, presided over by Mao Zedong, established the Fifth Research Academy of the Ministry of National Defense to develop the country's space effort. This was the official beginning of the People's Republic of China's (PRC) space programme. After four years, on 5 November 1960, China launched its first rocket, becoming the fourth country after Germany, the US and the USSR to enter space.

Since then, China has aimed to become a recognized international space power, thereby advancing its military capabilities. With the successful completion of the Shenzhou-4 flight on 15 October 2003 China's ambitious space programme developed dramatically with its first manned orbit of the earth. This flight, which was a milestone in China's space development, should not be considered an end in itself, but rather the entry ticket to the space power club of the USA and Russia (Liao, 2005).

According to Liao (2005) China's space programme has gone through five distinct periods. In the first period, 1956–1966, the Chinese established a space programme despite the trauma caused by Mao Zedong's "Great Leap Forward". Mao sought to push China to follow the USSR and the USA in seeking missile and space-launch capabilities. At that time China had few resources, either technological or economic, and was a far poorer nation than either the USA or USSR (Farclough, 2007).

In the second period, 1966–1976, after China had launched its first rocket in 1960, it began to devote significant resources to the development of satellites. China's space programme maintained a progressive course, even though sectors of Chinese society were being torn apart by the Cultural Revolution. China launched its first satellite, the Long March-1 (Dongfanghong (DFH)-1), on 24 April 1970, making it the sixth nation to launch its own satellite into orbit (after the USSR (Sputnik-1957), the USA (Explorer-1, 1958), Canada (Alouette, 1962), France (Asterix-scienti.c satellite, 1965) and Japan (Ohsumi-test satellites, 1966)). Since the DFH-1 in 1970, by 2005 China had launched some 60 satellites in five primary categories, which support both civil and military efforts. These are namely: retrievable remote sensing satellites Fanhui Shin Weixing (FSW), communication satellites Dong Fang Hong (DFH), meteorological satellites Feng Yun (FY), scientific and technological experimental satellites Shi Jian (SJ) and earth-imaging satellites Ziyuan. During the second period China developed an indigenous family of liquid-fueled space launch vehicles that are competitive with Western launchers, a large national space research effort and an extensive satellite industry. In addition, it made space remote sensing a priority and has developed its own communications and navigational satellites. And, although China's satellite industry lags behind that of the USA and Europe, joint ventures with foreign firms over this decade have helped it improve its satellite manufacturing capabilities (Liao, 2005).

The third period, 1976–1986, was an ambivalent period for the space programme, as China's recovery from the Cultural Revolution proceeded slowly under Deng Xiaoping's leadership. Mao had focused the programme on national prestige and national security. However, Deng's Four Modernizations programme placed the highest priority on economic and scientific efforts to help develop the economy. Therefore China's space budget was trimmed to meet more modest ambitions. With the reductions in space spending in the early 1980s came Beijing's authorization for China's space agencies to generate income from external sources. On 29 January 1984 the Long March-3 launch vehicle inaugurated the Xichang facility in south-central China. Following this successful launch China began offering Long March launchers to the West. In effect, China's space programme was shifting its orientation from the defense sector to the civilian and commercial sector. For example, the National High Technology Research and Development Project of China (Project 863) was launched in March 1986 by the central government with the aim of enhancing China's international competitiveness and improving its overall R&D capability in high technology. Project 863 focused on the leading strategic and upcoming high technologies that would benefit China's long- and medium-term development and security. In addition, the creation of Project 863 was an effort to position China to concentrate its space programme on practical applied satellites. Since then high technology development has served not only military and political purposes, but also civilian and commercial uses.

At the start of the fourth period, from 1986 to 1996, China was getting little response to the launch services it offered until a series of events occurred in 1986, starting with the disastrous loss of the US Space Shuttle Challenger. Then two of the US's other leading rocket launchers, a Titan and a Delta, spectacularly exploded, and Europe's Ariane went down. The China Great Wall Industry Corporation (CGWIC) had been actively marketing Chinese launch services in the hope that the flexible Long March family of launch vehicles would prove attractive to the international market (Liao, 2005).

The first launches for paying customers involved experimental payloads using the Long March-2 – first for a French company (Matra) in 1987 and then for a German consortium (Intospace) in 1988. China's Space Leading Group (SLG) was established in 1991 and has overseen and coordinated all space activities in a broad policy-making role. The Chinese National Space Administration (CNSA), established in 1993, is the executive agency for space functions, responsible to the State Council. In this period aerospace technology was able to contribute significantly to other national economic development efforts and was highlighted in the Five-Year Plan (1991–1995).

The fifth period started in 1996 with the Five-Year Plan (1996–2000). Since then China's commercial launches have been shared between two government organizations, the Commission of Science, Technology and Industry for National Defense (COSTIND) and the China Aerospace Corporation (CASC). During the above period China clearly benefited from US, Russian and European openness in space technology (Liao, 2005). For example, China and the EU have recently agreed on Chinese participation in the Galileo navigation satellite programme (alongside Canada and Israel). This collaboration enables China to develop a more sophisticated understanding of navigational satellites. Galileo is an example of how China has used foreign partnerships to speed up its indigenous space effort – not through pirating technology, but by participating in and learning from the experience of other programmes.

It is clear that a great deal of the technology now being applied to commercial space systems can be carried over to military systems. In this regard, the USA is concerned that China will employ dual-use and pirated or transformed technologies in both commercial and military space programmes. As a result the US does not engage in any collaboration with China on space. This period culminated in the historic Shenzou-4 launch. The first Chinese manned space flight program took place with Yang Liwei's successful 2003 flight aboard Shenzhou 5. This success made China the third country to independently send humans into space. But what is the next space development for China after manned space flight? The first feasibility study for lunar exploration was completed in 1995, and the development of lunar exploration technology was spelled out in China's first White Paper on space. The China State Council ruling cabinet leadership approved the eleventh Five Year plan 2006–2010 for space on 10 May 2007 (Vick, 2009).

It had already previously released a White Paper report on the results of the previous Five Year Plan 2001–2005 and the immediate future plans for this Five Year plan 2006–2010. Within that report emphasis was placed on satellite remote sensing expansion, direct broadcast satellites, meteorological satellites and navigation satellite developments. They also emphasized the development of a new sea monitoring satellite series in addition to a small constellation satellite series. The space plans were subsequently approved by the Chinese communist party central committer of about 350 members before the final five year Party congress of 2,000 approved it. China's space programme is to emphasize three areas of development: navigation, remote sensing and communication satellites all having dual-purpose requirements for the civil and military sectors of the national space effort. One of the efforts is concentrated around the Bediou GPS class satellite competitor to the GPS, GLONASS, and planned Galileo satellite systems.

China has launched multiple vehicles to the moon in the past decade. A series of Chang'e spacecraft (1–3) were sent to the Moon to orbit and to explore the surface, including a robotic rover landing successfully by the end of 2013. The *Chang'e 4* and *5* spacecraft will be sent to explore the dark side of the moon. It is expected that a mission to land on the dark side would be attempted by 2020, a feat that no other nation has attempted so far. There is concern that China's progress will translate into dominance over resources on the moon, including helium 3, a gas than could be used to provide nuclear power without radioactive waste, as well as an abundance of rare minerals and precious metals that are extremely high in price that can be used for a variety of electronics and industrial applications (Dawson, 2017). China has also focued on developing a space station, a heavy-lift booster rocket and a new launch site. These can all be seen as peaceful use of space, however, China's demonstrated ability to destroy a satellite in orbit by using an interceptor raised not only security concerns but also the possible destruction of property caused by the space debris generated from this type of explosion. In May 2015, China also tested part of a new anti-satellite ballistic missile system. These aggressive military actions are part of a larger military posturing by China, and many nations are watching as these events unfold.

A white paper on space was released in December 2016. According to the white paper, the Chinese government takes the space industry as an important part of the nation's overall development strategy, and adheres to the principle of exploration and utilization of outer space for peaceful purposes. Over the past 60 years of remarkable development since its space industry was established in 1956, China has made great achievements in this sphere, including the development of atomic and hydrogen bombs, missiles, man-made satellites, manned spaceflight and lunar probe. It has opened up a path of self-reliance and independent innovation, and has created the spirit of China's space industry. To carry forward this spirit and stimulate enthusiasm for innovation, the Chinese government set 24 April as China's Space Day in 2016. A series of achievements in China's space programme over the last 12 months has set the stage to start construction of the country's first space station in 2019, a year later than previously scheduled in 2016. Since 2016, China has successfully launched the Long March 7 carrier rocket, the Tiangong 2 space lab, the Shenzhou 11 manned spacecraft and the Tianzhou 1 cargo spacecraft. The four flights achieved success in China's manned space programme, and laid a solid foundation for the building and long-term operation of a space station. The Long March 7 rocket is vital for launching supply ships, and eventually crews, to China's future space station. It has now flown twice successfully. The Tiangong 2 orbital module launched in September

2016, welcoming two Chinese astronauts on the Shenzhou 11 spacecraft in October for a one-month expedition, the country's longest human spaceflight to date. The heavy-lifting Long March 5 rocket took off on its maiden flight in November. The powerful launcher is needed to place heavy space station modules into orbit. And the Tianzhou 1 robotic cargo craft launched on a Long March 7 rocket on 20 April, linked up with Tiangong 2 two days later and accomplished China's first in-space refueling test. The rapid-fire launch campaign has bolstered confidence that the key components needed for China's space station programme will be ready when construction begins, officials said (Clark, 2017). A core module, named Tianhe 1, is scheduled for launch in 2019 to begin assembly of the space station. Two support sections will launch by 2022 to complete construction of the space station, which should be operational for at least 20 years. Three-person crews will live on the space station for three-to-six months. The finished outpost will have a mass of more than 60 metric tons, about one-seventh that of the International Space Station, and comparable to the mass of NASA's Skylab station in the 1970s.

India

Despite being a developing economy with its attendant problems, India has effectively developed space technology and has applied it successfully for its rapid development and today is offering a variety of space services globally (Morring & Neelam, 2004).

During the formative decade of 1960s, space research was conducted by India mainly with the help of sounding rockets. The Indian Space Research Organisation (ISRO) was formed in 1969. Space research activities were provided further impetus with the formation of the Space Commission and the Department of Space by the government of India in 1972. ISRO was brought under the Department of Space in the same year. In the history of the Indian space programme, the 1970s was the era of experimentation during which experimental satellite programmes were conducted. The success of those programmes, led to era of operationalization in the 1980s during which operational satellite programmes like INSAT and IRS came into being. Today, INSAT and IRS are the major programmes of ISRO (Organisation, 2009).

To launch its spacecraft independently, India has a robust launch vehicle programme, which has matured to the state of offering launch services to the outside world. Antrix, the commercial arm of the Department of Space, is marketing India's space services globally. Fruitful co-operation with other space faring nations, international bodies and the developing world is one of the main characteristics of India's space programme (Morring & Neelam, 2004).

The most significant milestone of the Indian Space Programme during the year 2005–2006 was the successful launch of PSLV-C6. On 5 May 2005, the ninth flight of Polar Satellite Launch Vehicle (PSLV-C6) successfully placed two satellites – the 1560 kg CARTOSTAR-1 and 42 kg HAMSAT – into a predetermined polar Sun Synchronous Orbit (SSO). Coming after seven launch successes in a row, the success of PSLV-C6 further demonstrated the reliability of PSLV and its capability to place payloads weighing up to 1600 kg satellites into a 600 km high polar SSO.

The successful launch on 22 December 2005 of INSAT-4A, the heaviest and most powerful satellite built by India so far was the other major event of the year 2005–06. INSAT-4A is capable of providing Direct-To-Home (DTH) television broadcasting services (Organisation, 2009).

In addition, the setting up of the second cluster of nine Village Resource Centres (VRCs) was an important ongoing initiative of the Department of Space during the year. The VRC concept integrates the capabilities of communications and earth observation satellites to provide a variety of information emanating from space systems and other IT tools to address the changing and critical needs of rural communities.

India convincingly demonstrated its capability for a deep space mission with the smooth insertion in November of its maiden lunar probe Chandrayaan-1 – launched in October, 2008 – into a 100km (60 miles) orbit around the moon (Indian Space Research Organisation, 2009).

For a developing nation that began its space journey with the test firing of a 9kg (20lb) sounding rocket from the fishing hamlet of Thumba near Thiruvananthapuram in November 1963, Chandrayaan-1 was success on a shoestring budget. With a cost of less than Rp4 billion (USD 83 million), Chandrayaan-1 is considered the most inexpensive lunar probe ever launched – its cost is nearly one-third of China's Chang'e-1 and one-sixth of Japan's Kaguya. "With a minuscule budget, we have mastered cutting-edge technology in space," says Indian Space Research Organisation chairman Madhavan Nair.

Two moon missions are on ISRO's space agenda for early 2018. The first one will be the Chandrayaan-2 mission, an advanced version of its previous mission with the objective of deeper lunar surface probe, and the second mission will be an initiative by Team Indus, a group of space enthusiasts that wants to unfurl the tricolour on the moon's surface as part of a global lunar competition. Roping in investors like Infosys co-founder and former UIDAI chairman Nandan Nilekani and space experts such as former ISRO chairman K Kasturirangan and many experienced old hands from the Indian space agency, Team Indus is leaving no stone unturned to achieve its goal. Comprising mostly young engineers and led by IIT-Delhi alumnus Rahul Narayan, Team Indus is planning the mission as part of a global contest to win USD 30 million Google Lunar XPRIZE, which requires the rover of a competing team to move 500 metres on the moon's surface and should be able to beam back high-definition images back to earth.

For Bangalore-based Antrix, the commercial arm of the Indian space programme, the successful launch of Chandrayaan-1 by an augmented version of the Polar Satellite Launch Vehicle promises more customers for its PSLV cost-effective launch service. In April 2008, the PSLV set a record by launching ten satellites in one go. Eight were nanosatellites, weighing from 3–16kg, from Canada, Europe and Japan. Recent contracts won by Antrix include launching

Algeria's Alsat-2A and Italy's IMSAT spacecraft on board PSLV in 2009. The company also has in hand contracts to launch a micro satellite from Singapore's Nanyang Technological University and Cubesat, a three-satellite package from the Netherlands, on the PSLV. The launch of GSLV with an Indian upper cryogenic stage and GSLV-MkIII promises further commercial opportunities for Antrix. ISRO is planning a GSLV flight with a homegrown cryogenic engine – as a replacement for the Russian-supplied stage – this year.

Antrix, which has been supplying components and subsystems to global satellite builders, has also delivered the W2M satellite to Eutelsat, while sales of satellite images is a growth area for the company. Revenue from satellite data sales accounted for 10% of its turnover of Rp9.4 billion in 2007–8, with its market expanding beyond Europe and USA to include Australia and Russia. Asian and African countries now source remote sensing data from Antrix.

More than 400 Village Resources Centres (VRCs) have been set up to provide rural communities with information on natural resources, land and water resources management, teleducation and telemedicine. Using Insat, around 400 hospitals in remote and difficult to reach locations have been integrated into the telemedicine network.

Unlike many other space agencies, ISRO is still the main space manufacturer in India (OECD, 2014). It assembles satellites and launch vehicles from parts provided by ISRO's eleven centres spread around the country, with production mainly carried out in the southern part of India, in Thiruvananthapuram (launchers), Bangalore (satellites) and Sriharikota. Important centres are also the Space Applications Centre in Ahmedabad and National Remote Sensing Centre in Hyderabad. ISRO had 14,716 employees in 2012, distributed between the different centres, and its commercial branch, Antrix, located in Bangalore. It sells remote sensing data imagery, ground station services, satellite launches and exports of satellite components and other products. Antrix is also responsible for selling transponder leases on Indian telecommunications satellites, a market that has seen considerable growth in the last years (turnover in 2011 amounted to about USD 200 million). Private space manufacturers are expected to become more important as the demand for PSLV launch vehicles currently surpasses ISRO's production capacity. About 80% of the parts of the PSLV are now produced by industry. The twelfth Five Year Plan clearly states the need to increase the capabilities of private industry to take over some production and assembly tasks (Indian Planning Commission, 2013).

In September 2016, India sent a rocket into space that successfully launched eight satellites in one go. The main purpose of the launch which took place at the Sriharikota space centre off India's eastern coast, was to put into orbit SCATSAT-1, a satellite that will help weather forecasting. Five of the other satellites that were on board are foreign, from the US, Canada and Algeria. The launch took the number of foreign satellites launched by India to 79. This has earned the country more than USD 120 million (£92 million). And India's space agency has already secured deals to launch dozens more foreign satellites. In June of the same year India launched 20 satellites in a single mission, the most in the history of the country's ambitious space programme. Seventeen of those were foreign.

India's ability to launch multiple satellites in a single mission has also put it on firm footing in the global market. Many private companies are developing satellites that they need for their operations, but most cannot afford to launch these independently. Thus they need to piggyback on missions from agencies like ISRO that have launch facilities. Another aspect that could be making India an attractive proposition is the frequency of its launches and its ability to meet deadlines.

India now plans to have as many as twelve launches a year, a pace that's more than doubled since 2015. Still, getting foreign satellites on board is not simple. Additionally, there is competition too, not only from other space-faring countries but also increasingly from private firms like Elon Musk's SpaceX. So far India has only been launching small and light foreign satellites, using the PSLV, which has become its most reliable launch vehicle, with 36 consecutive successful launches so far.

However launching heavier satellites is the most profitable market, which is why many players are reducing the price of their rocket launches to obtain more deals. India has been launching heavy satellites on its Geosynchronous Satellite Launch Vehicle (GSLV) but so far it has only been used for domestic satellites. In recent months though, there have been queries from foreign companies for launches on the GSLV. If India can successfully start taking more heavy satellites to space, it could really enhance its position in a market that is worth billions of dollars.

Brazil

The Brazilian Space Agency (abbreviated in Brazilian Portuguese as AEB) was established in 1994 as a civilian authority within the direct purview of the Executive Office of the President of Brazil. It is responsible for pushing forward Brazil's space activities and for coordinating the national and international cooperation necessary to help further the country's strategic goals in space.

The National Policy on the Development of Space Activities (PNDAE) establishes the major principles, objectives and guidelines for Brazilian space activities. The policy outlines several specific objectives, namely: to establish within Brazil the scientific and technical competence in the space area which will make it possible for the country to act with real autonomy in some well identified situations, including the selection of technological solutions to Brazilian problems, and pursuing its national obligations under relevant international negotiations, agreements and treaties; to promote the development of space systems, and related ground infrastructure, that may provide data and services desired by the country; and to prepare the Brazilian industry to participate and become competitive in the global market for space related goods, services and applications (Silva, 2005).

The National Institute for Space Research (INPE) was founded in 1961 in order for Brazil to benefit from new developments in space science and technology and in particular, to increase Brazil's autonomy in strategic areas, by providing a means for industry to become competitive in the space sector and by encouraging the development of a national space technology capability. INPE's main goals are the fostering of scientific research, technological applications and to qualify personnel in the fields of space and atmospheric sciences, space engineering and technology.

The budget for the Brazilian space activities has been steadily increasing, albeit from a low base, as part of a long-term governmental policy to increase the country's investment returns on science and technology (Zhao, 2005).

Commercial activities include Embratel's BRAZILSAT telecommunications network, developed by Spar (of Canada) and launched on Ariane in the mid 1980s. A second generation of satellites was launched in the early to mid 1990s. A constellation of twelve EO satellites (ECO-8) has been developed. In 1993 the Brazilian Aerospace Industries Association was established to represent the interests of those Brazilian companies working in the aerospace (and space) engineering. Although Empresa Brasileira de Aeronbutica – usually known as EMBRAER – dominates the Brazilian aerospace/space industry, other companies have established expertise in key areas including rockets and missiles, avionics and other electronics and composite materials (Silva, 2005).

Compared with other countries, Brazil is a modest player on the global space scene. As available resources have not allowed the nation to advance in this sector, partnerships open a window of opportunity for Brazil to take part in a much wider range of projects than would be possible if these had to be funded by the country alone. International cooperation is considered to be the best way to participate in strategic projects for lower costs, and to have access to new technologies developed abroad. To keep these objectives on track, the Brazilian government established a national space policy, with the following priorities: "emphasis on applied sciences and applications, in particular microgravity research; participation in the ISS and in projects of space infrastructure, aiming at carrying out scientific and technological experiments" (Zhao 2005).

The PNDAE covered a ten-year period from 1998 to 2007. The programme currently consists of eight major initiatives: Space Applications, Satellites and Payloads, Satellite Launching Vehicles and Sounding Rockets, Space Infrastructure, Space Sciences, R&D on Space Technologies, Training and Development of Human Resources and Support to the Qualification of the National Space Industry.

Notable activities of the Brazilian National Space Programme include the four small data collection satellites developed by Brazilian engineers. SCD-1, was launched in 1993 and remains operational, with SCD-2 lost on the first VLS launch, and SCD-3 having been launched in 2000.

Also, since 1988 China and Brazil have been collaborating on a programme to develop two remote sensing satellites. The first CBERS (China-Brazil Earth Resources Satellite) satellite, CBERS-1 was launched in 1999 and is the first in a series of remote sensing satellites designed for global coverage using optical visible and infrared cameras. Initially a two satellite system, China and Brazil agreed to develop two second generation satellites CBERS-3 and -4. China and

Brazil have also agreed to explore the feasibility of the joint development of a Geo-stationary meteorological satellite and a telecommunications satellite, based on the CBERS satellite bus (Zhao 2005).

In addition, SACI a micro-satellite launched in 1999 carrying four experiments conceived by Brazilian scientists and their foreign partners is providing much useful information and other small scientific satellites are expected in the short and medium term. Finally, two small earth observation satellites, SSR-1 and SSR-2, projected to operate in equatorial circular orbit at an altitude of 900 km, were developed. The first was launched in 2000, while the second was scheduled for launch in 2003. A low earth orbit equatorial satellite constellation, aimed towards providing low cost communications to remote areas around the equator is also now under consideration.

As a result of the co-operation agreement signed between NASA and AEB, AEB will be responsible for the development and provision to NASA of equipment for the International Space Station (ISS) programme. In exchange, AEB will receive rights from NASA's allocation to utilise the ISS (Zhao, 2005).

Since the early 1970s Brazil has been engaged in a long-term launcher development programme which started with the development of a successful family of sounding rockets named SONDA. The Alcantara Launch Centre (CLA) is capable of launching solid fuel sounding rockets and research vehicles, as well as satellites into low earth orbit. Located on the Brazilian North Eastern Coast, near the equator, CLA's geographical position increases the Centre safety conditions and allows for lower launching costs. In the coming years the Centre is expected to enlarge its capacity and become commercially competitive both for national and international users. Infraero, the organization responsible for managing Brazil's airports, has been appointed to administer those areas of CLA that will be open to foreign launchers and operators.

Brazil suffered three major failures at the Alcantara Launch Center in the late 1990s and early 2000s, including a launch pad explosion which killed 21 engineers and technicians in 2003. In 2010, Brazil successfully launched a midsized rocket from Alcantara with ten microgravity experiments as a part of its payload. Ground broke on a long-delayed joint venture between Ukraine and Brazil in September 2011 for the Ukranian Cyclone-4 launcher project. The joint venture began in 2003, but money and the Alcantara launch pad explosion delayed the project for nearly a decade. Israel is in talks with Brazil to launch satellites from Alcântara, as Israel's geographic position makes domestic launches difficult. An eastward launch from Israel taking advantage of the rotation of the planet would cause the booster to drop in Jordan or Iraq. A 2000 agreement between Brazil and the United States also allows for private US corporations to launch from Alcantara if they desire. In 2009, Brazil and Russia agreed to create and launch five different rockets as part of the Southern Cross Project. The largest of the rockets, Epsilon, will carry a payload weight of four tons. The Southern Cross project will create five additional launch pads and oversee up to a dozen launches a year. The project is on pace to make its first launch in 2022. While lacking a manned shuttle initiative, Brazil is poised as a hotbed for space exploration along with private and joint government launches in the coming decades. Additionally, Brazil's Science without Borders programs aimed to spend USD 2 billion to educate 75,000 students pursuing advanced degrees in engineering and physical sciences at home and abroad, with hope that some of those students would return to work in Brazil. Brazil, thanks to its location and initiative, could very well become the planet's spaceport of choice in the late 21st Century (Veronese, 2012).

Other players

Israel

Until recently, Israel enjoyed a regional monopoly in outer space (Kass, 2006) being the only state in the Middle East region who could deploy satellites onboard indigenously-manufactured SLVs. The Shavit SLV is a modified Jericho MRBM that placed numerous civilian and military systems in space. Hayim Eshed, head of the Israeli Defense Ministry Space Administration, boasted that "With the exception of the Americans, we are superior to all other countries in two fields of satellite technology – resolution of photographs and picture quality." Israel further enhanced its satellite technologies with the 25 April 2006 launch of its arth Remote Observation Satellite (EROS)-B photo reconnaissance system. The system can also photograph activities in ballistic launch sites to obtain advanced warning of potential strikes and study future missile tests. Israel has an edge over others in the region in satellite technology, which Iran seeks to overcome.

Israel officially entered the space age with the lift-off of its first satellite, Ofeq-1, from the locally built Shavit launch vehicle on 19 September 1988. With that launch, Israel joined an exclusive club of countries that have developed, produced and launched their own satellites.

The next step was taken in early 2003 when NASA launched the 28th flight of space shuttle Columbia, on mission STS-107. The seven crew members on board included the first Israeli astronaut, Ilan Ramon. The sixteen-day mission of Ramon and his colleagues was devoted to research, with over 80 experiments in earth and space sciences, human physiology, fire suppression and the effect of microgravity on a wide variety of natural phenomena.

The 1988 launch of Ofeq-1 was coordinated by the Israel Space Agency (ISA), established five years earlier to support and coordinate private and academic space-related research into areas such as electronics, computers, electro-optics and imaging techniques, which had already been in progress for some 20 years under the management of the National Committee for Space Research (Paikowsky, 2007).

Designed as a technological satellite, Ofeq-1 spurred Israel's capability to send a satellite into orbit. Both Ofeq-1 and its successor, Ofeq-2, launched in April 1990, were very successful, sending back a stream of vital technical information. The two satellites reentered the earth's atmosphere within six months of their launching. Ofeq-3 was launched in 1995 with an advanced electro-optical payload. It more than doubled its expected lifespan, down-loading images of superior quality. The unbroken success of Israel's satellite programme was, however, brought to an abrupt halt with Ofeq-4. This fourth satellite in the series encountered problems in the second stage of its Janu-ary 1998 launch. It burned up, setting back Israel's satellite reconnaissance programme by several years. However, Ofeq-5, was successfully launched by a Shavit launcher in May 2002. Circling the earth every hour and a half, Ofeq-5 is a reconnaissance satellite capable of delivering color images with an extraordinarily high resolution of less than a metre. Underlying the success of the Ofeq satellites and their comparatively inexpensive launch capability are Israeli developments in the field of miniaturization. Lighter satellites are more efficient and save hundreds of thousands of dollars per launch (Israel Minister of Foreign Affairs, 2010).

Israel launched a micro-satellite into orbit in June 1998. Developed at the Technion – Israel Institute of Technology in Haifa – for a mere USD 3.5 million, TechSat II is a marvel of miniaturization. The satellite is an 18-inch cube that weighs just 106 lbs. It orbits 516 miles above the earth, generating its own energy from the sun and is packed with miniature cameras, computers and other locally manufactured space hardware used in communications technology, remote sens-ing, astronomy and geoscience. TechSat II comes within photographing distance of earth a dozen times a day. The ground-monitoring station at the Technion's Asher Space Research Institute downloads regular measurements of the atmo-sphere's ozone content from its ultraviolet sensors. From its charged-particle detector, scientists gauge the frequency with which such particles impact on the satellite and the potential damage they could cause to sensitive equipment such as computers. They also study the photographs recorded by its tiny camera (Paikowsky, 2007).

Begun in the 1980s as a student project, TechSat rapidly extended its bound-aries into a professional satellite programme. With the arrival of immigrant scientists from the former Soviet Union, the project took on its current form, making the Technion one of the few universities worldwide to have designed, built and launched a satellite.

As well as developing space hardware, Israel is using space as a platform to find out more about life on our own planet. In October 1996, ISA and NASA signed an active umbrella cooperation agreement, which allows Israeli life sci-ences experiments to be integrated into NASA space flights. The experiments conducted have led to greater understanding in the fields of embryogenesis (the early development of mammals), osteoporosis (loss of bone density) and the set-ting up of "space farms" in order to supply spaceships and space stations of the future with food.

Many international space programs have taken an interest in Israel's space achievements (Paikowsky, 2007). In addition to NASA, Israel has formal space research cooperation agreements with France, Germany, Russia, the Ukraine and the Netherlands. Israel recently signed a similar agreement with India, which provides for the installation of an Israeli-produced telescope on an Indian satellite due to be launched in the next two years.

In June 2003, Israel was accepted into the European Space Agency (ESA) as a participating member. The agreement will allow Israel to participate in European space projects and to submit proposals for joint development projects.

Israel sent its first geostationary telecommunications satellite into orbit on 16 May 1996. The Afro-Mediterranean Orbital System (AMOS) was built by Israel Aircraft Industries in partnership with Alcatel Espace of France and Daimler-Benz Aerospace of Germany. Launched by the French-built Ariane-4 launch vehicle, the AMOS communications satellite continues to provide high quality broadcasting and communication services for the growing markets of Eastern Europe and the Middle East.

The TAUVEX (Tel Aviv University Ultra-Violet Explorer) scientific instrument constructed by El-Op (Electro Optical Industries, Ltd.) is one cornerstone of a major international space research project in which Israel is an important player. The three-telescope array is designed to image astronomical objects in the ultraviolet range, including different types of hot stars (such as white dwarfs and mixed-type binaries), and young massive stars, which emit large amounts of ultraviolet radiation and ionize the interstellar medium and are thus important in star formation processes and in the evolution of galaxies. TAUVEX operates in a spectral region with reduced sky background, thus can detect relatively faint objects with a modest observing time per target. TAUVEX is slated to fly on the Indian satellite GSAT-4 as part of the India-Israel Agreement on Space Exploration. Its multi-year mission will yield a very deep survey of part of the sky; this will enhance considerably our knowledge about evolution in the universe.

A spin-off of TAUVEX is a small telescope with a resolution of five metres that will be used on the DAVID, a small commercial remote sensing satellite. Developed jointly by an Israeli hi-tech company and a German firm, the project is supported by the EU and ISA. Israel will participate in the European Global Navigation Overlay System (EGNOS), as well as the new Galileo project.

Israel's space activities today are highly focussed on High-Resolution-Imaging satellites in Low Earth Orbits. The funding levels for Israel's space programme are relatively modest. Nevertheless, the programme's achievements are among the most impressive of Israel's high-tech industries. On the basis of cost-to-performance and weight-to-performance, there is no doubt that Israel's imaging satellites are among the best in the world (Bhattacharjee, 2016). At present, there are five earth observation active satellites and eight reconnaissance satellites in orbit. EROS A operates as a commercial venture supplying imagery to the international market. This is followed by OFEQ 5, EROS B, OFEQ 7 (the second generation of Electro-Optical Remote Sensing satellites) and TecSAR launched in 2007, employing a state-of-the-art Synthetic-Aperture-Radar payload. It enables night images and penetration through clouds. In the coming years (under development and construction) the next generation of satellites will include OPTSAT–3rd, a new generation of high-resolution Electro-Optical remote sensing satellites and VENUS – a joint Israel/France Multi-spectral Mission to monitor vegetation and coasts with partners ISA (Israel Space Agency) and CNES, the space agency of France.

The State of Israel has been engaged with Communication Satellites since the early 1990s. Two satellites were launched to a geosynchronous orbit, Amos-1 in mid-1996 and Amos-2 in late 2003. Amos-1 and Amos-2 provide communication services to the Middle East, Central Europe and the East Coast of the United States. Amos-3 was launched in April 2008, to replace Amos-1. The Amos-1, 2, 3 series is of small-class (up to 1.5 ton) satellites. Currently, various countries are approaching Israel to acquire such satellites to strengthen their military infrastructure. Five years ago, Meir Nissim-Nir, the then Head of the Department for Satellite Control and Command for Israel Aircraft Industries stated that Israel possesses strategic capabilities in space satellites that produce targets for the Air Force. In Israel, ISA's partners include industry and academia. In general, some 30 industries nationwide are involved in the space programme, Israel Aerospace Industries being its prime contractor. In academia, Israeli universities lead in astrophysics, space research and space engineering. As a government agency, ISA also coordinates external relations and collaborations with foreign countries and other space agencies. These activities include developing space systems and subsystems, running the "ground segment" systems that communicate with space missions from Earth, scientific research and exploration initiatives that involve Israeli academic institutions and industry.

As a long-standing space-faring nation, Israel has established cooperation with leading space-faring nations. For example, ISA is currently developing Vegetation and Environment New Micro Spacecraft (VENuS) together with the French Space Agency: Centre national d'etudes spatiales (CNES), exploring the SHALOM project with the Italian Space Agency, Agenzia Spaziale Italiana (ASI), which involves a hyperspectral satellite. ISA also collaborates with NASA in the Mediterranean Israel Dust Experiment or the MEIDEX project, which studied the Mediterranean region and its influence on the weather and climate, the European Space Agency and others. The ongoing projects under the Israeli space programme are: the Samson (Space Autonomous Mission for Swarming and Geolocation with Nanosatellites) which has been designed to make small satellites; ULTRASAT, a small space mission designed to carry out a wide-filed UV transient survey, which is being jointly carried out by Weizmann Institute of Science, Israel Aircraft Industries (IAI) and Elbit Systems Electro-optics, Elop, in collaboration with NASA AMES and CALTEC and the Space IL project, which aims to successfully launch, fly and land a robotic spacecraft on the moon, operate the spacecraft across the lunar surface and transmit video, images and data back to earth by using a micro satellite. There are multiple private satellite companies in Israel and Europe that operate in tandem with the Israeli Space Program assisting ISA: Gilat Satellite Networks, Global TT Satellite provider (based in Brussels), Elbit Systems, Satlink Communications and Spacecom under Eurocom to name a few.

Iran

Iranian efforts to exploit space began under the Shah who tried to improve his country's scientific standing. In 1959, Tehran became a founding member of the United Nations' Committee on the Peaceful Uses of Outer Space (UNCOPUOS). Iran has viewed becoming a space power as a vehicle for modernity. Some of the goals it enumerated at a 2002 UNCOPUOS meeting reinforces this perception:

1   Commercializing space programmes for earth observation, and predicting environmental changes;
2   Promoting international cooperation based on concepts of joint benefits;
3   Encouraging space efforts in the private sector to increase awareness within the public of space and incorporate related initiatives into daily lives;
4   Developing a mastery of space science and technology directed to assist in the development of space programmes and commercial projects;
5   Increasing interest in space programs among the youth, who will play a notable role in the country's future.

Iran sought to accomplish these and other broad objectives in order to become more technologically advanced. On 5 January 2003, Rear Admiral Ali Shamkhani, the country's former defense minister, stated that within eighteen months, "Iran will be the first Islamic country to penetrate the stratosphere with its own satellite and with its own launch system." Iran has sought a space capability partly because of America's growing regional presence. Developing these programmes in response to the increased United States presence indicates that Iran feels threatened and partly seeks to exploit space to safeguard its own national security (Kass, 2006).

Iran apparently attempted to meet some of the above-noted goals starting in April 2003. The legislature approved a bill to create the Iranian Space Agency (ISA) to serve as a policy-formulating organization for space initiatives. The ISA performs research on technology, remote sensing projects, develops national space equipment and participates in the development of national and international space endeavours. It also coordinates various space-related activities within the country's research institutes, administrative agencies and universities. These efforts also help the ISA to execute decisions from the Supreme Aerospace Council.

It has been observed that Iranian efforts to advance its space programme follow an unsettling pattern seen elsewhere. In slightly different ways and to varying degrees of success, China, North Korea and Pakistan use a civil space programme clandestinely to manufacture longer-range missiles to further safeguard national security. Iran seeks to become a space power for similar reasons (Kass, 2006).

The Iranian defence ministry plays a prominent role in shaping the space effort, managing the Shahab ballistic missile programme, which Iran modified into a space launch vehicle (SLV). Successfully testing a launch vehicle has allowed Iran to boast that it is a space power (Kass, 2006). In September 2000, an Iranian government spokesperson stated that the nation developed a modified missile, the Shahab-3D, to launch communication satellites. The Shahab-3D is a two-stage projectile that underwent a flight test in September 2000 using a combination of solid and liquid propellants. The Shahab system resembles North Korea's liquid propellant No-dong, which both countries agreed to develop jointly (Kass, 2006).

The Iranian SLV initiative advanced further with North Korean assistance (Kass, 2006). On 31 August 1998, North Korea attempted to launch a satellite by reengineering a ballistic missile. The Taepo-dong 1 failed to place its satellite into orbit due to a mechanical failure. Nonetheless, the event marked an important advancement in North Korea's missile programme. The country showcased some key requisites for developing longer-ranged missiles – multi-stage separation and advanced guidance mechanisms. Moreover, Pyongyang now owned a multi-stage rocket capable of hitting targets much further than its more publicized cousin, the shorter-range and single-stage No-dong. Iran and Pakistan sent delegations to witness the 1998 launch. Their presence indicates that both nations could use Taepo-dong 1 technologies for their indigenous SLV efforts. Perhaps this event motivated Iran to conduct the September 2000 Shahab test using solid and liquid stages (Kass, 2006).

On 27 October 2005, Iran met a key aerospace objective by becoming the 43rd nation to own a satellite. The Sinah-1 spacecraft entered orbit onboard a Russian rocket to monitor natural disasters and observe agricultural trends. Moscow provided Iran with support. The Sinah-1's primary mission was to demonstrate that Iran could possess an operational satellite.

Manufacturing an independent satellite is likely to occur through development of the 60-kilogram (130 pound) Mesbah spacecraft. The system is initially intended to obtain pictures for a variety of civilian purposes, to include greater data collection and distribution, assisting in efforts to find natural resources and to more accurately predict the weather. Eventually, Iran will modify the satellite for remote sensing. The military could benefit from this technology, because it could obtain knowledge of where to build suitable facilities. The Iran Telecommunications Research Center (ITRC) and the Iran Science Organization of Science and Technology (IROST) are jointly building this micro-satellite with the Italian company Carlo Gavazzi Space (Kass, 2006).

Construction of Mesbah began in 1997, just before the start of then-Iranian President Muhammad Khatami's second term. On 4 August 2005, the day after Ahmadinejad succeeded Khatami, Tehran showcased Mesbah in an unveiling ceremony. Mesbah was scheduled to enter orbit in early 2006 onboard a Russian rocket but may have also been exploring other options, to include using an indigenously-developed SLV, to launch Mesbah or other systems (Kass, 2006).

There is widespread concern that Mesbah could serve as a springboard for Iran to manufacture more sophisticated reconnaissance satellites (Kass, 2006). The Iranian Defense Ministry initiated an endeavour to manufacture the Sepehr satellite. Furthermore, Iran contracted with the Russian company

M.F. Reshetnev Scientific-Production Association of Applied Mechanics (NPO PM, Zheleznogorsk) to build the USD 132 million Zohreh satellite. Zohreh is designed to provide Iranians with numerous services to include television and radio broadcasts, Internet and email access. Possessing advanced reconnaissance spacecraft could greatly help Iran, particularly after a natural disaster, because emergency personnel could effectively coordinate relief efforts. The military can also exploit this technology by rapidly distributing orders to forces to neutralize potential threats. Sending and receiving data quickly throughout the theatre is a key characteristic of a sophisticated military, which Iran seeks to further modernize with space assets.

Iran fervently believes that it has a sovereign right to sophisticated technologies, to include a space and nuclear programme. Iran's return to space with an indigenously-produced SLV in 2009 made the country the first in the Islamic world with this capability (Kass, 2006).

Iran frequently announces technological breakthroughs that are difficult to verify independently (Vahdat and Schreck, 2017). It has carried out multiple tests of ballistic missiles as well as other domestically produced weapons over the years. The Simorgh, for instance, is a two-stage rocket first revealed in 2010. It is larger than an earlier model known as the Safir, or "ambassador", that Iran has used to launch satellites on several previous occasions. The launch came as the US criticized Iran's ballistic missile tests, which American officials argue violate the spirit of the 2015 nuclear deal that Iran struck with world powers. Under the agreement, which does not expressly prohibit missile tests, Iran agreed to limit its uranium enrichment programme in exchange for the lifting of economic sanctions. With Iran pursuing a satellite launch programme for years, the US and its allies are concerned that the same technology could be used to develop long-range missiles. The country has sent several short-lived satellites into orbit over the past decade and, in 2013, it launched a monkey into space. However, it recently abandoned plans to send humans into orbit, saying in late May that the cost of doing so was prohibitive. The US National Air and Space Intelligence Center claimed that the Simorgh could act as a test bed for developing the technologies needed to produce an intercontinental ballistic missile, or ICBM. Iran's satellite-launch programme falls under the responsibility of the defence ministry, which has denied that the space programme is a cover for weapons development. The head of Iran's space agency in October expressed for the very first time some interest in cooperating with NASA. Iran has offered to share its scientific findings and satellite data with other countries. Iran's most recent known successful satellite rocket launch was in February 2015, when it sent an imaging satellite known as "Fajr" into orbit. That launch happened while Iran was negotiating the nuclear deal and it is believed to have carried out at least a partial test of the Simorgh rocket last year, though the exact details of that attempt were never made public.

In July 2017, Iran successfully launched its most advanced satellite-carrying rocket into space, in what is likely the most significant step yet for the launch vehicle. A confirmed launch of the "Simorgh" rocket would mark another step forward for the Islamic Republic's young space programme, but is likely to raise alarm among its adversaries, who fear the same technology could be used to produce long-range missiles. Iranian state television said the rocket, which means "phoenix" in Persian, is capable of carrying a satellite weighing 550 pounds. The report did not elaborate on the rocket's payload. Other state-linked agencies including the semi-official Fars news agency also described the launch as successful. Media reports did not say when the launch took place at the Imam Khomeini National Space Station in Semnan, some 138 miles east of Tehran.

South Korea

Korea started to participate in the space sector only in the early 1990s. Its first project was a micro-satellite named KITSAT-1. Almost at the same time, the first project that sounded like a rocket project, KSR-1, with first stage solid propellant, was started in 1989. With the above two small scientific projects, Korea began to step into the sophisticated and technology-intensive space industry.

The space industry is a symbolic industry through which Korea can prove its national technological capability as well as its national power (Hwang, 2006). Korea is a latecomer in this particular industry, deciding to participate almost 50 years after the launch of the first artificial satellite. The space industry has very different characteristics from the other conventional mass production industries with which Korea has successfully caught up. Technology accumulation through learning by doing is very lengthy, as the production unit remains almost one per project. However, during the past ten years Korea has improved its technological capabilities in satellite development, and has also made progress in space launch vehicle technology.

According to the Space Development Promotion Act enacted in May 2005, the supreme government body for deciding space policy in Korea is the National Space Committee, which is placed under the control of the president and chaired by the Minister of Science and Technology. The committee consists of around fifteen committee members, including nine ministers of related ministries. Among the related ministries, the Ministry of Science and Technology (MOST) is the major government body for formulating and executing the national space development plan. The Ministry of Commerce, Industry and Trade (MOCIE) is mainly concerned with fostering manufacturing industries, and the Ministry of Information and Communication (MIC) is concerned with the information and communications sector, including satellite broadcasting and communication. The Ministry of Construction and Transportation (MOCT) is responsible for CNS/ ATM (Communications, Navigation and Surveillance Systems for Air Traffic Management) and land development while the Ministry of Maritime Affairs and Fisheries (MOMAF) is involved in monitoring the ocean environment and marine ecosystem, production of fisheries information, etc.

The main space development research institute in Korea is the Korea Aerospace Research Institute (KARI). It was established in 1989 under the supervision of MOST. Space activities in Korea have mainly been carried out by government research institutes in cooperation with foreign companies (Hwang, 2006). Furthermore, the number of development projects connected to production units has been very limited thus far. For this reason Korean industries have been relatively less developed. Recently Korean satellite development projects have been growing fast in terms of number of projects as well as monetary base and this provides more opportunities for Korean companies to be involved in space development projects. Korean companies have been participating in satellite development projects and have increased their technological capabilities through learning by doing. Other Korean companies have been working as subcontractors for the development of the Korean Sounding Rocket and Space Launch Vehicle Program.

The SaTReC-I is a technology-oriented venture company which developed and delivered Lazak-Sat, a 100kg class microsatellite for remote sensing, for Malaysia in 2005. It is the only Korean company thus far to have developed and exported a satellite independently of outside technological assistance.

Korea established its first National Space Development Mid- and Long-Term Basic Plan in 1996 and revised it in 2000 and 2005. The plan incorporated basic activities in space up to 2015. The long-term objectives of space development were to acquire the independent technological capabilities for space development and to join the top ten countries in the space industry by competing in the global market (Hwang, 2006).

The mid-term objectives were more specific. First, Korea acquired the capability to launch micro-satellites by the year 2007. Second, by the year 2010, a Low Earth Orbit (LEO) multipurpose satellite was developed independently. Finally, the technical basis to compete in the global space market was established. In order to accomplish these objectives, Korea developed thirteen satellites (four satellites in the initial phase) by the year 2010 (seven multipurpose satellites, four scientific satellites, two geostationary satellites). When the mid-term plan was completed, Korea acquired the capability to develop LEO multipurpose satellites domestically. Multipurpose satellites meet the national needs for monitoring the ground, ocean and the environment as well as satisfying public needs for continuous satellite data. Science and technology satellites perform the preliminary research in core technologies necessary for the development of the multipurpose satellites, as well as performing space science experiments. The Communication, Ocean and Meteorological Satellite (COMS) is currently used to acquire the technology to develop a geostationary satellite locally and satisfy needs for satellite communications, ocean monitoring and meteorology services.

According to the OECD (2014), the Korean government plans to develop a rocket built entirely with Korean technology by 2018–20. The First Space Development Basic Plan allocated some KRW (Korean Won) 1,546.9 billion for the period 2007 to 2011. In 2012, the Second Basic Plan for 2012–16 was launched, with an estimated total allocation of KRW 2,133.1 billion for the five-year period. It was revised in November 2013 with a budget increase towards an earlier development of Korea's Space Launch Vehicle 2. From 2007 to 2012, the Korean space budget actually fell, but saw a substantial increase from 2012 to 2013. When adjusted for inflation, the budget decreased by 20% between 2007 and 2013 in local currency. In 2013, Korea's space budget amounted to KRW 348.2 billion (around USD 318 million), with the allocation to launcher development and the Naro space centre accounting for 40% of the total budget. Satellite operation and development was the second-biggest budget item, with KRW 105 billion (USD 96 million), more than 30% of the total budget.

Saudi Arabia

Saudi Arabia uses Russia to launch their spacecrafts. Saudi Arabia's six satellites entered orbit onboard Russian rockets. It has many SLVs that can carry small satellites, which is beneficial to Saudi Arabia because engineers have greater flexibility in picking the launch date. The Kingdom views space as a source of national pride (Kass, 2006). The engineers who built the Saudisat-1 and Saudisat-2 satellites obtained specialized knowledge, which will serve as a springboard for other related initiatives.

The spacecrafts that Russia hoisted were indigenously-constructed at the Space Research Institute (SRI). SRI also supports the spread and advancement of space technology. The country's other notable space facility is the Saudi Center for Remote Sensing (SCRS). Saudi Arabia established the center in 1986, because it recognized that remote sensing had numerous civil benefits. Enhancements to SCRS allow it to obtain and distribute imagery simultaneously from multiple foreign remote sensing systems.

Saudi Arabia's space effort is far more mature than that of Iran, yet generates significantly less international concern. According to Turki bin Sa'ud bin Muhammad al-Sa'ud, head of KAAST, his facility completely financed the Saudisat-1 and Saudisat-2 satellites without assistance from the defense ministry or any other government entity. The director called any claims that the two systems had a military purpose "baseless". The satellites are intended solely for telecommunications and research purposes. KAAST's ability to completely fund this initiative demonstrates Saudi Arabia's desire to exploit space solely for civil purposes (Kass, 2006).

Sheldon (2016) outlines how Prince Mohammed bin Salman and Deputy Crown Prince of Saudi Arabia, has launched an ambitious social and economic reform initiative called "Vision 2030". The initiative was developed by Prince Mohammed in order to promote reforms as the Kingdom faces record-low oil prices, unprecedented regional instability as well as looming social problems ranging from youth unemployment to inefficient government. Commentators have welcomed the reform as necessary, however they have also cautioned that it is ambitious in such a short period of time and it is imperative that it delivers if the Kingdom of Saudi Arabia is to maintain its status as a regional power and thrive in an interconnected, competitive and uncertain world. One way to help ensure success, however, is for Saudi Arabia to harness the technologies and exploit the full potential of space systems.

Pakistan

For the purpose of space science research and development, the Space and Upper Atmosphere Research Commission (SUPARCO) was established by Pakistan in 1961, and it started functioning in 1964. This national organization has a high degree of autonomy, implements the space policy of Pakistan and was established by the Space Research Council (SRC), whose president is the Prime Minister. The commission comprises the chairman and four members for space technology, space research, space electronics and finance.

It was granted the status of a Commission in 1981. SUPARCO is devoted to Research and Development work in Space Sciences and Space Technology and their applications for the peaceful uses of outer space. It works towards developing indigenous capabilities in space technology and to promote space applications for socio-economic uplift of the country (Lele, 2013).

Badr-1 was Pakistan's first indigenously developed satellite and was launched from the Xichang Launch Center, China on July 16, 1990 aboard a Chinese Long March 2E rocket. Badr-1 weighed 150 pounds. Originally designed for a circular orbit at 250–300 miles altitude, Badr-1 actually was inserted by the Long March rocket into an elliptical orbit of 127–615 miles. The satellite successfully completed its designed life.

SUPARCO started building the small amateur radio satellite in late 1986 with support from the Pakistan Amateur Radio Society. The satellite was named Badr inspired from the Urdu language word for "new moon". Badr-1 was planned to be launched on the US Space Shuttle, but the 1986 Challenger explosion and consequent delay in American flights changed the plan (Lele, 2005).

Paksat 1 was Pakistan's first geostationary satellite. The satellite was originally known as Palapa C1 and was designed to serve Indonesia. After an electronics failure, it was renamed Anatolia 1 and then renamed Paksat 1 again in 2002. It was originally manufactured by Boeing and used the HS 601 spacecraft design. It was launched on 1 February 1996.

Paksat-1R satellite replaced the existing Paksat-1 in 2010. Pakistan's national space agency signed a consulting deal with Telesat in March 2007 for advice on the purchase, manufacture and launch of the Paksat-1R satellite. Under the agreement Telesat helped the Pakistani agency find a manufacturer and provide technical and commercial advice during the negotiation process. Telesat also helped oversee the construction of the new satellite and monitor the launch and in-orbit testing services.

Today, Suparco continues to suffer from education funding that is the lowest in south Asia and continued military supervision (Jyoti, 2017). Its current chairman, Qaiser Anees Khurrum, is a former high-ranking general. The agency has suffered a series of embarrassing failures in recent decades. It has had to cancel several orbital slots because it could not launch in time. The agency is now placing its hopes on a Mission in 2040 by when it aims to have indigenous satellite making and launching capabilities.

Space service economy country players

Luxembourg

In the 1980s, during the nascent days of the satellite communications industry, Luxembourg foresaw the opportunities it could bring. The tiny European nation, known for steel manufacturing and tax breaks, provided financial support and passed regulations that allowed its homegrown satellite company, SES, to thrive. And because it provided that early support, one of the globe's smallest countries came to host the world's second-largest commercial satellite operator. And now, 30 years later, the country is positioning itself in a different off-earth industry: asteroid mining.

Bold forecasters such as Scoles (2017) speak of a full-on celestial supply-chain. In that version of the future, the entities that control that supply chain – doing the mining and selling the resources – will become very rich. They will, in a way, rule that final frontier. In 2016, Luxembourg began taking steps toward dominating the industry, and so potentially the flow of cash and commodities beyond earth. Luxembourg stepped on to space mining's ground floor early last year, when the Ministry of Economy announced the Space Resources initiative.

Key to the programme, said the official statement, "will be the development of a legal and regulatory framework confirming certainty about the future ownership of minerals extracted in space from Near Earth Objects such as asteroids." In November, the country drafted a law permitting companies to own the resources they obtain from space. It has also pledged an investment of at least 200 million euros in forms like R&D grants and purchasing equity in companies. Deputy Prime Minister Etienne Schneider has said that the country can also reimburse companies up to 45% of what they invest in R&D. The two major mining players based in the US, Planetary Resources and Deep Space Industries, have now established, or will soon, legal offices within Luxembourg. The country has purchased equity in and given grants to it. Along with the European Space Agency, Luxembourg has also collaborated on Deep Space Industries' Prospector-X mission, which will use a nano-spacecraft to test some of its asteroid technologies.

On the occasion of the 2017 Paris Air Show in Le Bourget, Luxembourg's Deputy Prime Minister and Minister of the Economy Etienne Schneider visited the ESA pavilion and, together with ESA Director General, Jan Wörner, signed a joint statement on future activities concerning missions to the asteroids, related technologies and space resources exploration and utilization. The Grand Duchy of Luxembourg and the European Space Agency jointly agreed on the opportunity to further study technical and scientific aspects of space resources exploration and utilization activities. To this aim ESA will undertake an analysis of the feasibility assessment and technical maturity of asteroids exploration and utilization.

Furthermore, this analysis will also contribute to Near Earth Asteroids classification, define methods to study the interiors of asteroids, look at multi-sampling technology and address technologies for in-situ extraction and operations on asteroidal surfaces. It may also consider laboratory experiments with meteorites/analogues as well as the conception of a virtual institute devoted to the science of asteroids and related technologies. Luxembourg will be associated to the analysis as an element of its "SpaceResources.lu" initiative that aims to offer an attractive overall framework for the exploration and exploitation of space resources. By signing the joint statement, Luxembourg and ESA jointly recognized the benefits achieved by space exploration to the whole of humankind by furthering scientific knowledge, fostering technical innovation, inspiring the people and enhancing peaceful international cooperation. Moreover European accomplishments in space exploration foster European cohesion and identity and position Europe as an inspiring force globally. In this context, the important role of asteroids as potential resources to extend human presence in space as well as their potential risk of impacting earth is jointly recognized.

Luxembourg has been cooperating with ESA for nearly 20 years now and has been an ESA Member State since 2005. At the latest ESA Council meeting at ministerial level Luxembourg increased its subscriptions in fields associated with missions to Near Earth Objects (NEOs) and related technologies. ESA has been following with interest the Luxembourg's SpaceResources.lu initiative. A joint Luxembourg/ESA working group has been meeting regularly to exchange information and prepare potential joint activities. The Asteroid Science Intersections with In-Space Mine Engineering (ASIME) workshop held in September 2016 in Luxembourg with the support of the Luxembourg Ministry of the Economy, Europlanet, the University of Luxembourg and ESA was an emblematic example of cooperation to advance the understanding of the issues related to asteroid missions and the exploration and future utilization of space resources.

Isle of Man

The Isle of Man is increasingly being recognized as a leading location for the space sector. With the support of a pro-space government, the Isle of Man plays host to a number of global satellite companies, new space start-ups and international space associations as well as being able to offer orbital slots and launch licences via the UK Space Agency (SpaceIsle.com, 2016). It offers an established industrial cluster of space, aerospace and high-tech industries along with an established professional infrastructure which includes many of the world's leading companies in finance and insurance.

The Isle of Man Communications Commission, which licenses and regulates all telecommunications for the Isle of Man, works with the UK regulator, Ofcom, via ManSat and the UK Space Agency, when authorizing space sector activities in the Island, as for or example in the case of geo-stationary satellite filings and telemetry, tracking and control under international treaties. The Isle of Man's professional services sector has developed strong expertise in the global space and satellite industry, reinforcing its ability to enter and operate successfully in niche sectors. Four of the world's top ten satellite companies have a presence in the Isle of Man that include SES, Inmarsat, Avanti and Telesat. The Isle of Man is home to the Space Data Association, which is the first satellite operator-led association dedicated to sharing critical operational data in support of satellite operations, improving flight safety and preserving the space environment. The Satellite Interference Reduction Group has also recently set up in the Isle of Man.

The International Space University (ISU) is located in Strasbourg, France and specializes in the education of postgraduates and professionals to prepare them for work in Space-related activities. The ISU is in a partnership with the Isle of Man government and has developed the International Institute of Space Commerce (IISC), which is based in the Isle of Man. It is intended to be the intellectual home for the space industry and for space academia around the world with the ultimate aim to promote and enhance world's space commerce to the general public. IISC's vision is to act as a resource for all, being an international and non partisan "Think Tank" drawing upon new ideas and solutions to existing and future problems the space industry faces by drawing together experts from academia, government, the media, business, international and non-governmental organizations.

The Isle of Man had its first brush with the international commercial space industry in 2001, and less than ten years later it was named the fifth most likely nation to put the next person on the moon. Only the United States, Russia, China and India were ranked ahead in a report released by industry analyst Ascend. The island's meteoric rise in the space sector may have seemed unlikely to many, but another publication confirmed a growing reputation in the space economy. A report in May 2012 by business research organization the Institute of Directors (IoD) said: "In the new space economy, you can be small and succeed. You don't need astronauts to be in the space business. The Isle of Man has built a powerful industry niche for other countries to follow." The island's emerging status in an international industry worth about USD 300 billion a year has come as a surprise for many, even for those at the helm (Supple, 2012).

The island's journey into space began in 2001, when the government entered into an agreement with local firm Mann Sat to file for select orbital positions and radio frequencies with the International Telecommunications Union in Geneva. The director of this firm was Isle of Man resident Chris Stott, husband of NASA astronaut Nicole. He brought the island into close contact with the global space sector in preparation for the introduction of the zero rate of corporate tax in 2006. As a result, the island has hosted more than 30 space companies and so far the industry has pulled £35 million directly into the Manx exchequer – a figure set to rise to over the billion mark in five years.

Conclusion

While the previous chapter provides an analysis of the space sector in the US, this chapter primarily focuses on the other space nations starting from the more established players (i.e. Russia, ESA and Japan), the fast growing emerging economy players (i.e. China, India and Brazil), others players (i.e. Israel, Iran, Korea, Saudi Arabia and Pakistan) to the space service economy country players (i.e. Luxembourg and the Isle of Man). From the chapter it emerges that international politics today is very different from politics in the 1950s and 1960s. The conflicts that the world faces today are multi-faceted, with threats that are no longer defined by geographic location. In the past, as described in Chapter 1, space achievements were mainly restricted to the US and the Soviet Union and were a sign of their political power and military prestige. Today many more countries are interested in space exploration not only to demonstrate prestige but to discover more about the universe and to provide the technology for better communication, navigation and business opportunities for their countries. Several countries have begun to cooperate on space missions, and ultimately the International Space Station is increasingly becoming a testimony of this international effort. Dawson (2017) argues that countries with power and a natural competition with each other consider space as another platform to demonstrate excellence with advantages that are not necessarily focused on the military. Overall, the international level of effort of space exploration today is remarkable both in terms of interest and level of planning and development. In the light of this evidence, the next chapter will consider some scenarios for the future of the space sector.

References

Bhattacharjee, D., 2016. Israeli Space Program – The Challenges Ahead. Indian Council of World Affairs, 17 October 2016. Available at: http://icwa.in/pdfs/IB/2014/IsraeliSpaceProgramIB17102016.pdf.

Clark, S., 2017. China's space station plan bolstered by year of successes. Available at: https://spaceflightnow.com/2017/04/29/chinas-space-station-plan-bolstered-by-year-of-successes/.

Corporation, F., 2009. *Resource Center*. Available at: http://www.futron.com/resource_center/resource_center.htm.

Dawson, L., 2017. The Politics and Perils of Space Exploration. Springer, New York.

European Space Agency, 2017. ESA Budget 2017. Available at: http://www.esa.int/spaceinimages/Images/2017/01/ESA_budget_2017.

Eurospace, 1995. Space: a challenge for Europe 1. *Space Policy*, 11(4), 227–232.

Fairclough, G., 2007. China's Long March to the Moon. wsj.com. Available at: http://online.wsj.com/article/SB119308504660267440.html.

Furtron Corporation, 2009. Space Competitiveness Index 2009.

Furtron Corporation, 2014. Space Competitiveness Index 2014.

Hwang, C.Y., 2006. Space activities in Korea – History, current programs and future plans. *Space Policy*, 22(3), 194–199.

Indian Planning Commission, 2013. Twelfth Five Year Plan (2012–2017). Available at: http://planningcommission.gov.in/plans/planrel/12thplan/pdf/12fyp_vol1.pdf.

Israel Minister of Foreign Affair, 2010. Focus on Israel: Israel in Space. Available at: http://www.mfa.gov.il/mfa/mfaarchive/2000_2009/2003/1/focus%20on%20israel-%20israel%20in%20space.

Jaxa, 2010. Annual Report 2010. Available at: https://repository.exst.jaxa.jp/dspace/jaxapress?select=jaxapress.

Jaxa, 2017. Annual Report 2017. Available at: https://repository.exst.jaxa.jp/dspace/jaxapress?select=jaxapress.

Jyoti, D., 2017. Pakistan began space programme 8 years before India, but ISRO is galaxies ahead now. Available at: http://www.hindustantimes.com/india-news/pakistan-started-space-programme-8-years-before-india-today-isro-is-galaxies-ahead/story-uZW0NQG5Qmxa1o2QM8M8SL.html.

Kass, L., 2006. Iran's Space Program: The Next Genie in a Bottle? *The Middle East Review of International Affairs*, 10(3). Available at: http://meria.idc.ac.il/journal/2006/issue3/jv10no3a2.html.

Lele, A., 2013. Pakistan's Space Capabilities. In Asian Space Race: Rhetoric or Reality? Springer India, 43–58.

Liao, S., 2005. Will China become a military space superpower? *Space Policy*, 21(3), 205–212.

Morring, J. & Neelam, M., 2004. Third world rising (India's space program). *Aviation Week & Space Technology*, 161(20), 46–49.

Moskvitch, K., 2010. Glonass: Has Russia's sat-nav system came to an age? Available at: http://news.bbc.co.uk/2/hi/8595704.stm.

OECD, 2014. The Space Economy at a Glance. Available at: http://www.keepeek.com/Digital-Asset-Management/oecd/economics/the-space-economy-at-a-glance-2014_9789264217294-en#.WleREqjiZPY.

Organisation, I.S.R., 2009. Indian Space Research Organisation. Available at: http://www.isro.org/.

Owen, J., 2015. Shooting for the Moon: time called on Isle of Man space race. Available at: http://www.independent.co.uk/news/science/shooting-for-the-moon-time-called-on-isle-of-man-space-race-10101750.html.

Paikowsky, D., 2007. Israel's space program as a national asset. Space Policy, 23(2), 90–96.

Russian Space Web, 2017. Available at: http://www.russianspaceweb.com/2017.html.

Scoles, S., 2017. Luxemburg's bid to become the silicon valley of space mining. Available at: https://www.wired.com/2017/01/luxembourg-setting-silicon-valley-space-mining/.

Sheldon, 2016. Saudi Arabia's Vision 2030. Available at: https://spacewatchme.com/2016/05/saudi-arabias-vision-2030-golden-opportunity-space-2/.

Silva, D.H.D., 2005. Brazilian participation in the International Space Station (ISS) program: commitment or bargain struck? *Space Policy*, 21(1), 55–63.

SpaceIsle.com, 2016. Available at: https://www.gov.im/lib/docs/ded/locatingyourspacebusinessinthe.pdf.

Supple, S., 2012. One giant leap for Isle of Man-kind. Available at: https://www.ft.com/content/2ee8fc32-115b-11e2-a637-00144feabdc0.

Tarasenko, M.V., 1996a. Current status of the Russian space programme. *Space Policy*, 12(1), 19–28.

Tarasenko, M.V., 1996b. Evolution of the Soviet space industry. *Acta Astronautica*, 38(4–8), 667–673.

Vahdat, A., and Schreck, A., 2017. Iran rocket test: space program boon or nuclear hand-wringer? Available at: https://www.csmonitor.com/World/Middle-East/2017/0727/Iran-rocket-test-space-program-boon-or-nuclear-handwringer.

Vannin, E., 2012. Isle of Man: A small nation's race to the moon. Available at: http://www.bbc.com/news/world-europe-isle-of-man-18769463.

Veronese, K., 2012. Could Brazil be the next space superpower? Available at: https://io9.gizmodo.com/5891721/could-brazil-be-the-next-space-superpower.

Vick, C., 2009. North Korea's Space, Ballistic Missile Administration, Development Infrastructure. Available at: http://www.globalsecurity.org/space/world/dprk/agencies.htm.

Yip, G. S., 2003. Total global strategy II, 2. Aufl., Upper Saddle River.

Zak, A., 2008. Russian space program in the first decade of the 21st century, Available at: http://www.russianspaceweb.com/russia_2000_2010.html.

Zhao, Y., 2005. The 2002 Space Cooperation Protocol between China and Brazil: An excellent example of South–South cooperation. *Space Policy*, 21(3), 213–219.

Section III
Looking ahead

7 Future trajectories

Scenarios for the future of the space sector

To explore the future, analysts can choose among various techniques, depending on the nature of the exercise involved. Forecasting is perhaps the most prevalent technique. It employs forecasting models that provide a simplified description of reality and of the relations that are believed to exist between independent or exogenous variables (the values of which are determined outside the model) and dependent or endogenous variables (the values of which are generated by the model). Forecasting models are useful for short-term projections, but they are of little value for exploring the long-term future. This is because such models implicitly assume that the underlying structure of the model (more specifically the relation between the dependent and independent variables) does not vary over the forecasting period.

While this assumption may be reasonable for the short term, it is unlikely to hold in the longer term. Attempts can be made to deal with this problem by developing several forecasts based on alternative values of some of the structural parameters. However, in this approach, uncertainty is treated as an excursion around a "preferred" or "most likely" path or destination. For futures that are inherently unpredictable, a range of scenarios offers a superior alternative for decision-making, contingency planning or mere exploration, since uncertainty is an essential feature of scenario analysis. Individual scenarios provide a rich characterization of alternative futures. Their goal is to describe a coherent future world by means of a credible narrative. Taken together, several scenarios are likely to contain the future state, although no individual scenario would describe it. In this section, the scenario approach is clearly preferable, since the drivers are broadly defined and involve complex interactions with a wide range of variables over a long period of time.

This section analyses three alternative future visions of the world, and their implications for the evolution of the space sector. For each likely scenario, the political, economic, social, energy, environment and technology aspects are presented, and the consequences for the space sector (considering military, civil and commercial components) are predicted. These forecasts are based on the main trends and factors likely to influence over the next 30 years the drivers of change, according to the opinions expressed by experts in the recent literature and collected in the OECD's publication "Space 2030: Exploring the future of Space Application" (2004).

Scenario 1: "Smooth Sailing'

This is an optimistic scenario where the world is at peace, multilateralism and international cooperation prevail, globalization brings prosperity to the world, notably the developing world. Poverty is significantly reduced, energy supplies are adequate to meet demand and effective measures to clean up the environment are taken collectively. There is a pacific global world order, guided by international organizations, in which free markets and democracy gradually become the universal model for social organization. International co-operation allows the rapid growth of space industry.

Main features

- Political: Strong spirit of co-operation. The USA, the European Union, Japan, Russia, China and India have good relations and are more interdependent. However, they still face the threat of the use of weapons of mass effect by terrorists and criminal groups.
- Economic: Strengthening of the WTO. Foreign Direct Investment is better protected. High rates of growth worldwide, as developing countries gradually catch up with the West. Demand for transport and communication, and educational services, increases rapidly.
- Social: Prosperity growth helps to lighten the adverse consequences of demographic trends. In the developed economies, economic growth provides the money to deal with the costs of an ageing population. In the developing countries, it generates jobs for the rapidly growing labour force. As a result, migration flows from the South to the North increase moderately. More effective public health and education programmes are implemented worldwide.
- Energy: International tensions over energy remain, as alternative sources of energy are developed. It is not easy to meet rising demand, and big efforts must be made for exploration and extraction.
- Environment: environmental problems tend to increase in the medium term. The EU takes the lead in seeking solutions, and a new world treaty substituting Kyoto protocol is put in place.
- Technology: new advances spur economic growth and help to fight environmental threats. Fast diffusion of new technologies to the developing world helps these countries to catch up with the West. Technology is increasingly developed at international level, as co-operation among national research teams is getting tighter and tighter.

Implications for the space industry

Major progress is achieved in applying space technology to the solution of global social and environmental problems.

In the field of military space, a more peaceful world order puts less priority on military expenditure. As tensions among the space powers are reduced, co-operation among them increases. The focus is put on military space infrastructure in the areas of telecommunications, earth observation and navigation.

In the field of civil space, space exploration and investments in science will increase significantly. An increasing number of countries decide to join the International Space Station (ISS). By 2020, a permanent international station is established on the moon; by 2025, the first manned mission to Mars is launched. In terms of development of civil space infrastructure, the International Space Agency (ISA) will support international efforts in space-based solutions to global problems. The World Health Organization (WHO) will support the use of telemedicine in the developing world; UNESCO will promote distance learning as a way to reduce educational backwardness. Space assets will be used for monitoring crops, pest control and precision farming. Private Western firms will participate in these programmes. A world environment protection agency will be created, and it will use space-based resources for monitoring the enforcement of environmental agreements.

In the field of commercial space, we will witness the creation of an even more open business environment. WTO discipline will be extended and space firms will benefit from FDI protection. Similarly, UN conventions on space will provide clearer definitions and better reflect commercial property rights. The role of the International Telecommunications Union (ITU) allocating orbital slots will be enforced. All space nations will adopt space legislation following a uniform, model code. Regulations of operators of space assets will be harmonized. There will be a significant expansion of the space infrastructure as the result of the establishment of a global broadband telecommunications infrastructure as well as truly global positioning and navigation infrastructure for civil and commercial use. Global earth observation system will be used for civil security and commercial purposes. In terms of development of the space industry, space firms will be able restructure globally to take full advantage of economies of scale and scope. Space firms will engage in fierce competition. Major efforts will be made to significantly cut costs and improve services. Large R&D budgets will be devoted to innovative space products and services. The cost of access to space will be significantly reduced. The cost of manufacturing launchers will decrease substantially and major advances will be made in micro- and nano-satellites. Space tourism will begin first on a suborbital basis, and then on an orbital basis by 2020s.

Scenario 2: "Back to the Future"

This is a "middle of the road" scenario that describes a return to a bipolar world where international relations are dominated by the uneasy interaction between the two blocs: the United States and Europe, on the one hand, and a coalition of China and Russia, on the other. Despite the political difficulties, economic growth remains reasonably under an economic regionalization scenario involving closer co-operation between the United States and Europe. However tensions are on the rise on several fronts, notably over the environment and energy security. According to the scenario, as it was in the Cold War era, a bipolar world gradually emerges. US predominance is challenged by a growing China, who rejects Western values and is supported by a recovered Russia. Europe strengthens its ties with the US and co-ordinates its military forces. Conflicts between the two blocs are constants.

Main features

- Political: China is keen to take advantage of its new strength and its national politics brings about conflicts with the Western countries, mainly about energy and natural resources. It is helped by Russia, because the two economies become complementary. Both blocs respond to tensions by strengthening their military capability.
- Economic: Poor economic growth is achieved in the West, as the USA cannot improve its trade deficit and Europe cannot undertake the necessary structural reforms to spur growth. On the contrary, China enjoys high rates of growth; its attempts to satisfy its huge demand of supplies result in confrontation with the West, who respond by closing their markets to Chinese products, thus broking world economy into two rival blocs.
- Social: As economic growth is poor, social tensions emerge. Immigrants are viewed with hostility; more emphasis is placed in order and security in ageing societies.
- Energy: Heavy dependence on fossil fuels continues. Concerns about security of supply rise, and major efforts are put on develop new sources of energy.
- Environment: International agreements disappear, as the environment deteriorates. Agreements on controlling the pollution are only at regional level.
- Technology: The rate of innovation in the West is affected by the slow economic growth. Priority is given to military research.

Implications for the space industry

Three co-operative blocs emerge: USA-Europe-Japan, China-Russia and India-other emerging countries (e.g. Brazil). Space firms benefit from higher military effort, but on the contrary suffer from a less open trade and investment environment.

In the field of military space: a new type of space race and the "weaponization" of space spur the competition among blocs about military use of space technology. Budgets are mainly spent in developing anti-satellite systems and space-based lasers, capable of attacking both satellites and missiles. The military space industry of the USA and Europe becomes integrated, and so with China and Russia.

In the field of civil space, main civil space projects are devoted to create "soft power": prestige, influence. Particularly in terms of space exploration and science, the Western bloc launches an unmanned Mars exploration programme, with the target being to put humans on Mars by mid-century. China and Russia start a moon project, with the target being to exploit the moon's potential mineral and energy resources, establishing a manned outpost. India promotes co-operative space projects among developing countries like Indonesia, Brazil, establishing a third axis in the new space race. As for the development of civil space infrastructure, space applications increase and provide government-sponsored solutions. Telemedicine and efforts focused on the environment are the main projects. Private actors develop suborbital launchers, spurring space tourism. Main infrastructures are military devoted: energy relay satellites, space-plane technologies.

In the field of commercial space, a return to protectionism in the space sector is encouraged out of security concerns. In terms of the business environment, emphasis on military applications tends to slow the development of commercial space, as space firms devote a higher proportion of their resources to military contracts. Many new space-related products are developed regionally. But trade restrictions reduce the diffusion of new technologies. Restrictions on information flows negatively affect the telecommunications sector. The growing demand for energy results in further exploration and greater need for space-based technologies (to monitor pipelines or to improve exploring techniques). Suborbital space tourism is developed to a certain extent by private firms. Semi-private firms integrate their activities and develop dual-use applications under public-private partnerships, taking advance of the military efforts.

Scenario 3: "Stormy weather"

This relatively pessimistic scenario describes a world where a breakdown in multilateralism, caused by strong divergence of views among key actors, precipitates an economic crisis that further exacerbates international relations. Economic growth is likely to be slow and concern about the environment low. The worst nightmares come true. International institutions are gradually eroded and ignored. International co-operation is replaced by bilateralism, as ethnic conflicts multiply leading to massive migrations and terrorism. Economic conditions deteriorate as the world returns to protectionism.

Main features

- Political: Confronted with terrorism and other threats, the USA becomes gradually isolationist. Tensions between the USA and other countries, including its European allies, are frequent. A confusing web of shifting partial agreements/alliances among like-minded countries emerges.
- Economic: Slower growth and gradual erosion of the WTO discipline. Tariff and non-tariff barriers emerge, flows of FDI dry, as the globalization process is gradually reversed.
- Social: Security concerns move to the top of the policy agenda. Poverty rises in the South, as migration flows to North increase dramatically.

- Energy: Security of supply is the primary concern for most countries, exacerbating tensions among importing countries.
- Environment: Is not paramount in the policy agenda, as security and energy takes all the attention. Anti-pollution measures are taken at a national level, as international agreements are difficult to reach.
- Technology: Depressed economies and lack of co-operation bring about a low rate of innovation, except in the military sector.

Implications for the space industry

Security and defence uses of space become paramount, in a divided world with no clear alliances. The impact on space business is mixed: on the one hand, space firms benefit from government contracts; on the other hand, markets become more fragmented.

In the field of military space, the military space budget rises worldwide. The USA, which maintains the lead in the space industry, develops an unmanned reusable hypersonic cruise vehicle for military purposes. Europe launches a major military space programme in the 2010s, in order not to be left behind in military capability by the USA and the emerging countries as China. The same happens in China.

In the field of civil space, space exploration and science, no major common international exploration programmes are pursued. Some countries try to strengthen their soft power through a number of spectacular initiatives. However, the scientific value of these space ventures is weakened by duplication of effort and by the priority given to technology over science. In terms of civil space infrastructure, China and India are the leaders in the development of space-based telemedicine and distance education applications, ready to be exported to other developing countries.

In the field of commercial space, given that the business environment is one in which protectionism tends to be strong, this limits technology transfers and export opportunities. Private investment in space is reduced, as the economic conditions are depressed. This is partly counterbalanced by the decision of a number of governments to purchase space services directly from private sources, rather than to create them. There will be a limited expansion of the commercial space infrastructure as a result of strong regional barriers to information that will have a damaging impact on telecommunications. Space assets will be used for monitoring the production and distribution of oil and gas. A civil and commercial version of the small launch vehicle will give the USA advantage in launching small satellites. Suborbital space tourism will be hardly developed.

New trends in space innovation

Once defined, the likely scenarios for the space industry, the OECD report on Space and Innovation (OECD, 2016) focuses on the drivers of space innovation and its likely trajectories for the future by identifying several themes. According to the report, the space sector is currently facing a paradigm shift, like many other economic sectors. Innovations are currently taking place throughout the space sector's value chain, from fundamental research to distanced applications, like groundbreaking mass-market uses of satellite signals in smartphones. A combination of factors is leading these evolutions. In line with the information presented by the OECD report (2016), this section first reviews the major overarching thrusts for space innovation; then the new state of affairs in industrial processes and technologies, with the involvement of non-space actors; and finally the key role of downstream space applications in pushing for ever-more innovation.

Major overarching thrusts

The space sector is facing a new cycle in its development (Table 7.1). Three overarching thrusts are driving innovations in the space sector and will probably

Table 7.1 Cycles of space development

Cycles	Dates	Description
Pre-space age "-1"	**1926–42**	First rockets (from Goddard the V2)
Pre-space age "0"	**1943–57**	Military race for intercontinental ballistic missiles, first satellire on orbit (i.e. Sputnik)
Cycle 1	**1958–72**	Space race (from Sputnik to the end of Apollo era), beginning of military applicantions (e.g. spy sartellites), humans in space, robotic space exploration
Cycle 2	**1973–86**	First space stations (Skylab, Salyut) and shuttles (US space shuttle, Buran), further development of military applications (GPS, Glonass), beginning of civilian and commercial applications (Earth observation, telecommunications), emergence of new actors (Europe, China (People's Republic of), Japan)
Cycle 3	**1987–2002**	Second generation of space stations (Mir, ISS), stronger role of space applications in militaries, strong development of civilian and commercial applications
Cycle 4	**2003–18**	Ubiquitous use of space applications in various fields thanks to digitalisation (rise of downstream activities), new generation of space systems (small satellites) prompted by integration of breakthroughs in micro-electronics, computers and material sciences, globalisation of space activities (large and very small national space programmes coexist, development of global value chains)
Cycle 5	**2018–33**	Growing uses of satellite infrastructure outputs (signals, data) in mass-market prosucts and for treaties' global monitoring, third generation of space stations, extensive mapping of solar system and beyond thanks to new telescopes and robotic missions, new space activities coming of age (e.g. new human-rated space launchers, in-orbit servicing)

Source: OECD, 2016.

continue to do so over the next decade: the persistence of national security and science objectives, the expansion of downstream space applications, and the pursuit of human space exploration. One undetermined factor will be the role of commercial actors in leading efforts in human space exploration.

More governmental research for national security and science. Since the beginning of the space age, geopolitical considerations have played a dominant role in shaping space programmes. This is likely to continue into the future. As is the case in other high-tech sectors, the role of governmental research for national security reasons will remain a major source of future innovations that will eventually trickle down into the civilian and commercial. Many of the known programmes in OECD countries point to potential breakthroughs over the next decade in terms of ever-improved satellite data analytics and space access, as space technologies converge with other advances in information technologies, materials, robotic and artificial intelligence, to name a few. Science and space exploration supported by governments should also remain key drivers for much of the fundamental space research and R&D. Space missions bring also national prestige and technological know-how. Space telescopes and robotic exploration have already considerably increased our understanding of the universe and of the earth itself.

The expansion of downstream space applications. Further development of space applications will be pursued to solve problems on earth and/or to make a profit. Civil and commercial space systems have seen an exponential expansion all over the world, with sophisticated and diverse applications, as many space technologies have been gradually transferred from scientific and military applications to civil and commercial ones. Recent innovations, like small satellites development and enhanced uses, are only starting to impact the value chains in space manufacturing, contributing to develop cheaper access to space solutions and possible new mass-market downstream applications (e.g. live video feeds from space). Although competing terrestrial technologies may affect the uptake of some applications (e.g. fibre rollout in selected large cities), the advances in digitalization and further technology convergence could contribute to bring about new applications (e.g. building on the expected user-centric 5G mobile telecommunications standards).

Humans in space. Although criticized at times for its high costs, many regard the exploration of space by humans as another foremost thrust of future space programmes and innovations. One major change, as compared to only a decade ago, is that such a vision is not only articulated by scientists in space agencies with more or less support from policy makers, but it is also an objective of some entrepreneurs and large commercial firms. NASA's concept of the Low Earth Orbit economy (i.e. the "LEO economy") envisages a possible strong role of the private sector in developing future human spaceflight activities in orbit, with a major role for space agencies in building the technological blocks for human exploration beyond the Earth's orbit (NASA, 2016). As part of this vision, NASA's Space Launch System (SLS), a heavy-lift launcher (the largest rocket ever built) and its Orion capsule are under development, with the aim to launch humans by the mid-2020s on missions to an asteroid and eventually to Mars. In parallel, several long-term space exploration proposals call for setting up permanent scientific and commercial outposts on the moon (e.g. the ESA's suggestion for a moon village by 2040) and landing eventually humans on Mars. As earth's orbit, and potentially the moon, continue to serve as test-beds for human spaceflight programmes in the next decade, with strong necessary institutional involvement, some commercial ventures may also make their mark, before future attempts to reach asteroids and Mars.

Industrial processes and technologies

The sources of innovation in the space sector can be traced to recent evolutions in industrial processes (advanced manufacturing, new processes) and technologies.

Advanced manufacturing. Technological advances in materials and advanced manufacturing techniques are gaining ground in the space sector. One example is the increased interest in additive manufacturing technologies, such as 3D printing and direct-write processes. Different manufacturing techniques are already in use in the space sector, mainly to fabricate models and prototypes, but increasingly also to produce space-related components on active missions. Preliminary experiences indicate significant savings of cost and time. This is also an interesting technology for future space exploration, where one could imagine 3D printing of spare parts and other equipment directly in space. Experiments with plastic 3D printing have already taken place on the International Space Station to test the technology in a micro-gravity environment. Constructing 3D-printed habitats with materials that can be found on Mars was one recent NASA Centennial Challenge, where monetary prizes are offered to teams that come up with the best ideas. Another additive manufacturing technology is direct-write processes with conductive materials, which makes it possible to deposit sensors or antennas directly on the surface of the equipment, including hard-to-reach places, which would again lead to reduced weight and improved functionalities.

New industrial processes. Although often deemed conservative, most organizations involved in space programmes regularly update their industrial processes to take advantage of processing efficiencies to reduce production. For instance, design (CAD) software was developed in the aerospace industry in the 1990s and then was transferred to other sectors. But the main game-changer in recent years is the influence of new entrants, hard-pressing new processes for space manufacturing throughout the industry. To lower the costs of production, the adaptation of new industrial qualification procedures is being pursued, using existing experience and data from high volume industries, typically from the automobile and aeronautics industries, to mass produce spacecraft and launchers. This process has been promoted by SpaceX, a California-based US company founded by the billionaire Elon Musk (also founder of the PayPal and Tesla companies). This relatively new entrant in the space manufacturing industry was at first not taken seriously by incumbents, before imposing a model followed by many of them. The production is based on vertical industrial processes (i.e. more than 70% of each Falcon launch vehicle is manufactured at the SpaceX production facility), and mass production inspired by the automobile sector, not used before in the space industry. It has also benefited from supportive US institutional grants and then procurement to develop the activity. The company's fabrication volumes keep increasing, with production to grow more than five times year over year, with two Falcon rocket cores produced in 2012 and 17 produced in 2015. The resulting rocket systems have been tested and are now regularly launching satellites for commercial and governmental customers. The company's factory is configured to achieve a production rate of up to 40 cores annually (OECD, 2014). As a comparison, two to eight rockets are produced per year in other organizations (e.g. six launches of Ariane 5 in 2015), which has been until recently more than enough to cover institutional and commercial demand for access to space. The exceptions are China and India, where the number of satellite launches with indigenous rockets has accelerated in recent years. This success has shaken the industry and other actors are adapting to this new competition. The US manufacturer Blue Origin plans, for example, to produce its entire space vehicle at its new production facility in Florida, with the exception of the engine, which is produced at a different location. The joint venture of Airbus and Safran, which will be producing the future European Ariane 6 and light launcher Vega-C with Arianespace, will also be consolidating its production supply chain, which is currently spread across 25 different European industrial sites. Other manufacturers, in contrast, are spreading out their supply chain, using cheaper international suppliers to cut costs, despite higher risks of delay. New industrial processes are also affecting the design and manufacture of satellites. Small satellites in particular benefit from advances in miniaturization technologies. Larger satellites still have a major role to play, as they carry more instruments and have longer lifetimes, which allows important commercial and governmental missions to be carried out. However, recent advances in miniaturization and satellite integration technologies have dramatically reduced the scale of the trade-off.

Space technologies. Many specific developments in space technologies seem to have accelerated in the past three years and more breakthroughs may be on the horizon:

- *Reusability of space systems*: Space systems reusability may be on the verge of becoming a reality. Several companies are in the testing or planning phase to recover and reuse the most valuable parts of their launch vehicles. For example: the vertical landing of first stage engine and reuse of entire launcher stages (SpaceX, Blue Origin); the horizontal landing of first stage (Arianespace's Ariane 6); or incremental and partial first-stage recovery and reuse of the first-stage engine power plants (United Launch Alliance). Ongoing efforts are also taking place in governmental programmes, with India's winged reusable launch vehicle technology demonstrator, which realized its first supersonic flight; the US Air Force's X-37B spaceplane programme, with already more than a year in orbit; or DARPA's reusable spaceplane XS-1 programme with a planned 24-hour turnaround time, with a flight potentially in 2020.

- *Electric propulsion*: Another trend is the increased use of electrical satellite propulsion on commercial satellites. In-space electric propulsion for satellites and space exploration probes has been the focus of targeted R&D efforts for decades, and the technology is now becoming economically viable on commercial telecommunication satellites. Electric propulsion considerably lowers mass formerly occupied by chemical fuel and frees space for more transponder capacity or other instruments, in addition to allowing the use of a smaller and cheaper launch vehicle. Different electric propulsion technologies have been used for decades, either in combination with chemical propulsion or as the main propulsion on explorative probes. This was first used on NASA's Deep Space 1 launched in 1998. The downside is that its thrust is less powerful, so that orbit-raising with electric propulsion lasts months instead of weeks, which had, until recently, disqualified it for commercial operations. The biggest satellite manufacturers in the US and Europe now all propose partial or all-electric propulsion solutions, with both Boeing and Airbus being contracted for five satellites each as of spring 2016. In addition, the 648 planned satellites in the forthcoming OneWeb constellation, which Airbus will be producing, will be all electric.

- *In-orbit servicing*: Several governmental agencies and commercial companies have developed, or are in the process of acquiring, some capabilities for in-orbit servicing. In-orbit servicing involves a number of complex operations in space: the servicing of space platforms (e.g. satellite, space station) to replenish consumables and degradables (e.g. propellants, batteries, solar array); replacing failed functionality (e.g. payload and bus electronics, mechanical components); and/or enhancing the mission (e.g. software and hardware upgrades). This is a major challenge as, when in orbit, space platforms can move at speeds of several kilometres a minute, depending on their altitude, and it is quite challenging to have several spacecraft "flying" very close to each other. One important step includes automated and autonomous rendezvous and docking capabilities, mastered today by organizations in Canada, China, Europe, the Russian Federation and the US. The first International Docking System Standard is now being used on the International Space Station, to allow a diversity of spacecraft from different countries and companies to dock. Recent developments include the next generation of in-orbit habitation modules, including for example the docking of Bigelow Aerospace's first experimental inflatable module to the International Space Station (ISS) in 2016. In terms of in-orbit refuelling, some long-term R&D programmes are underway, supported increasingly by satellite communication operators as final customers. They have interest in extending the commercial life of future commercial spacecraft, which would allow postponing the sizeable investment needed each time to completely replace satellites in orbit. In-orbit servicing also requires, by definition, the capacity to conduct proximity operations. This not only involves robots able to perform the required tasks technically, but also the capability of remaining close enough to the spacecraft to be effectively serviced or repaired. Advances in this area are promising for future commercial in-orbit servicing ventures and orbital space debris cleaning initiatives, but they also cause some security concerns.

The (r)evolution of downstream space activities

Advances in computer processing power and analytics are contributing to a string of innovations at the end of the space sector's value chain: a real (r)evolution in downstream space applications. Innovative and sometimes baffling uses of satellite signals and data by entrepreneurs are contributing to create new businesses (e.g. the successful Pokemon Go smartphone application uses satellite positioning). The availability of satellite positioning, navigation and timing signals, telecommunications connections in very isolated places and on mobile platforms (ships at sea, aircrafts), and the growing access to satellite imagery is leading to new innovations in products and services, like never before. None of these downstream products and services would function without satellite signals or data. Some years ago, GPS devices were expensive, often costing several hundred US dollars for the most advanced ones (OECD, 2004). Today, location information derived from satellite data has become more of a feature than a stand-alone product. Services and technology are constantly evolving and becoming integrated in smartphone applications and other mobile devices. In the case of satellite imagery, it has become possible in only a few years to develop thousands of new applications, thanks to faster computer processing, cloud computing, allowing the handling of very heavy datasets and machine learning techniques. In terms of satellite telecommunications, operators are competing to make their networks ever more accessible and to tailor connectivity for their customers' needs. Some are providing tools, like application programming interfaces, to help developers create new applications using satellites capacities. Although expertise is still essential to make sense of the diversity of existing data, the digitalization tools that have become available to even small companies are game changers. The innovators that make use of satellite capacity in the downstream community are increasingly thriving on mobility needs and new digitalization tools. Based on a very preliminary mapping of downstream space activities (OECD, 2016), some of the most active companies using satellite data for their business do not own large infrastructure. They rely on analytics, quasi real-time big data, including satellite data, and visualization tools for their businesses. They invest time and money in developing and sustaining entire communities of users, and creating new business models. The successful commercialization of their products and services depends indeed on inventing constantly new products or improving existing ones, but also on other complementary capabilities in design, marketing, production and distribution. As an illustration, the company Democrata

Maritime was founded in 2014, and supported by one of the European Space Agency's business incubation centres (BIC). It relies on constant streams of satellite data and it developed original algorithmic models to provide customers in the shipping and insurance industry with information to help them measure and insure against collision risks and other risks at sea. Although registered as a data processing company under the standard industrial classification codes, and not at all as a space firm, the company would not function without satellite capacity. As another example, an increasing number of start-ups and established consulting firms in North America are now regularly producing early predictions of yield across a range of crops, using satellite imaging, weather and climate data, and powerful machine learning algorithms. They sell their forecasts to hedge fund managers, livestock feeders or to businesses linked to individual farmers. In terms of satellite telecommunications, many important developments are ongoing in the space sector, including in the diffusion of innovations to other sectors. At the European Space Agency, the Advanced Research in Telecommunications Systems (ARTES) programme, based on co-funding of projects by public and private actors, has led to many innovative applications (ARTES Apps) in a wide diversity of economic sectors (Figure 7.1). Out of the 192 downstream projects developed so far under ARTES, 40% reached successful commercial exploitation, 18% became operational but were not commercialized, and almost a quarter did not have any follow up. The rest is still at the seed stage.

But in addition to new businesses, one very important trend in new downstream space activities is the increasing uses of satellite-based information. Access to satellite-based information opens the door for new unexpected uses. One business opportunity, as well as a challenge for all these downstream firms, will be to harness future data management challenges. Big data refers to the amount, complexity and variety of digital data generated from an ever-growing number

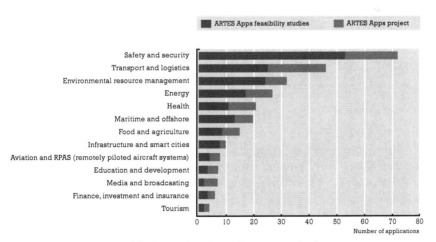

Figure 7.1 Sectors impacted by innovations in satellite communications

Source: OECD, 2016.

of sensors and devices, as well as the technologies used to manage and generate value from this data, e.g. for processing, storage, distribution, analytics, etc. (OECD, 2016). The volume and variety of data generated from increasingly performant satellite instruments (i.e. earth observation and navigation satellites), and a growing number of sensors and devices, pose the same challenges as in other sectors in terms of processing and storage, most concretely, but also in distribution and analysis. Furthermore, with the growing importance of timely, and in some cases real-time data flows, the rapid down- or uplink of information, as well as processing and distribution, will be equally important, and essential for commercial sustainability. The ever-improved machine-to-machine communications with fixed or mobile devices (e.g. boats, pipelines, oil wells) should provide new business opportunities.

Comparison with other industry sectors: from aviation to space tourism

Another way to forecast the future of the space industry is to look at the evolutionary patterns of more mature industries such as the aviation industry. Following the delineation of the parallels between the two industries we ultimately hope to be able to forecast some more accurate projections for the future of the commercial space industry both in terms of an overall strategy internationally and in terms of the future of the industry in general.

Aviation industry

There are some similarities in the evolutionary process of the space industry and the aviation industry; we have outlined some of these similarities below. Following the delineation of the parallels between both industries we ultimately hope to be able to forecast some projections for the future of the commercial space industry both in terms of an overall strategy internationally and in terms of the future of the industry in general.

Stage I: Military beginnings

Aviation industry

World War I was the catalyst that prompted aviation industry advancement (Pritchard & MacPherson, 2005). Two cycles emerged which in steady rotation promoted the future of aviation. One cycle was the "parry and thrust" between adversaries – as one side gained a competitive advantage the other required better planes to counter that advantage. The other cycle was a similar form of competition between the makers of fighters and bombers – the better a fighter, the better a bomber required to offset the adversaries gain and vice-versa. Military aviation began with the use of reconnaissance aircrafts – aircrafts used to establish the position and activities of the enemy. The French army purchased its first planes in 1910 and a year later introduced armament into these reconnaissance crafts. In 1912 the French military began aerial bombing experimentation, followed by the British in 1913. Meanwhile, Igor Sikorsky built the "air giant" in Russia, a four-engine aircraft that became the prototype of the multi-engine strategic bombers of the Great War.

Space industry

The space industry, like the aviation industry before it, finds its roots in military motivations. The cold war which lasted from the mid 1940s until the early 1990s spurred the "Space Race" which involved the informal competition between the USSR and the United States to be the first to exploit space exploration and technology for military defence purposes. The term "Space Race" in fact emerged as an analogy for the "Arms Race": "From the Start, the Space Race Was an Arms Race" (Broad, 2007). As a result the Cold War period became an era of outstanding success for emerging space programmes (Hughes, 1990). The Soviet Union's launch of Sputnik I in 1957 was the catalyst that spurred the "Space Race". Sputnik I the world's first artificial satellite, the size of a basketball and weighing only 183 pounds took about 98 minutes to orbit the earth on its elliptical path. Subsequently between 1958 and 1960 the US army for their part: placed four earth satellites into orbit; launched the free world's first lunar probe and first solar satellite; launched three primates into space, two of which were recovered alive; initiated effort on a 1.5-million-pound- thrust booster being designed for a lunar exploration vehicle; began work on the launch vehicle which would carry the first men into space.

Stage II: Mail delivery

Aviation industry

Through its use of airmail contracts during World War I, the US Post Office Department has long been praised for promoting aviation and its respective technologies. In 1918 the US Post Office Department took over the airmail service from the USAAS (US Army Air Service). Initially the Department used surplus World War I planes which were for the most part flimsy and not built for long cross-country flights. Consequently for the purposes of airmail, planes with a larger operational range and payload capacity were introduced, such as the Airco and the Junkers JL-6. Better planes were not the only improvements in the aviation industry to come out of the US Post Office Department; in 1921 ten radio stations were installed along the New York–San Francisco routes to transmit weather forecasts and by 1924 flights were guided by a transcontinental airway with rotating beacons and lit emergency land-ing fields along the way. NASA chief administrator Michael Griffin has been known to compare the forecasted role of NASA in the commercialization of space to the role played by the US Post Office Department in the advancement of aviation. Despite this comparison, Griffin has expressed concern that the current stability of the state market may be the fork in the road where the similarities of the two industries part ways: "What we have not had is a stable, predictable government market for space services sufficient to stimulate the development of a commercial space industry analogous to that which was seen in the growth of aviation", Michael Griffin, NASA Chief Administrator (Pritchard & MacPherson, 2005).

Space industry

In 1994, the Commercial Space Transport Study was released by a group of leading aerospace contractors. The study documented the need for faster package transportation globally in today's worldwide market and included interviews with Federal Express and many other courier services. Several of these companies expressed confidence that there would certainly be a market for the fast package delivery that a suborbital rocket plane could offer (Zuprin, 1998). A rocket plane, made possible by the recent availability of reusable rocket engines, has the capacity to take off and land from conventional airports, but flies up and out of the atmosphere at a supersonic speed, zooms through sub-orbital space before re-entering the earth's atmosphere and landing as a conventional plane would land at an airport (Zuprin, 1998). These space planes have already made package delivery possible; In August 2007 an unmanned Russian cargo ship carried more than 2.5 tons of supplies to the International Space Station, including books, movies and gifts for the crew.

Commercialization of both industries

Now that we have briefly discussed the similarities of the aviation and the space industry, we will spend a little more time analyzing the commercialization of the aviation industry in an effort to understand what might happen within the space industry in terms of overall strategy and commercial structure.

The commercialization of the aviation industry

In 1926 the Air Commerce Act was introduced; this Act was the foundation of state regulation of civil aviation in the US. The Act came about as a result of pressure from the aviation industry, who believed that air transport could not reach its full potential without government intervention to help improve and maintain safety standards. The Air Commerce Act encouraged the formation of new commercial airlines including:

- Northwest (1926)
- Eastern (1927)
- Pan Am (1927)
- Boeing Air Transport (1927) – subsequently became United (1931)

- Delta (1928)
- American (1930)
- TWA (1930)

This commercialization was facilitated by the emergence of automobile manufacturer Ford's all metal Tri-Motor Aircraft – the "Tin Goose". The "Tin Goose" could fly at 110mph and hold twelve passengers. Between 1926 and 1935, flying boats (seaplanes) opened new markets for air travel. Pan Am, with the use of these crafts cleared the path for the first scheduled Trans Ocean travel. The first Trans-Pacific flight took place in 1935 and the first Trans-Atlantic flight took place in 1938. Commercial aircrafts of the 1940s consisted of derivatives of military transport and bomber aircrafts. Subsequently the 1950s saw the development of the turboprop engine that led to the first propeller-driven aircrafts. Shortly after, the turbojet engine emerged which consequently led to the large commercial jet aircraft of the 1960s that is still widely used today. Subsequent to the deregulation of many services sectors, the 1990s saw a dramatic increase in the number of strategic alliances between airline companies, a pattern which we believe may repeat itself in the space industry. Before putting forward our projections for the space industry, we will briefly recapitulate the history of some of the major strategic alliances that have shaped the airline industry into the form that it holds today. Throughout the 1990s national governments reduced their control over route allocation and pricing. As a result many of the large air carriers chose to enter into agreements with competitors in an effort to reap the benefits of cooperation which allowed them to extend their international reach by facilitating a wider mass and global presence, creating value through knowledge and quickly learning about unfamiliar markets (Hertrich & Mayrhofer, 2005). Despite the new freedom that comes with deregulation, there were certain barriers to entry which resulted in the formation of alliances as opposed to mergers or acquisitions. Some of these barriers included the fact that established major air carriers, more specifically those from the US typically dominated the market because of the importance of their domestic market. Also certain government bilateral agreements limited several airlines' ability to serve a number of markets. Finally prohibitive antitrust rules and strong corporate cultures often acted as barriers to mergers and acquisitions (Hertrich and Mayrhofer, 2005). As a result most airlines opted for strategic alliances which allowed them to gain access to new markets without heavy investment, and so the 1990s saw a series of interlining and code-sharing activities (code-sharing is the process of one airline selling seats provided by another airline) (Hertrich and Mayrhofer, 2005). Below we can see some of the alliances that were formed throughout the 1990s:

- 1994: "European Quality Alliance" /(Qualifier) made up of Austrian airlines, SAS, Swissair.
- 1997: "Star Alliance" made up of Air Canada, United Airlines, Lufthansa, SAS (who left the "European Quality Alliance") and Thai Airways.

- 1999: "One World Alliance" made up of AA, BA, Cathay Pacific, Canadian Airlines and Qantas.
- 2000: "Sky Team" made up of Aero Mexico, Air France, Alitalia, CSA Czech Airlines, Delta Airlines and Korean Air.

All of these exceeded their bilateral inter-lining and code-sharing agreements, engaging in a number of supplementary activities including using their membership as a marketing and communication tool.

The commercialization of the space industry

As we have come to discover, the commercialization of space has only come about after a long period whereby the industry was reserved solely for the purposes of interests at a national level. Space related organizations were traditionally owned and run for reasons of national prestige, bearing a striking similarity once again to the aviation industry. As a result of the similarities that have been identified between the two industries we feel it likely that the commercial space industry will see some major consolidation over the next few years. In an effort to compete, many of the smaller companies may join forces and it could end up that but a few large and dominant groups, perhaps specialising in different competencies (i.e. space tourism, space internet, extracting precious metals etc.) will remain.

There has already been much collaboration on a small scale, particularly on the part of NASA, as we have seen previously. However NASA has been in contact with Virgin already in an effort to purchase flights for microgravity experiments (Morring, 2006). We feel that it is this type of partnership that is bound to initially surface and that will characterize the first stages of collaboration in the commercial space industry. It is likely that in this early stage many partnerships will be formed on the grounds of leveraging technological capabilities as opposed to quickly learning about unfamiliar markets which was one of the primary reasons for the strategic alliances that took place within the airline industry. As we have already stated, there exists potential within the space tourism industry for an oligopoly, however, if this was ever to become a likely event, one would imagine that relevant regulatory bodies would intervene to prevent such an outcome. If that was the case, then consolidation would provide a viable means for companies to increase their market share. There are many benefits to having significant market share in the space tourism industry. These arise from the cost advantages that arise out of such a market position and the opportunities to reinforce existing barriers to entry. This is partially due to the fact that the aviation industry only evolved commercially after the best part of a century, while the commercial space industry came about much faster and so the technology is still relatively young. Also the different cultures involved in the aviation industry are far more diverse as virtually every country in the world has, if not an airline, an airport. The space industry however seems to be dispersed more by region. The EU and NAFTA are the regions with the highest concentration of space related commercial activity, thus minimizing the number of cultures involved. Furthermore the general offering is undoubtedly going to be highly standardized given the inherently risky nature of the activity, which further quashes issues of cultural arbitrage.

Convergence between the two industries

There is a possibility of convergence between the airline industry and the burgeoning space tourism industry. The underlying forces behind this potential convergence are two-fold. Firstly, supply-led convergence could result from changes in the external business environment of firms in either industry, specifically in the areas of regulation and deregulation. Supply led convergence occurs where organizations begin to behave as though there are linkages between the separate industries (Johnson et al., 2008). A positive change in the level of deregulation in the airline industry led to a wave of alliances and consolidation, the likes of which could be repeated in the space tourism industry given the current low level of regulation present in the industry. The space tourism industry is still in its infancy, with real competition yet to get fully underway, and yet, already the favourable legislation laws in place could attract the attention

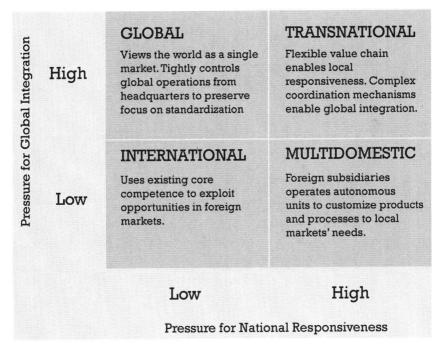

Figure 7.2 The integration/responsiveness grid and strategy types
Source: Radebaugh and Daniels, 1986.

of experienced players in the airline industry. The possibility of an oligopoly in the space tourism industry is a very real one if the industry continues to adhere to the stable market conditions.

Secondly, demand led forces could lead to the convergence of the airline and space tourism industries. When customers begin to behave as though industries have converged, convergence is said to have been led by demand forces (Johnson et al., 2008). The key element of demand led convergence between the space tourism and airline industries will centre around the substitution of one product for another, in this case sub-orbital flight for airline flight. This is a distinct possibility, especially for a company such as the Virgin Group, which has a presence in both the airline and space tourism industries. The convergence of these separate industries could be brought about in the initial stages by the use of chartered flights using spacecraft for point to point travel across the planet, an issue that we will address further on in this section. Certainly it seems that Virgin Galactic, the major player in the sub-orbital space tourism industry has an interest in such an outcome.

Looking at the integration/responsiveness grid and the associated industry types in figures 7.2 and 7.3, it is apparent that the civil aircraft industry needs high global integration and low local responsiveness.

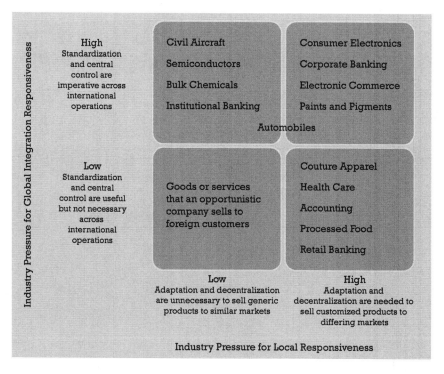

Figure 7.3 The integration/responsiveness grid and industry types

Source: Radebaugh and Daniels, 1986.

This form of international strategy is associated with a global orientation (as illustrated below). A global strategy most commonly involves a high degree of standardization with an emphasis on centralizing decisions at headquarters and creating value by designing an offering for a world market while maximizing economies of scale through effective and efficient execution of manufacturing and marketing activities.

As discussed in relation to Virgin Galactic, minimizing costs is certainly an objective for those competing in the commercial space industry and as global strategy dictates there will likely be a large amount of standardization involved in the offering. This will most likely be the case for Virgin Galactic's competitors, who, in attempting to catch up with the market share captured by Virgin Galactic as a result of its first-mover advantage, and because of the emerging nature of the space tourism industry, will be pressurised into imitating the market leader, which will lead to homogeneity and standardization throughout the sub-orbital space tourism industry (Porter, 1996). As such it is probable that the commercial space tourism industry will also adopt a global strategy as it not only is the strategy adopted by civil aviation but it also corresponds to the type of operation best suited to the commercial space industry.

The future of the commercial space industry

Our primary reason for examining the link between aviation and space as analogous industries was due in part to our final projection as regards the next step forward for commercial space. Aviation has already evolved from military aircraft to postal aircraft to its final stage of the global passenger service. We feel that commercialized space travel will probably share the same terminus, but in doing so will render traditional aviation obsolete. The reason behind this shift from the aviation industry to the commercial space industry lies primarily in the cost and scarcity of jet fuel. On the other hand, liquid oxygen, which constitutes most of a rocket-planes' propellant fuel costs 10c per Kg − a quarter of the price of jet fuel which a conventional aircraft consumes − and some estimations reveal that the cost of a ride on a suborbital rocket plane to get from one country to another is likely to be less than double that of a traditional subsonic aircraft ride (Zuprin, 1998). The premium paid by the customer would cover the benefit of such convenient rapid travel − which thanks to the supersonic speeds made possible by sub-orbital voyaging, would have the capacity to offer a flight from New York to Paris in under an hour − as well as the experience of the suborbital flight itself which would include the view of black starry space and the feeling of weightlessness as the craft enters the free-fall of the earth's orbit on descent (Zuprin, 1998). Yet fuel, due to its dependence on the ever-dwindling fossil fuel oil, is becoming increasingly expensive, not to mention unavailable. In August 2016, Merrill Lynch announced expectations for a 46% jump in the cost of oil by June 2018, with these increases projected to last through 2020 if current oil prices remain below USD 80 a barrel. The estimated price fluctuations raise two big questions to those in the aerospace industry: what factors are projected to contribute to the price spike? And how will an increase in aviation fuel prices ultimately affect aerospace? To understand the projected price spike, it is essential to have a grasp on the global affairs that have kept barrel prices low. According to the *New York Times*, these price trends are directly related to the industry's massive surplus. Canada, Iraq and Russia have seen drastic increases in production, and an end to sanctions on Iran has contributed to an influx of oil by the country. Meanwhile, the United States has nearly doubled its oil production thanks to the use of fracking technology, and OPEC has done little to limit oil surpluses due to economic competition between the feuding countries of Saudi Arabia and Iran, all of which has forced oil-reliant nations facing economic hardships, like Venezuela, Nigeria, Ecuador and Brazil, to keep prices competitively low. However, this oil surplus has begun to slow. Low barrel prices eventually equate to a drop in oil production. When oil becomes less profitable, companies cannot continue expanded extraction efforts. These slows have already started, with the US beginning to see a small decline in domestic oil production versus last year and OPEC threatening to pull back supplies soon. For other oil producers, sustaining record lows comes at a cost that cannot be continued. As aviation fuel prices rise, airlines must adjust their budgets accordingly; with more funding funneled toward gas, less is available for overall growth. One of the benefits of the drop in oil prices for airlines has been the ability to regain ground following major upsets such as profit losses following 9/11 and the 2008 recession. Expensive operation costs due to a spike in oil would have a direct impact on the continued growth of airlines. In a similar vein, a rise in oil prices has played a historic part in economic recessions. As the cost of daily necessities rise, extras, like vacations involving air travel, are sacrificed. Thus, airlines may end up paying more for fuel with fewer passengers per flight. And that means further cuts to profits. Of note, one positive side effect due to an increase in aviation fuel prices has been the resulting advancements to ecological considerations. Airline demands resulting from high fuel costs in the early 2000s have been partially responsible for ecological strides, like Boeing's 737 MAX and the ecoDemonstrator 757. With more fuel-efficient aircraft now available to airlines, spikes in fuel prices may cut into profits less than they have historically. Liquid Oxygen on the other hand, which is the primary propellant of the rocket plane is extracted from the oxygen found in the air through a process of fractional distillation. Consequently, one could argue that the merger of aviation and space could come about not only as a result of increasing wealth and therefore demand for rapid travel, but actually out of a functional need brought on by the obsolescence of aviation. Alex Tai, Virgin Galactic's chief operating officer has already said that the commercial suborbital space flight operation that they are currently putting together is to be a stepping stone to the next stage of space activity that they wish to explore – point-to-point travel on planet earth (Roach, 2007). There have already been talks between Virgin and NASA regarding the feasibility of a hypersonic passenger service, and both parties are exploring their options as regards a collaboration whereby Virgin would pay for the project and NASA would take care of the requisite research (Roach, 2007). "The long-term goal – going from A to B – is probably where the larger market is." Alex Tai, Virgin Galactic Chief Operating Officer seems confident that a global passenger service is going to be the big money-spinner in the future of the commercial space industry and due to the arguments we have put forward, as well as the enthusiasm of some of the biggest players in the industry, we are inclined to agree.

Forces affecting the industry

To better understand the space industry Porters Five Force Framework Model (Porter, 1996) will be used. Porters Five Forces mainly focus on the industry structure analysis in the organizations external environment. It reveals the source of competition in the industry and external influences including the threats and opportunities of the industry to obtain competitive advantage. In the dynamic and competitive space environment, survival, growth and profitability are of the essence for all involved. This section presents an overview of Porters Five Force Model with a look at the space industry as a whole.

Existing competitive rivalry between suppliers

There have been significant advancements in civil space programmes, which have fostered both international cooperation and technical and scientific achievement but also driven geo-strategic competition. In recent years, changes in funding and policy priorities of several space programmes indicate the growing rivalry in space, particularly in human space flight and lunar exploration. In 2003 China became the third country to launch a human into space, and India has since proposed a human spaceflight programme. The US, Russia, Japan, India, China and the European Space Agency have each announced plans for future lunar exploration. Whether or not these announcements will bear fruit, or if the new space race is real or imagined, the military tensions that drove the first space race cannot be ignored. Cooperation and rivalry in space tend to follow the geo-political patterns on earth, and there are indications that strategic partnerships are strengthening. Of note is the relaxation of US trade restrictions on sensitive space technologies to India at the same time that China is working with key allies such as Pakistan, Nigeria and Venezuela. There is an aim to reduce the potential for confrontation in space, but as the number of players increases and the stakes get higher, it becomes more difficult to manage political and military tensions (Foust, 2003). The EU and Japan have the economic and technological means to deploy weapons in space, but they lack both the political will to challenge the USA and the ability to fund the costs of an independent defence policy. That said, the ESDP (European Security and Defence Policy) and the satellite plan Galileo (the alternative to the American Global Positioning Satellite GPS) have provoked irritation inn their main ally (Garibaldi, 2004). Russia has the know-how to compete militarily in space but lacks the financial resources. If it had the means, Russia would presumably put into effect a space policy aimed at filling the power gap with the US and attempt to re-establish a multi-polar international order.

Threat of new market entrants

The number of countries involved in space exploration has grown from a small, select group beginning in the 1950s to more than 80 nations that today have organized efforts to use space exploration to benefit their societies. The future of space exploration will be grounded in such international involvement and, more importantly, in collaboration among nations to benefit people everywhere. Nations that are capable of increasing competition in space exploration are notably Japan, China and India. Although China's funding is not in the same league with ESA or NASA, the successful manned space flights of Shenzhou 5 and Shenzhou 6 and plans for a space station by the Chinese space programme of the People's Republic of China have shown what the country can accomplish. The United States military is evidently keeping a close watch on China's space aspirations. China's 2007 ballistic missile launch to destroy a satellite was taken as some token that the space race had not really ever ended and actually had only expanded.

Bargaining power of buyers

Thus far governments have played a primary role in the space industry, therefore the bargaining power of buyers has been low. Governments are the leading advocators and financers of space discovery especially in the BRIC nations, the ESA member states all contribute according to set budget specifications, and NASA bureaucratic desire to monopolize space has been well documented. However, following harsh criticisms over huge budgets and red tape fiascos, there have been avocations towards privatization of NASA in the near future, where the private sector may offer lower costs and greater innovation than the government. The United States, in the light of recent continuing developments and innovations by China and Russia, can ill afford to remain to be passive in an economy dependent upon satellites and aerospace. Therefore, if NASA is no longer in the business of being on the cutting edge, then it should be turned over to those who are, namely the private sector. An Asian space race is providing new competition to NASA, reigniting a spark that was once considered stagnant. Perhaps this is the new lease of life that NASA needs to become innovative once again. The US had planned a manned lunar mission by 2025, but there remain other countries with designs on the moon. After two successful manned-missions into space in 2005, the moon is in China's sights. Japan, the US's old rival Russia, and India all have active space programmes, with national pride, national security and even commercial gain all at stake. "There's a mini-space race going on in Asia with Japan, China and even India claiming an interest in sending astronauts to the moon," Bill Read of the Royal Aeronautical Society told CNN. For NASA, a Chinese "taikonaut" reaching the moon before them would be an embarrassment. In a speech marking the space agency's 50th anniversary on 1 October, NASA's Administrator Michael Griffin said that he expected China to get to the moon before the US. So while private interest is continually growing in the space arena, government's predominant position of control has meant that bargaining power remains relatively low for buyers.

Power of suppliers

Power of suppliers in the space industry is high – especially in the highly developed nations. NASA's technological capabilities are unmatched by any other space player, but their source of competitive edge may be slipping, as the emerging players like China and India are all developing their technological departments at alarming rates. The fact that a wide range of technological transfers are outsourced to India has allowed for vast improvements and learning for their own technological capabilities. Their development of a probe to scan the moon's surface in greater detail than ever before, has resulted in a huge amount of interest from all key space players. Russia's outstanding experience and capabilities in the space sector, and also recent economic resurgence has meant they are technologically sound, and capable of giving the US a run for their money in space development, reducing significantly their supplying power. China in particular will emerge as a major space player, mastering the full range of space technologies and is likely to generate the world's largest demand for space infrastructures. There is money to be made in space. According to a report by the Space Foundation released in 2006, the "space economy" is estimated to be worth about USD 180 billion, with more than 60% of space-related economic activity coming from commercial goods and services. "Space has always been commercial. Two-thirds of the satellites today are commercial so big money has been made from space technology. Space tourism is a new part of space's business sector that might be small now, but it will grow." (Norris, 2007).

Threat of substitutes

The threat of substitutes will affect different parts of the industry in varying ways. Solar power energy is of huge interest to countries wishing to harness energy and distance themselves from the recent oil crisis that has hit the western economies. Solar power is just one of the energy resources that can be chosen to fulfil energy requirements on earth. Other, perhaps more appealing options include wind-power, geo-thermal, gas, oil – all of which are more readily accessible on earth. In relation to the space tourism industry, there is a colossal threat of substitution. Obvious to state but – not everyone's dream vacation is to orbit around earth, and spend USD 20 million in the process. Space tourism is conspicuous consumption at its highest! As of 2007, space tourism opportunities are limited and expensive, with only the Russian Space Agency providing transport. Virgin Galactic is one of the leading potential space tourism groups today. Galactic will be the first private space tourism company to regularly send civilians into space. There has been considerable interest shown in the 2009 space adventures – however, space tourism will not make Branson a sizeable income for some time to come.

Key strategic issues facing the industry: PESTEL analysis

In order to gain a slightly deeper insight into the future of the space industry we adopted a PESTEL analysis: Political, Economic, Social, Technological, Environmental and Legal analysis.

Political

Traditionally the space industry is a government area of spending. This has been changing over recent years but governments across the world have been investing heavily in the industry.

This could be due to the fact that governments see a successful future for themselves within the industry of space. However, another factor to consider is, with all this government interest and spending is there a potential for a battle of the superpowers within the industry? There are many powerful and large countries and states involved United States, Russia, Europe, China, Japan and India. They are all competing within the one industry and the potential for major competition is a factor to be considered.

Economic

With regard to the space industry it is the stronger economies that have more money to invest in the industry which in turn leads to them making more successful discoveries and with these discoveries, their economies become stronger again. This is a trend that most governments seem aware very aware of. Emerging economies such as China and India are using their economic growth to break into the space industry and make technological advances. They too seem to be aware that this industry has a huge potential.

Social

Cultural Change: There are more and more people from across the world getting involved in the space industry and want to be involved in the industry's growth. This could be an indicator that the space industry could be a uniting front for the world as there is no precedent. The industry has an effect on people the world over.

Expectations: It seems more people want to be involved because of their expectations regarding the idea of space tourism. People seem to be of the belief at this point that there will be a possibility for all to take part in this aspect of the industry.

Demographics: The demographics of the space industry have been changing over the years. Increasing numbers of people without major technological backgrounds are becoming involved, particularly with regard to the aspect of space tourism. However, at the moment this is only available to the super-rich who have the money to invest. This could be the cause of more social divides and social stratification in the short-term.

Technological

Within this industry there are technological advances at all times. Without these the industry growth would otherwise grind to a halt. There are however, major safety concerns surrounding these advances. There is also a call for more reusable space products, for example with regard to launch testing. This in turn would be more economic. The transport from earth into orbit requires huge investments in technology, training and financial resources. In the majority of cases these technologies are highly specific as space technology involves an enormous degree of complexity. Therefore, the development of all new technology is extremely costly and time consuming. Each step forward in the industry can take many months, even years to occur and accidents like that of Columbia, which halted the operation of NASA's space shuttle for months, can be detrimental to the progress of the industry. If the future of the space industry is in fact space tourism, rapid developments in technology need to take place. At the moment human space flight is still considered relatively dangerous; a lot of this risk needs to be eliminated before the first human tourists enter space. Simply getting the public to space safely is the challenge in the immediate future as far as technological advancements in the industry are concerned. However the idea of hotels, leisure facilities and tourist resorts raises a whole other technological difficulty. Thus the development of the space tourism industry is going to be a long and costly process. The highly specific complex technology is however necessary for the industry to succeed. Since safety is the number one priority in this case it is unlikely that the technological advancements will be rushed. There is also the issue of financing all these developments.

Environmental

It is highly likely that many environmental issues will arise in relation to space travel. There is little information currently on the effects of space exploration on the environment but it is unlikely that they will be positive. In 2003 NASA developed and tested an environmentally friendly rocket fuel that may increase operational safety and reduce costs over current solid fuels. It is unclear however if this fuel is now used for all rockets launched or if it was sidelined. In the future of the space industry a much greater amount of fuel will be used so it would be in the interest of the space industry and the environment that an environmentally friendly fuel was produced and used. Also the fact that many of the spacecraft parts are largely only used once and are generally unable to be recycled will raise environmental issues. Focusing on manufacturing products that could be used numerous times or that are recyclable at least would be a huge step forward in reducing the carbon footprint of the industry. This would also provide huge competitive advantage for the firm to develop this product first. As we have seen in recent years in the airline industry the environmental issue has become more important than ever. Customers will now be more aware of the environmental impact of going into space. In order to combat any negative attention in regard to environmental safety it is necessary that as the industry develops products that are as friendly to the environments of both earth and space as soon as possible.

Legal

Legislation concerning space activities is a hazy area. International competition laws are a particular area that many countries have not even considered yet. As the industry continues to grow and develop the lack of competition laws will give rise to international disagreements. Intellectual property rights are another area of concern for this new area of business. In the space industry the leakage of knowledge and skills and the poaching of professionals is a growing problem. Intellectual property rights help regulate the area and stop the illegal flow of resources. There is also the issue of safety legislation, which thus far has not been addressed thoroughly enough for this rapidly growing industry. Security standards as well as compensation for injuries or death need to be clarified. Penalties or litigation could do enormous harm to the companies within the industry. The stakeholders of a space company have to bear that in mind when deciding whether or not they intend to invest in a space venture. As we can see there is little or no legislation governing space. In the future this lack of regulation is bound to lead to problems. As more and more nations venture into the realm of space the issue of legal ownership is going to arise. As on earth, where different states have different political and social regulations our institutionalized world is going to demand some kind of legal structure in relation to space. If tourism becomes as prominent in the future of space as we believe it will, there will have to be a legal framework in place. One of the solutions could perhaps be an international committee that sets out this framework. If this international regulating board did emerge it would indicate that the society of space would be truly globalized.

Further potential

The effects of globalization are indeed bringing about a new evolution in the industry. A brief SWOT analysis was undertaken to gain an insight into current strengths and weaknesses and determine their potential for the future as opportunities or threats.

Strengths

The governmental agencies traditionally involved in the industry have built a solid infrastructure. They have provided much needed resources, funding, knowledge and experience. These factors have all contributed to the social approval and success of the space industry.

Weaknesses

There are currently high barriers to entry within the industry. This is evident following the Porter evaluation of the industry structure. Legislation surrounding the industry is very hazy. Safety issues are a major concern as are leakages of knowledge and protection of the environment. There is the perception of a high level of risk around the activities of the industry.

Opportunities

As state involvement is weakening, it is providing the opportunity for private firms to become involved in the space industry. The potential for high returns on investment, low regulation by governments, many potential customers and new market areas for growth and expansions may very well confirm the prophecy; "the first trillionaires are going to be made in space". There is now an opportunity to eliminate previous gaps in legislation and address areas such as safety, intellectual property rights and environmental issues. The introduction of private firms to the industry could bring about much needed changes faster such as the introduction of cheaper and reusable materials, decreasing levels of uncertainty and higher efficiency rates. There are also more opportunities for cooperation and collaboration between governmental and non-governmental agencies.

Threats

With increased competition however, there is a threat of potential hostility among the major state players, turning the industry into a battle of the superpowers perhaps. There are also increasing danger levels as attempts are made to make bigger breakthroughs and faster.

International business perspective

In the forecast of the future directions of the space industry, three different likely scenarios have been identified, each of which is related with a different perspective in international business today.

- The first scenario foresees the final success of globalization. International co-operation among countries is complete, and triggers the inexorable integration of markets, economies and technologies, at least as far as space sector. That is the best environment for the space industry to develop and become profitable. Space businesses can have a global strategy, as they can provide its products and services worldwide without trade restrictions.

- The second scenario sees how regionalism prevails, as in the old era of the Cold War. The world is split up into two blocs, and space industry cannot grow as fast as with international multilateralism. It is hard for space business to become profitable due to the distorting effect of barriers to trade among countries, based on differing tariffs, rules-of-origin requirements etc.
- The third scenario shows the collapse of the globalization process, and international relationships become a continuous competition among countries without any co-operation. This is the worst possible business environment for the space sector, which then cannot develop to the fullest its commercial possibilities.

A space firm should engage in international business due to the complexity a space-based economic activity requires. A space firm only operating at a national level is likely to fail, because it does not take advantage of the benefits of going international:

- To expand sales: space-based products and services can be standardized, as its technological components do not need to fit national tastes – they are not cars, clothes or food.
- To acquire resources: the amazing technological knowledge a space firm requires can be best acquired at an international level, searching for components, technologies, information anywhere they could be found/located.
- To minimize risk: diversify suppliers across countries, or counter competitor's advantages.

A successful space firm should follow a global strategy. It should expand into foreign operations that champion worldwide consistency, standardization and cost competitiveness. Value is created by designing products for a world market and manufacturing and marketing them as effectively as possible.

With regard to the space industry, research and development, innovation, funding and risk taking were the key success factors identified.

Research and development is work directed on a large scale towards the discovery of new knowledge around products, processes and services. Before the first space shuttle and satellite in the 20th century, space was a largely unexplored and mostly undiscovered part of the universe. Scientists were largely unaware of the chemical make up of the area and space exploration was an alien concept. It was through intense research and development that the impossible became possible. In the space industry a large amount of resources are spent on researching new types of materials for satellites and spacecraft and also on the developing of new processes and products. Constant research and development is what is needed if this young industry is to flourish and if its future in tourism is to be realized.

Innovation is defined as the alteration of what is established by the introduction of new elements or forms. It can be thought of as a follow on of the research and development process. In the space industry it is probably the main key success factor. Since the industry is very young and is constantly evolving, innovation is what keeps it from stagnating. Constant invention, experimentation and creation of new products are what drives and what will continue to drive the space industry forward. Innovation allows the space industry to improve its methods, to become safer, more successful and ultimately more accessible. It is through innovation that the first satellite and the first spaceship were created and due to continuing innovation that there will be further developments in spacecraft. It is through creating spacecraft that are reusable or that have reusable or at least recyclable components that the space industry will be revolutionized. Innovation is what will make this creation possible. Innovation is what gives firms in the industry competitive advantage over each other. The most innovative firm is the most successful.

As for funding, the space industry is extremely expensive to finance. Currently it is only really possible for state bodies or extremely wealthy private individuals to finance firms in the industry. Research and development, new product development, raw materials and human capital are only some of the expenses that need to be met on a daily basis. The fact that all the components for the products are so costly and can only be used once means that financially there is a huge barrier to entry for people thinking of entering the space race. A fully reusable launch vehicle can cut the cost of launch by 90% immediately and by more as operating and manufacturing experience accumulate. But only by continued funding can this happen. It is thanks to the continued financial backing from both governments and private individuals that the industry has been able to thrive. As we have seen funding is a key success factor of the industry but it is also a key strategic issue. Slowly but steadily government funding for the industry is slowing down, although this leaves a gap for private firms and individuals to participate in the industry, it also raises problems for the industry. Some countries that rely heavily on state funding will have to start cutting back on some areas of development. Those countries may not have private parties that are interested in entering the space industry. The high barriers to entry are a deterrent to those non-state bodies who are interested. To achieve successful entry into space tourism the industry is going to need to attract a considerable amount of investment. Research and development, materials and technological innovation are only some of the processes that are going to require a lot of capital investment in the near future. Certain developments in methodologies and products are likely to create significant cuts in costs for the industry; however these developments have not yet taken place. The decrease in state funding that is likely in the Western world will be a blow to the industry but the increased interest from private parties will hopefully help to curb the negative consequences of any such decrease. The space industry must now try and attract more investment from private sources rather than continuing to rely on a likely dwindling state support.

All industries, especially developing industries, have a degree of risk involved. However everything that makes the space industry successful is about taking risks. Safety is not guaranteed in human spaceflight. In fact the process is still considered exceptionally risky and even the most highly qualified experienced individuals can run into difficulties when on a spacecraft. This is illustrated by the demise of the Challenger and Columbia space shuttles in 1986 and 2003. Without the willingness of scientists to experiment and of astronauts to explore the unknown it is highly unlikely that the space industry could be as successful as it is today. There is also the case of financial risk; the space industry is young and relatively unstable, investment in the area is not guaranteed any return. However as we saw above funding is a vital factor for this industry's success so, without the willingness of both governments and some private individuals to take the risk to invest, the industry would have been unable to grow and flourish. Even the development of new products and new markets has a degree of risk. There is no precedent in this industry since space exploration is such a new phenomenon. It is a risk to assume that the idea of space tourism will be a successful one and to invest so many resources into making it a viable option but without taking these risks there would be no growth in the industry and no possible creation of new markets. Risk taking has been and will continue to be the basis for realizing the space industry's potential.

References

Broad, W. J., 2007. From the Start, the Space Race Was an Arms Race. The New York Times. Available at: http://www.nytimes.com/2007/09/25/science/space/25mili.html?ref=space.

Foust, J., 2003. The Space Review: What is the "space industry"?. Available at: http://www.thespacereview.com/article/34/1.

Garibaldi, 2004. The Chinese Threat to American Leadership in Space. Security Dialogue, 35(3), 392–396.

Hertrich & Mayrhofer, 2005. Strategic Alliances in the Global Airline Industry: From Bilateral Agreements to Integrated Networks. In International Marketing. London: McGraw Hill.

Hughes, K., 1990. Pioneering Efforts in Space. Available at: http://www.redstone.army.mil/history/pioneer/welcome.html.

Johnson, G., Scholes, K. & Whittington, R., 2008. Exploring Corporate Strategy: Text & Cases 8° ed., Prentice Hall.

Manufacturing Technology to Japan: Surrendering the US Aircraft Industry for Foreign Financial Support. Canada–United States Trade Center occasional paper (30).

Morring, 2006. Dream Teams. *Aviation Week & Space Technology*, 165(17), 22–25.

NASA, 2016. U.S. Human Spaceflight History. Available at: http://www.jsc.nasa.gov/history/hsf_history.htm.

Norris (2007) quoted by Irvine, Shooting for the moon: The new space race, CNN, 2007. Available at http://edition.cnn.com/2007/WORLD/europe/10/05/ww.spacerace/index.html.

OECD, 2004. Space 2030: Exploring the Future of Space Applications. Available at: http://www.oecd.org/document/18/0,3343,en_2649_34815_34726866_1_1_1_1,00.html.

OECD, 2014. The Space Economy at a Glance. Available at: http://www.keepeek.com/Digital-Asset-Management/oecd/economics/the-space-economy-at-a-glance-2014_9789264217294-en#.WleREqjiZPY.

OECD, 2016. Space and Innovation. Available at http://www.keepeek.com/Digital-Asset-Management/oecd/science-and-technology/space-and-innovation_9789264264014-en#.WleX-KjiZPY.

Porter, M. E., 1996. Competitive advantage, agglomeration economies, and regional policy. International regional science review, 19(1–2), 85–90.

Pritchard & MacPherson, 2005. Boeing's Diffusion of Commercial Aircraft Design and Manufacturing Technology to Japan: Surrendering the US Aircraft Industry for Foreign Financial Support. Canada – United States Trade Center Occasional Paper.

Radebaugh, L.H. & Daniels, J.D., 1986. International business: Environments and operations, Addison-Wesley.

Roach, J., 2007. Virgin Galactic, NASA Team Up to Develop Space-Plane Travel. National Geographic. Available at: http://news.nationalgeographic.com/news/2007/03/070320-virgin-space.html.

Zuprin R, 1998. Aviations next great leap. *MIT's Technology Review*, 101(1), 30–36.

8   Epilogue

The Business of Space has seen substantial development since the turn of the century and especially in recent years. However, it is still in its infancy. Space competition is no longer simply one between competing superpowers but involves a myriad of actors that include national governments and their agencies, both civil and military, and increasingly private sector players including (high net-worth) entrepreneurs.

At the same time, technological advances have been evident in both the upstream and downstream segments of the industry. In the upstream segment, the most striking advance has been the mastery of rocket reusability by the likes of Blue Origin and SpaceX leading to significant reductions in launch costs and accelerating the overall launch cycle. With the advances in satellite design, the provision of additional services in the downstream segment of the industry has become possible.

Historically, space related endeavours had tended to be focused on the exploration of space rather than the exploitation of space. Such exploration was undertaken through terrestrial observation or human missions in space or through the journeying of craft in space equipped with instruments directed towards exploring our neighbouring planets and beyond. Still, the exploitation of space has been undertaken by means of space satellites in earth orbit for activities such as communications, earth observation and navigation, weather and climate monitoring. With the increasing proliferation of smaller sized satellites, the downstream segment of the space sector is continuously expanding such exploitation of space, driving growth in the business of space.

Yet the exploitation of space has barely begun. In terms of accessing energy or mineral resources, developments are still largely at the drawing boards. Likewise, in terms of manufacturing in space and the potential for additive manufacturing there, the process has only just started with NASA's experiments on the International Space Station. And while space travel and tourism have been the subject of much anticipation for some time now, there is still some distance to be travelled before they materialize at a significant level. However, it is only a matter of time before the rich potential for greatly expanded exploitation of space starts to be realized. As such, business in space will in the future account for an increasing share of the business of space.

Humans have always sought the next frontier. Today the mystique and potential of space makes it an alluring frontier for humans to pursue. While the rewards of doing so are potentially great, it is not without risk. As in any pioneering endeavour there will be winners and losers. Nonetheless with research and development, innovation and risk-taking including risk capital, and collaboration between state and non-state actors, the business of space beckons as the next frontier of today.

Index